Farewell—We're Good and Gone

BLACKS IN THE DIASPORA

Darlene Clark Hine, John McCluskey, Jr., and
David Barry Gaspar, *General Editors*

Farewell—We're Good and Gone

THE GREAT BLACK MIGRATION

❧

Carole Marks

INDIANA UNIVERSITY PRESS ❧ BLOOMINGTON AND INDIANAPOLIS

Manufactured in the United States of America

Library of Congress Cataloging-in-Publication Data
Marks, Carole.
Farewell, we're good and gone.
(Blacks in the diaspora)
Bibliography: p.
Includes index.
1. Afro-Americans—Economic conditions.   2. Afro-
Americans—Migrations.   3. Afro-Americans—Social
conditions—To 1964.   4. Migration, Internal—United
States—History—20th century.   5. Southern States—
Economic conditions.   I. Title.   II. Series.
E185.8.M22   1989   305.8'96073   88-45454
ISBN 0-253-33642-2
ISBN 0-253-20520-4 (pbk.)
1   2   3   4   5   93   92   91   90   89

For Mother and Dad

It true we love de South all right,
But, yes we love God, too.
An' when he comes ter help us out,
What's left for us ter do?

Den comes de North and wages high,
Saying, come on up de horn,
An' den you think we'll stay down here?
"Not us"—Good bye, we're gone.

An' let one race have all de South,
Where color lines are drawn,
For "Hagar's Child" done [stem] de tide
Farewell—we're good and gone.

Contents

Preface

It is beyond the scope of this book to chronicle a history of the South before World War I. There have in the past been many such laudable studies from Woodward's 1951 *Origins of the New South* to Ransome and Sutch's recent *One Kind of Freedom* and hundreds in between. What is of interest are the direct events from the 1880s to 1916 that created a deterioration in conditions and opportunities for southern blacks. It is usual to write a history of the black experience from slavery to the present as a progression of better times. Indeed, many gains were made over those years. But the time in question was filled with economic displacement, political disenfranchisement, and social isolation. Coming after substantial advances in the Reconstruction period, these retrogressions were bitter pills for many. As a child, I remember it said that my grandfather never voted for a Democrat a day in his life. Before this research, I had assumed it was primarily because the Republican party was the party of Lincoln, the great emancipator. But I understand now his frustration at a one-party system in the South that wiped out all semblances of progress attempted during those earlier years. My grandfather was a lawyer practicing in North Carolina in the early years of Redemption. His brother was a lawyer as well. But conditions were rapidly changing during the course of his professional career, and opportunities for blacks in the law in North Carolina were practically nil. To take the bar examination, his children would have had to go to law school, something my grandfather was not required to do. But there were no law schools for blacks in North Carolina in 1915. He looked upon a world in 1915 where he could not say, "Things will be better for my children." He looked upon a world of segregation and repression and could only advise his sons to keep silent. And so his children left during the Great Migration and my grandfather left soon after.

I wish to acknowledge the help of many people. I began my research as a postdoctoral fellow at Duke University's Program for the Comparative Study of Immigration and Ethnicity. Its directors, Alejandro Portes and Charles Hirschman, were instrumental in introducing me to new ideas and research and in guiding my work. I was able to continue as a Fellow at the W. E. B. DuBois Institute at Harvard University and wish also to thank Nathan Huggins, its director, for his help and support. At Brown University, Basil Zimmer, Martin Martel, and Rhett Jones were always ready to provide comment and criticism. Ida Harper Simpson, Edna Bonacich, and Johnnetta Cole's work and wise counsel have also been very important. Mary Cannady's generous help at the beginning made the effort possible. Gail Brittingham's typing of the final draft of the manuscript was a godsend. And finally, I wish to thank my husband, René, whose wisdom and understanding have always been a source of inspiration and comfort.

Farewell—We're Good and Gone

CHAPTER ONE

Migration in Historical and Theoretical Context

Why not say what happened?
—ROBERT LOWELL

IN THE SUMMER OF 1916, President Wilson was engaged in a heated campaign for reelection, a nation with a "passion for peace" was cautiously preparing for war, and women were applying new militancy to their quest for a national suffrage amendment. Hardly noticed in that unusually warm summer was the migration of a tiny stream of black workers from the South. Yet, over a period of the next fourteen years, there would occur one of the largest redistributions of population in the country—an event that would rival those mentioned above in historical importance.

"The Great Migration," wrote Ray Stannard Baker, "is the most noteworthy event, next to emancipation, which has happened to the Negro in America."[1] It began when the Pennsylvania Railroad Company, motivated by a shortage of labor and influenced by a venture to import black students to Connecticut tobacco fields, sent agents South to recruit new laborers. During its course, from 1916 to 1930, over one million blacks fled the southern states to seek haven in the North (see Table 1.1). It is conservatively estimated that over 400,000 left in the two-year period, 1916–1918. They left at an average rate of over 16,000 per month, 500 per day.

The Great Migration represents a "watershed" in the experience of blacks in the United States because it was the first mass movement out of the South, the beginning of significant industrial employment, and the initial exercising of the rights of citizenship.[2] Few migrations in history have held such promise. Yet, as this book will show, the black migrants going North found little to satisfy their search for economic equality or social justice.

Black migrants were induced and encouraged to move to the large industrial cities—Detroit, Pittsburgh, New York, and most of all, Chicago. They journeyed thousands of miles, sometimes alone, sometimes accom-

Table 1.1

Estimated Net Intercensal Migration of Blacks
from the South, 1870–1930

(in thousands; minus sign denotes net out-migration)

	Period	South
	1870–1880	−60
	1880–1890	−70
	1890–1900	−168
	1900–1910	−170
The Great	1910–1920	−454
Migration	1920–1930	−749

SOURCE: U.S. Department of Commerce, Bureau of the Census, *Current Population Reports,* Special Studies Series P–23, no. 80 (1978), p. 15.

panied by their families. Young men, poor and seeking greater opportunity, they were labor migrants much like the Poles and Italians who had traveled to these same centers some years before them and the Mexicans and Puerto Ricans who were to come some years later.

Rumors were said to be powerful in the exodus, and the devout saw it as a sign from heaven. Why else, they argued, would so many be "obsessed at once with the same impulse?" Some believed a great calamity, richly deserved, would finally befall the South. "Floods and destructive pests were seen as a sign of God's anger. Judgement day was coming."[3] For others, the migration was an unusual but worldly event:

> This abnormal movement among the colored people is striking in many ways. It seems to be a general response to the call of better economic and social opportunities. The movement is without organization or opportunities. The Negroes just quietly move away without taking their recognized leaders into their confidence any more than they do the white people about them. A Negro minister may have all his deacons with him at the mid week meeting but by Sunday every church officer is likely to be in the North. They write the minister that they forgot to tell him they were going away. They rarely consult the white people, and never those who may exercise some control over their actions.[4]

Most scholarly accounts agree that the migrants were drawn into moving by the concurrence of four forces. First, the boll weevil invasion in the South destroyed the single-crop dependency and threw hundreds of thousands of agricultural laborers off the land and into southern cities. Second, disenfranchisement and the legal legitimation of separation through a myriad of Jim Crow provisions in state legislatures gave the southern black populace little or no recourse for any wrong done them. Third, the war in Europe cut off the supply of immigrant labor that had previously been used to operate northern factories at the very time when, because of the war, more manpower was needed. And finally, northern investment in a South rich in resources and poor in capital, had transformed a region in the early stages of industrialization into a dependent colony where development was strong but jobs were scarce.

Black workers made up a considerable portion of emigrés not only because of their economic position but because of their political one as well. Once jobs were redefined into the limited but more lucrative pool of the industrial sector, white workers were unwilling to write them off as "negro work" as they had in the past. Their superior political situation, solidified by their positioning within the all-white, one-party Democratic South, helped make their desires reality. The impact of the Great Migration did not end when migrants entered the factories of Chicago and Detroit. Instead, the exodus is said to mark the beginning of the proletarianization of the population. Once urbanized and employed in the industrial North, it was merely a matter of time, the argument goes, before blacks would take their rightful place in the building of American society.

Reality never matched the dream of the Great Migration. Black workers were recruited for the lowest-level jobs—dirty work shunned by the native white population. They worked in vulnerable positions from which they were laid off at the first sign of economic downturn and moved into positions from which there was no upward mobility. It is because of these outcomes that the period of the Great Migration makes a compelling subject for investigation.

Three major propositions will be advanced in this work that contradict much that has been written about the migration in the past. First, a majority of the migrants of the Great Migration were urban, nonagricultural laborers, not the rural peasant usually assumed. Second, black migrants left the South not simply to raise their wages but because they were the displaced mudsills of southern industrial development. Third, much of the mobilization of the migration was orchestrated in the board rooms of northern industrial enterprises.

In addition, this work will challenge two major, widely held beliefs about the incorporation of black workers into the industrial North. First, it will show that black workers did not, as usually claimed, suffer disadvantages as unskilled laborers entering an increasingly skilled labor market. Second, it will document that personal characteristics such as level of skill were less important in any case than institutional barriers in determining migrant assimilation and mobility.

The optimism claimed for the Great Migration was misplaced. The prediction made by many that over time blacks, like the Irish, Italians, and Poles before them, would take their rightful place in American society was unfounded and unsupported. Still, the Great Migration was a necessity. It moved out of an economic and political abyss hundreds of thousands of nonagricultural laborers who could in truth say about their place in the North, "Home was never like this." It made possible the adequate and proper education of hundreds of thousands of black children. And it freed a southern group under threat of becoming in 1916, what they were in 1619, chattels of a peculiar institution. But to those who hoped for so much more, the Great Migration was a disappointment.

A General Theory of Labor Migration

Labor migrations represent a modern form of population movement in which workers, in search of employment, are encouraged to move from less developed peripheries to more developed cores. In historical terms, labor migrations replace a more traditional form of population movement where individuals leave settled areas for the frontier. Labor migrations evolve from advanced forms of development where core and peripheral societies represent essentially interdependent sectors of a single world system.

Labor migrations must be studied in the context of specific transformations unique to the core and periphery under study. The details may vary as some represent international movements of labor, others internal migrations; some involve essentially cheap labor, others are called "brain drains." The Great Migration was basically an internal labor migration of low-wage labor, yet its similarity to recent international and even brain-drain migrations will become evident. Even in their distinctiveness, labor migrations display many attributes in common.

The most prominent are the external forces that guide them. Ultimately, individuals decide to migrate but not for a host of individual reasons. The underlying causes of labor migration are found within the social structure. Such was the case of the Great Migration. Economic underdevelopment, state policy that subjugates a sector of the population, and a powerful ideology of racial or ethnic inferiority or both expand its significance from a unique historical event to results familiar to those who study current international movements of labor. These studies show that advanced industrial nations and sectors prosper through the importation of migrant labor that (1) fills low-wage, bottom-rung positions in the economy, (2) occupies jobs that native workers shun because of low remuneration and poor working conditions, and (3) is powerless, because of its migrant status, initially to overcome these disadvantages.

In such research, the assumption that labor migrants move merely "to raise wages" is rejected in favor of an explanation that includes an intricate interplay of economic and social forces.[5] The emergence of a mobile group of laborers who transport themselves to core areas where labor is needed, at little or no cost to employers, is seen as more than mere happenstance. Rather, it is viewed as the deliberate consequence of the penetration of a subordinate sector by a dominant one and of the unequal outcome of that penetration. Migrants leave areas characterized by high levels of unemployment, decline in traditional occupations, and increased competition from workers abandoning rural areas.[6] In short, they flee a developing periphery.

In the past, demographers in particular have differentiated between internal and international migrations, citing the less volatile nature of the short distance, rural-to-urban moves of the former. Labor migration theorists view the demand for labor and the disparity between regions as key elements in the migration process, considering issues of relative distance or volatility less significant. In such instances, it matters not whether a periphery is within a nation or between nations. The processes of labor recruitment and utilization are the same.

Yet, "modern" migrations may also be said to be of a different character from "traditional" internal migrations. In the latter, rural populations drift into cities at first on an occasional basis and only gradually become fully urbanized and acclimated. Employment is not really the focal point of the move, though populations are drawn, like labor migrants, to jobs at the bottom of the employment hierarchy. In labor migrations, on the other hand, migrants "represent expelled labor required to move to areas of centralized production where employment opportunities are opening."[7]

Labor migrations are created by "specific historical-structural transformations."[8] According to Alejandro Portes, "the progressive articulation of the global economic order during the last four centuries is the factor underlying the increasing dominance of labor migration."[9] The actual formation of labor migration is related to the numerous intricacies of labor shortages and market needs, fluctuations in business cycles and rates of profit, and struggles among and within classes. In the United States, the period of labor migration occurred in the second half of the nineteenth century, when masses of southern and eastern European laborers were recruited to fill unskilled positions at low wages and, in many instances, were encouraged to return home again. The volume and the flow of migration, the receptivity of the native population to the newcomers, and the ultimate success of the migrant experience were all influenced by the forces that gave rise to it in the first place.

Further, the conditions of labor migration continually readjust, though rarely alter, the basic order. No two are exactly the same. Yet, the factors of similarity are so striking that comparisons among seemingly disparate population movements are readily invited. Each has a core of centralized production and an undeveloped periphery rich in labor and extractive materials. Labor and market needs in both core and periphery initiate and contribute to population movements, making the relationship between the two neither accidental nor unrelated. The very process of development itself may be understood in terms of the growth needs of the core that are satisfied by the periphery. These needs are the twin pillars of advanced economies: cheap raw materials and cheap labor.[10]

Modern societies prosper through raw material extraction, production, and manufacture; the cheaper the raw materials, the greater the profit. Core areas gain first from the exploitation of their own resources. However, having depleted their own or having used up the cheaply extracted ones, a search for alternative sources is begun.[11] Raw materials found in less developed regions are likely to be cheaper because they are plentiful and untapped and because "the labor required to extract them is cheaper."[12]

Patterns of penetration of the core into the periphery in a quest for raw materials vary greatly. At the turn of the century, imperialist expansion created structures consistent with colonial domination. At the end of the Second World War, foreign investment and unequal trade agreements represented preferred strategies. Yet, regardless of the method of penetration, the effect is "usually to distort and subvert the development of the periphery by transferring wealth to the core and by creating unequal exchange." That is, goods beginning as raw materials are assembled, refined or extracted, and returned to the periphery where they "undersell local producers," withdraw wealth from the region, and impoverish many of its citizens.[13] As summarized by Portes, "the accumulation drive leads to a perpetual expansion of profit-seeking ventures and the coerced incorporation of outlying areas."[14]

But the core's success is not without peril. Its very prosperity leads to an increase in production and frequently a rise in the need for labor. The surrounding countryside provides the first source of additional workers. But its reserve is small, quickly absorbed, and possesses a potential political power that makes its use even more problematic. And if demand continues, the cost of labor increases, the rate of profit declines concomitantly, and the forces that challenge profit multiply. An urban and industrial work force, unable to supplement wages with subsistence once provided by agricultural contributions, adds more pressure to the rise in labor costs. Absorption itself reduces the safeguard of a reserve industrial army and increases the likelihood of worker organization. Being in demand, workers may form unions seeking both higher wages and protection in the form of unemployment, accident, and old-age compensation. The emergence of powerful unions also may act as a protection for workers against competition. In the face of this evolvement, employers seek redress, not only from the high price of labor but also from its potential power. The most "advanced" economies tend to experience the greatest threat from organized labor because advancement itself suggests high levels of absorption and depletion. For employers of the core, such conditions trigger an articulated search for cheaper alternatives. Alternatives, upon which profit and survival depend.[15]

There are several ways that employers can try to halt the decline in the rate of profit. According to Edna Bonacich, "lengthening work days, increasing productivity by increasing the intensity of labor or reducing real wages below subsistence" are prominent among them.[16] The high risk of strikes from organized workers as a result of such proposals, however, makes these plans questionable. Investing a proportion of capital in machinery as opposed to labor represents another alternative for capital. In the early twentieth century in the United States, the introduction of automated systems effectively controlled large segments of the work force by processes of homogenization and substitutability. But the short-run advantages of such schemes can be offset by long-term disadvantages. The introduction of machinery, for example, "may be associated with greater education and training needs on the part of the work force, contributing to higher costs for reproducing that work force."[17]

Such contributions within the system create pressure for a solution outside of it. The effort to gather the cheap labor of a less developed region was, until recently, the most effective strategy. Now, industries can export factories to the cheap labor. But before this technological innovation, labor was imported to the immobile factory site. The main reason for the lower cost of labor from less developed regions lies in the nature of the mode of production. In less developed industrializing systems, workers tend to combine new industrial labor with more traditional forms; for example, by working part-time in a factory and helping to maintain a family farm.[18] Employers, who in general provide health care, education, and housing benefits as a result of employees' pressure, save on such costs with more part-time and inexperienced workers. In some instances, they may establish paternalistic relations with populations who have low expectations about employer responsibilities and a "historic lack of organization" among workers to demand minimum requirements.[19]

Dividing the world into core and periphery and positing a continuum from expensive to cheap labor implies that core societies may select from an almost inexhaustible supply of workers. One must clarify the model, however, by suggesting that the process of cheap-worker recruitment centers on the previous relationship between core and peripheral societies. Workers are drawn from areas already within the orbit of core society political and economic relations through prior trade agreements or investments.

It should be emphasized that what is described is not a total exploitation of the periphery. Products, labor, and money flow out but not all peripheral groups lose in the penetration. Some, in fact, participate in the recruitment of workers and the management of industries and thus benefit from the rewards dispensed by the core society. Development of this petty bourgeois class is crucial to the maintenance and functioning of the dependent relationship between core and periphery.

Patterns of development within the periphery exacerbate the problem of surplus populations. As Robert L. Bach has noted, "penetration consists of familiar processes of removing peasants from the land and 'opening up' of the economy to the world market."[20] Particularly in the early stages of industrialization, the pace of economic activity is insufficient to absorb all the labor displaced in the new economy. The drawing off of some of this excess is another of the reciprocities established between core and periphery. According to Michael Piore, the selection of areas from which labor migrants are drawn is facilitated by just such factors of penetration. France, for example, gathered its labor from its dependent colony, Algeria; the United States has from time to time recruited workers from Puerto Rico, Mexico, and numerous "colonies" from which it established contact. Of significance, then, are the relationships between countries and regions rather than the desires or peculiar characteristics of migrants.[21]

Those at the bottom of the economic hierarchy within the periphery are subject to the most upheaval and loss. According to Bonacich, "the local craft workers are driven out of their trades in competition with cheap manufactured imports. Agricultural laborers are either forced off their land or retain an increasingly tenuous hold on it."[22] Often, rural families must "supplement their meager livelihood by sending members to work at least part-time" in urban-industrial enterprises. A fierce competition for a limited number of jobs results. Hence, high unemployment, a degree of desperation not previously experienced, and greater receptivity to labor migration inducements obtain.

Though all at the bottom experience decline and hardship in the face of development, those among them induced to migrate are highly selective. Age, gender, and health requirements characterize most recruitment schemes and are based on the types of available jobs. As suggested, because of absorption and depletion, the existing work force of the core may pick and choose among jobs, leaving the largest number of vacancies at the bottom. It is toward filling this set of unwanted jobs that recruitment is initially aimed.

This circumstance does not mean, however, that in all or even most instances migrants only fill vacant jobs. For one thing, labor migration to advanced centers undermines existing labor organization. Also, it infuses the "reserve industrial army with new blood" and creates jobs for this group even in the face of high unemployment among existing core populations. The general poverty of migrants from peripheral areas makes them ready to accept terms that workers in advanced societies would consider unacceptable. Recruits are often "bound to contracts for several years preventing them from exercising the right to search for the best paying jobs once they reached the country of immigration" and are used to depress the wages of existing workers.[23] Core societies play a dominant role in labor recruitment. Employers often send agents who are actively involved in worker selection. In some instances, they work alone. In most, however, they have the help and support of local business interests or other forms of local elites. Acting as intermediaries, these groups help to maintain precapitalist and dependent social relations with peripheral workers. For instance, they may offer loans to prospective migrants which stipulate that the workers repay the money by working for a specified employer. In these cases, "a semi-coercive element, not unlike debt peonage, enters into the condition of the worker, preventing him or her from becoming 'free wage labor.'"[24] In other cases, these groups merely act as conduits for the journey out of the sending areas, employing labor at ridiculously low prices or purchasing land or goods at fractions of their actual worth. But, again, these middlemen rarely act alone, operating instead under the constant influence and at least tacit support of core employers.

Nor do employers work alone in this process. State power ostensibly acts as a mediator in the secular struggle between classes. Yet, the state, in its role as mediator, is not independent of the economic order that sustains it; and so, in times of conflict, it most often intervenes on the side of capital. In the case of the migration policy in the United States, decisions have fairly consistently supported this assessment. In the early part of this century, unions pressed hard for restrictive legislation and were defeated regularly by one arm of the government or another. Only when employers had located an alternative supply of cheap labor were restrictions put in place. Even then, however, exceptions to redress regional shortages of low-wage labor were authorized by legislation or executive order. When, for example, the 1917 Immigration Act caused problems to growers in the Southwest, "the Secretary of Labor issued a departmental order waiving the literacy test, head tax and contract labor clause," sections most objectionable to them.[25] Immigration laws before Congress in 1987 introduced similar exceptions for farm labor.

The state's role evolves around several strategies that are at times contradictory. Bach notes that it must first "maintain the legitimacy of its claim to universal political representation and, hence, the legitimacy of the capitalist social relations of which it is part." Second, it "attempts to reduce the threat of working class struggles by narrowing the range of debate and in a more general way by creating and reproducing the powerlessness of the working class as a whole." Third, it operates in a protective function as military support in times of crisis to maintain order, supporting thereby in a consistent pattern employers over workers. And finally, it acts in a last resort, in a repressive manner toward migrants "treating them as criminals and thereby ensuring their submissiveness."[26]

The complementary interaction between the state and capital in migration serves further to the disadvantage of the working class, whose ire, more often than not, is directed against the new labor. It does not take long for organized labor to realize the threat suggested by their presence. As indicated, the role of migrants frequently has been to counteract the organizational efforts of domestic workers; hence, in a reciprocal pattern of action and reaction, as the migrant population swells, their opposition grows.[27]

Conditions in the core increase rather than diminish the vulnerability of the newcomers. A host of adjustment problems, including language comprehension and unfamiliarity with host society customs put migrants at a disadvantage. Under such conditions, they may be forced to accept any available job at the lowest pay, at least until they can establish minimum levels of incorporation into the host society.[28]

Even once settled, however, employers and the state keep migrant workers suppressed in several ways. As Bonacich notes, first, "they exercise selectivity in terms of whom they permit to enter."[29] Not only do they enforce rigid age, health, and gender requirements for work, but in some instances, immigration law may also exclude all dependent populations, such as wives, children, and elderly relatives. In other cases, the availability of employment for only a specific sector may at least necessitate a temporary family breakup.

Second, employers and the state encourage the political weakness of migrant workers by establishing a special legal category for them, withholding or delaying the rights of citizenship, and through perpetual raids and roundups, increasing their insecurity. As newcomers, they cling, uprooted and exploited, to tenuous but necessary employment. As noncitizens, "they are vulnerable to being shipped home at the slightest provocation."[30]

Third, and most directly, employers in migrant-importing societies may bind workers to contracts before they migrate. These workers are unaware that the contracts they are signing are "highly unfavorable" when compared with those of workers in the place of destination.[31]

Because of their vulnerability, immigrant workers "tend to be concentrated in jobs that are insecure, dirty, unskilled, and at the bottom of the hierarchy of authority where there is little possibility for advancement."[32] They are also much more subject to close police supervision and to arbitrary decisions by officials and employers.[33] As Portes suggests, "even domestic migrants can be made subject to forms of political exclusion."[34]

Immigrant workers are not distributed evenly within the labor markets to which they move. "They tend to be regionally concentrated, and to be over-represented in certain industries, firms and jobs." Immigrants concentrate in the "peripheral" sector of a dual or segmented economy and are likely to be excluded from most labor within the "center" sector industries.[35] This distinction between periphery and center within the core labor market is an important one. Center firms are large in size and influence. "Its organizations are corporate and bureaucratic; its production processes are vertically integrated through ownership and control of critical raw material suppliers and product distributors; its activities are diversified into many industries, regions, and nations."[36] Because of their size, influence, and wealth, these firms tend to use technologically progressive systems of production and, in general, to substitute capital for labor. Employment in this sector is small, highly trained, and well-organized.

Firms in the peripheral sector, by contrast, "have little capital and a high labor-to-capital ratio (labor intensity)."[37] They have low levels of "technological innovation" owing to insufficient capital and low labor productivity. These firms are generally small in scale and hire proportionally large numbers of seasonal and part-time workers. Further, their use of labor power rather than machinery leads to a minimal investment in the training of any particular worker. Moreover, worker circulation, the bane of center firms, represents in this sector a method of reducing labor costs. Worker productivity is, on the whole, much lower in these than in center firms. This characteristic relates not to "training differences" but to "the amount of capital applied to each worker." Center and peripheral workers may, in fact, "be substitutable in terms of their personal characteristics." But the nature and extent of the productivity of jobs is different.[38] This circumstance adds to the increased vulnerability of even organized workers. Suggests Manuel Castells, "The very presence of immigrant workers constitutes a permanent source of fragmentation within the working class, both inside and outside the firm."[39]

Peripheral firms, though the mirror images of center ones, do not represent a backward element in an otherwise progressive economy. The peripheral sector produces useful and even indispensable goods and services and provides employment for millions of people. Economist Paul A. Samuelson has in fact suggested that the most important thing about these firms is that "they make jobs."[40] They are, then, parts of the same dynamic; if one were to disappear, the other could not survive. According to Robert Averitt, "peripheral firms satisfy the residual need for domestic employment; center firms supply the nation with industrial might."[41]

What is problematic about this marriage of opposites is the placement of workers in the peripheral sector. The dilemma is both economic and political. No one willingly accepts the lower wages and greater insecurity of peripheral employment. Nor, as in the case of the United States, does the image of the "American dream" admit dead-end, non-mobility-producing employment. As black workers proved in the labor recruitment of the Great Migration and successive immigrant groups would sustain, bringing in workers from outside the system at low wages that are nonetheless higher than those they previously received, creates a solution acceptable, at least initially, to both sides. It is a resolution that fills bottom-level jobs with willing low-wage labor and perpetuates better paying positions in an upward pattern throughout the occupational structure. Labor migrants, then, to borrow from Karl Marx's more general comment on the large class or propertyless wage workers, "bear the burdens of society without enjoying its advantages, are excluded from society and forced into the most resolute opposition to all other classes."[42]

Focus on the structural processes of labor migration emphasize economic transformation, displacement, and exploitation. So far neglected in this discussion, however, have been assessments about the fate of migrants. Is there any way in which labor migrants can be said to benefit from the experience? Would they have been better off remaining in sending areas? Even in the context of exploitation, social scientists have answered these questions in the affirmative, defining three positive fates possible for migrants.

The first, and most familiar is assimilation. Robert Park outlines the process by discussing its stages from initial contact and conflict, through accommodation to assimilation, the complete absorption of the out-group into the dominant society.[43] Historically, assimilation characterized much of the early European immigration to the United States and was seen as an inevitable outcome of migration. However, assimilationist theory, once a major paradigm in sociology, has gone out of favor particularly with the current immigration of what appears to be unabsorbable groups into the dominant society.[44] Return migration is the second positive alternative for labor migrants. In this alternative, migrants view their time in receiving areas as temporary and their employment as instrumental. They intend to prosper in the host society and return home at the first opportunity. Piore has suggested that eventual return has been the dream of most migrants throughout history, though many never manage to do so.[45] However, improvements in transportation and the relative cheapness of travel obviously have made return migration now more possible. Portes points out that recent U.S.-bound Mexican workers seldom break their ties with places of origin, participating instead in a planned and articulated pattern of work in the United States, residence in Mexico.[46]

The final alternative is the development of an enclave society. In it, migrants sustain and support themselves through the development of ethnic enterprises. These firms provide employment and permit capital to stay within the immigrant community. The term *enclave* differs from the more general sociological notion of *ghetto* in that ghettos are rarely seen as having primarily an economic and employment function. It is not necessary for enclaves to cater exclusively to internal markets, although some do. Indeed, the most successful ones trade freely with the dominant society. However, self-sufficiency is the major ingredient of their prosperity.

Each of the described alternatives may operate as a "significant under current, running counter to dominant structures of exploitation." Adopting one of these alternatives, migrants may be said to benefit from migration. Yet, migrants, as a collective, do not choose among their fates. They are determined, rather, by the historical and at times idiosyncratic forces that give rise to the migration in the first place. As Robert Blauner observes, "All groups started at the bottom but the bottom has by no means been the same for all groups."[47]

The Great Migration: The Specific Case

The Great Migration was a mass population movement with significant social, economic, and political antecedents—a migration brought on by changes in the political economy. It was much more than "a general response to the call of better economic and social opportunities."[48] The South in the years just before the migration had become a full-fledged colony of the North, with its raw materials sent there for manufacture;

its local products undercut by cheaper, northern ones; its labor transformed from artisan to wage labor; and, in general, its terms of trade with
the North made unfavorable. With these changes in the economy, certain
sectors of the southern population became both expendable and superfluous. That is, they were displaced from previous employment and unabsorbable in an economy top heavy with labor. Between 1916 and 1918,
over 400,000 black migrants left the South. The mobilization was rapid
and orderly. The word was passed from relative to relative and from community member to community member. At times, an entire town would
be emptied. Thousands left despite the fact that many educated men and
respected leaders counseled against it. It was a mass migration and yet
a selective one as well. One letter writer from Florida reveals a common
pattern; an experienced nonagricultural worker, he seeks better wages
and educational opportunities for his children, and he is willing to pay
his own way:

> While reading the Defender I saw where you needed laborers in Chicago.
> I have children and I lost my wife a few years ago. I would like to properly
> educate them. I am a barber by trade, and have been barbering for twenty
> years. I have saved enough money for our fare.[49]

To the white South, the first thought was delight at the loss of the
"black problem." The *Nashville Banner* expressed the opinion that the migration might serve "to relieve the South of the entire burden and all of
the brunt of the race problem." Others described it more succinctly as
"the countervailing effect of getting rid of the Negro majority."[50]

But as the migration continued, alarm replaced joy and a suspicion
emerged that the region was being robbed of a valuable resource. Local
authorities began, unsuccessfully, to try to halt the emigration. At various times they stopped trains, arrested labor agents, arrested migrants,
and prevented recruitment by excessive license fees and residence requirements. Migrants suggest that the exodus from rural areas in particular had to be secretive. There were even proposals to stop the delivery
of mail. On the whole, however, the opposition was sporadic and often
relatively passive. The pattern of resistance on the part of southern employers was never uniform.

The reason was that the South was simultaneously experiencing an environmental calamity, the boll weevil, and industrialization and development. It was a region in the throes of "convulsive change." Once dependent on black labor for its very survival, farmers in rural areas were now
advising and encouraging their tenants to leave. Some had reorganized
on a mixed farming basis, with an emphasis on livestock, and no longer
needed as many laborers. Others merely threatened to do so. Typical was

one large planter in Lowndes County, Alabama, who "called together a group of his black tenants, showed them a Hereford bull which he had just unloaded from his car and threatened them that unless they worked harder he would, through cattle breeding, drive every one of them off his plantation."[51]

In the cities, change was even more dramatic. Before industrialization, black workers occupied a well-defined niche in the labor market, monopolizing since slavery many artisan trades and those unskilled and semi-skilled manufacturing jobs that white men did not want. Industrialization transformed all of these positions and created competition between racial groups where none had previously existed.

Laborers both forced and encouraged out of rural areas swelled urban labor markets at the heat of the competition, further exacerbating the problem. Blacks vied against whites, rural laborers against urban ones, and all with very little protection. The South had low levels of unionization and most workers, rural and urban, black and white, bargained on their own. What protection could be gained, then, accrued to white workers as a result of their superior caste position. White workers attempted to maintain this advantage by pressing for legislation to exclude blacks from certain trades like barbering, which the blacks had monopolized since slavery. But black exclusion did not raise white men's salaries. In fact, in some industries like the all-white cotton mills, it probably lowered them.

While whites paid dearly for the privilege of employment with lower wages, longer working hours, and worse working conditions in comparison with white workers in the North, blacks paid an even higher price. In the period before mass mobilization, an increasing number faced employment uncertainty even in jobs they had held for a long time. In addition, industrialization itself made obsolete many black-dominated occupations, such as blacksmithing and trucking. The importation of cheaper goods from the North eliminated many manufacturing firms that had previously catered to local markets and had consequently offered many jobs. And in new lines of industry opened up as a result of industrial expansion, like iron, steel, lumber, and tobacco, blacks were excluded by community consent.

The displaced laboring population of the South represented an ideal labor pool for the North. Although small levels of black populations existed in the North before the migration, as late as 1910, 7 million blacks resided in the South while less than 1 million lived in all other regions of the country combined.[52] The North had never been a promised land for blacks, but it had always "offered [them] more economic opportunity, more security as a citizen, and a greater freedom as a human being."[53]

Nevertheless, this difference precipitated only a small stream of north-ward migration for almost two generations after emancipation. In the 1880s when the North needed labor, it turned not to the southern re-serves but to the displaced populations of eastern and southern Europe. These populations were drawn to the United States at a rate of over 1 million a year right up until the First World War. Displacement itself was a key element in their recruitment because it created large and readily mobilized labor pools. The almost exclusive use of European immigrants in industry meant that in the North the small proportions of black labor were peripheral to the economy. However, in 1916, when the southern black reserves were tapped because of the cutoff of European immigra-tion, employers used them in the same manner European labor had been used.[54] Employers fostered ethnic antagonism by the use of ethnically dis-tinct labor, disciplined labor through the use of migrants as strikebreak-ers, and drew unorganized populations from regions where labor organi-zation was rare. Further, the large pool of southern black labor allowed employers to be selective as to age, health, and, in some instances, previ-ous manufacturing experience in order to collect competent workers to do tasks that "native" workers shunned. Finally, employers could benefit from populations ignorant of northern wage levels and willing to work for amounts well below those of the existing work force. It is little wonder that labor agents, employees of major northern industries, combed the South for this new labor supply and were reported in every community from which migrants were drawn.

For black migrants, the South had provided more than enough reason for the exodus with the legal legitimation of segregation. As early as the 1890s, blacks experienced a real decline in their political and social power. Poll taxes and grandfather and understanding clauses were made into law and took away their previously exercised right to vote. Jim Crow laws prohibited the right of free access in public transportation, in theaters, and in recreational areas. Segregation in housing and in the schools cre-ated for many black children vastly inferior environments that would have severe consequences throughout their working lives. But migration awaited economic development and, specifically, southern-worker con-tact with the North.

Thus, lines of communication between North and South had to be es-tablished to heighten awareness of the opportunities available in the North. Labor migrations are full of such instances of boosterism—sophisticated campaigns structured to entice the novice by fantastic promises. Migrants were touched by these appeals but cautious. "Pio-neers" who were sent North to "test the waters" confirmed to family and friends that there was indeed opportunity in the North. Said one, "of course everything they say about the North ain't true, but there's so much of it true don't mind the other." The *Chicago Defender*, the largest black newspaper in the country, produced issue after issue of persuasive articles admonishing blacks to throw off the bonds of the South and free themselves. Self-help organizations like the Urban League as well as governmental agencies like the Department of Labor became active employment agencies, gathering workers for northern war industries.

While the war in Europe and the boll weevil invasion ended, the mass migration did not. Instead, it grew even stronger in the decade 1920–1930 than it had been in the decade 1910–1920 (see Figure 1.1). The persistence of this large-scale exodus beyond the special circumstances of its initiation suggests the complexity of its operation. This migration was not simply a combination of fortuitous events.

Recent literature has supplied some questions useful for the study of labor migrations. Portes has suggested that "the problem of contemporary migration involves, in essence, the mobilization, transportation and utilization of a disposable labor force within territorial units that have been brought into the same economic system."[55] Following the basic categories suggested by Portes, I shall first examine migrant mobilization and

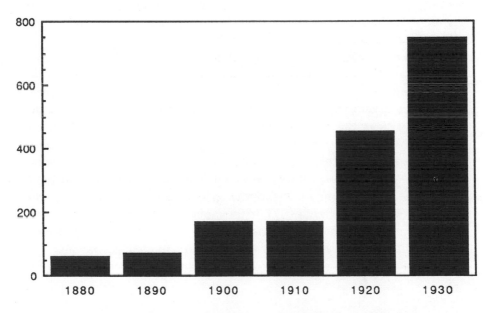

Fig. 1.1. Black outmigration from the South, 1880-1930.

Source: U.S. Census, 1976.

investigate the mechanisms of release and transport of the migrating population by identifying incentives, inducements, and costs associated with the exodus. Next, I shall identify economic transformations within the South as they affect class formations and conflict and worker employment and displacement.[56] I shall then examine changing patterns of worker incorporation in the North that necessitated the search for labor in the South. And, finally, I shall analyze the nature and extent of migrant incorporation into the core economy by exploring the actual work experience of southern migrants in northern cities and the historical transformations underway in society that gave meaning to those experiences.

In studying migration from the perspective of underlying structural rather than simply individual factors of change, one can avoid the pitfall of assigning motivations as numerous as the migrants themselves and, more importantly, provide the possibility for future comparison from one migration to another. Parallels between the Great Migration and modern international movements of labor demand more than reinterpretations of history. Much of the sociological study of race in America rests on the wisdom that blacks arrived in northern cities too unskilled to advance in the manner that other immigrants had used before them but nonetheless certain to advance over time. Experience has not proved this to be the case. Much research accepts the presence of a large black underclass that continued to fall further and further behind the dominant society as if it were a modern or ahistorical phenomenon. I suggest that the origins of that underclass are to be found in the very mode of incorporation of black workers during the Great Migration.

Investigation of the Great Migration also reveals the real connection between a number of seemingly disparate population movements. Many American workers, from the young girls brought from New England farms to work in the mills to the most recent migrants, have been recruited for the same purpose. All have been victims of changing economies, displaced in places of origins and inserted into places of destination only at the lowest level. All have met with ethnic antagonism and have been blamed for working for cheaper wages, for being antiunion, and for their strikebreaking activities. That they remain fighting among themselves rather than at the institutions that keep them at the bottom of society is probably the key to the prosperity of our time. This was also the fate of southern black workers incorporated into the northern economy.

CHAPTER TWO

The Great Migration

The unusual amounts of money coming
in, the glowing accounts from the
North, and the excitement and stir of
great crowds leaving, work upon the
feelings of most Negroes. They pull up
and follow almost without a reason.
They are stampeded into action. This
accounts in large part for the apparently
unreasonable doings of many who give
up good positions or sacrifice valuable
property or good businesses to go
North.
                    —Department of Labor, 1917

THE WORDS "Farewell—We're Good and Gone," the title of the familiar migration poem, were neatly chalked on one of the special trains heading North, symbolic of a collective hunger for deliverance. For many, the Great Migration was like a religious revival. After three hundred years of subjugation in the South, a taste of freedom was finally thought to be at hand. Wrote one migrant in Philadelphia, "I don't have to master every little white boy comes along. I haven't heard a white man call a colored a nigger you no now—since I been in the state of Pa. I can ride in the electric street and steam cars where I get a seat. I don't care to mix with white what I mean I am not crazy about being with white folks, but if I have to pay the same fare I have learn to want the same accomodation."[1]

The South in 1911 was an isolated region. It was not only that it was economically backward in comparison with the rest of the country; it also had fewer schools, lower levels of literacy, and less basic services than almost any other region. Rural areas of the South were particularly disadvantaged by lack of educational facilities and by lack of communication with the outside world. The absence of both radio and mail delivery meant that many rural residents knew of even major current events long after the fact.[2] Yet, in a matter of months, over 400,000 blacks were mobilized and transported from the farthest corners of the region. Given this improbable logistical feat, it is important to discover how migrants first found out about opportunities in the North. How does one get from Laurel, Mississippi, to the promised land? It is also important to understand the motivations for the move. Who were these people who had learned to want the same "accomodation"? By what incentives and inducements would they choose suddenly to leave an area their families had lived in for generations? How were they persuaded, and who financed the trip? In this chapter, such topics are addressed.

Lines of Communication

Migrations begin, it is suggested, not with well-established migration streams, but with the development of information links regarding the possibility of movement. Advanced economic centers to which migrants flock represent communications systems, to borrow a phrase from Melvin Webber, "vast complex switchboards through which messages [about migration] are routed."[3] Among the most important of these are recruitment messages: messages about job opportunities and transportation. Recruitment activities, according to Piore, explain both the timing of specific population movements and the particular areas between which migrant flows develop. It explains why "one region develops significant out-migration, and another, essentially comparable in terms of income, transportation costs, culture, and labor-force characteristics," does not.[4]

The assessment that such information is crucial to international migration was first made by Robert Park and Herbert Miller, who described the process of "migration chains." John MacDonald and Leatrice MacDonald have documented such processes for immigration to the United States. Sydney Goldstein has done so for migration within the United States.[5] The term "chain migration" has been used almost exclusively, however, for arrangements by means of primary social relationships, while the term "lines of communication" is broader in scope and includes both primary and secondary relationships. Lines of communication set up two-way channels of information between sending and receiving areas of employment, housing, education, climate, and general conditions of social life. These links are set up by (1) agents hired by employers in places of destination to recruit new workers, (2) "pioneers" who journey to sending areas and then correspond with family and friends, (3) organizations established either in receiving or sending areas with the special purpose of providing services (i.e., employment, housing, finance), who in the interest of expanding membership, also engage in recruitment, and (4) institutions, such as ethnic presses, that provide specialized information about job opportunities and social conditions for targeted populations.[6]

It is unlikely that any single line of communication would represent a sufficient linkage for the mobilization of migrating populations. Successful agents, to the extent that they remove available labor from sending areas, are often restricted by local governments in their activities and, in some cases, are prevented from carrying out their jobs. Service organizations must balance activities among the numbers of people they are equipped to handle, amounts of money available to them to provide services, and recruitment strategies that produce the most committed, knowledgeable client group. Institutions, such as the press, may represent the most extensive resource for providing information to potential migrants, though they, too, may be limited by local governmental restrictions and by their own acceptance in the community as a legitimate carrier of information. It is likely, then, that it is in combination that these lines of communication form the necessary links that make large numbers of individuals aware of opportunities in receiving areas.

Agents

In the Great Migration, the initial line of communication was established by agents of northern companies, acting as intermediaries between employers and potential labor migrants. Agents were paid a fee for each worker they were able to produce. Most "active in large cities where their presence [was less] conspicuous," some were paid merely to "walk briskly down the street through a group of black workers [and], without turning, say in a low tone," 'Anybody want to go to Chicago, see me.'"[7] According to Emmett Scott, "that was sufficient." Scott notes that "they were reported, at one time or another, in every section from which migrants went." Often, they got laborers to sign wage contracts at levels well below existing scales in the North. Agents were surprisingly selective of their recruits, considering they received a flat rate for each, favoring men over women, young over old, and healthy over infirm.[8] Frequently, stipulations as to age and health were written directly into the contracts. Misrepresentation was grounds for instant dismissal. Larger companies, in particular, made use of labor agents. In the summer of 1916, for example, the Pennsylvania Railroad used them to import "12,000 blacks to do unskilled labor."[9] The Illinois Central Railroad "also issued passes," through labor agents, "on which hundreds of blacks traveled to Chicago."[10] War-related industries like the steel mills, with contracts backing up and labor tight, did not hesitate to promise the moon to those who qualified, though they managed to pay low wages nonetheless.

In addition to agents of large, industrial firms, there were independent recruiters, "who charged migrants from $1.00 to $3.00 for placing them in jobs."[11] Independents also received fees from the smaller companies to which they directed the migrants.

The federal government was a less frequently mentioned though certainly active source of recruitment. In 1916, the "Immigration Bureau" of the Department of Labor, a bureau whose function was to place all Americans in jobs wherever they might be as a matter of patriotic duty, "helped hundreds of black workers to find jobs" in the booming war industries of the North.[12] An agency of the state itself was operating as an employment bureau in the interests of those who wanted to transport cheap labor from one region to another.

There was concern over all this activity in the South and resentment against the "conspiratorial" nature of the efforts to remove this labor, even among those who welcomed its exodus. In the winter of 1916, the Macon, Georgia, *Telegraph* urged the police to stop labor agents because:

> The invasion of the South for Negroes isn't just a temporary raiding of our labor market. It is a well-thought and skillfully executed plan to rifle the South out of its well-behaved, able-bodied labor.[13]

For many, a well-executed plan to extract black labor was more frightening than the loss of labor itself. A concerned state senator from Louisiana actually introduced legislation "to prohibit members of the race from going North." For others, the occasion, regardless of intent, provided a good opportunity to "generate revenue." Local officials in towns across the migration belt began to enact and enforce statutes either prohibiting labor agent activity or demanding license fees. Paying off these officials was a cost willingly incurred by some of the more established agents. The rest were forced to resort to more surreptitious measures. Some hired black stand-ins who could move, without notice, through the black community and gather workers. Others began working through the mails. Many sections were flooded with letters addressed to persons whose names had been obtained from migrants in the North.

Because of the constant activity of labor agents, many researchers have assumed that they paid for the trip North.[14] Yet, the volume of migration directly attributable to them seems to be minimal. Louise Kennedy concludes:

> During the first year or two of the European War, the direct appeal of labor agents from the North was responsible for the migration of members of colored laborers, but the activities of these agents were soon limited, as

many southern states attempted by legislation to prevent them from soliciting labor for northern industries.[15]

After initially providing "passes," the practice was soon abandoned in favor of one where transportation costs were advanced and later deducted from wages. Neither system, however, proved to be effective. Northern employers began to complain about the work force gathered by agents. Writes Kennedy:

> The earliest movements contained a large number who had not been economically successful in the South and were even greater failures in the North. They simply floated from one job and one place to the next, inevitably swelling the turnover rate for colored laborers as well as arousing the wrath and disgust of employers.[16]

Employers wanted to exercise more control. They demanded greater selectivity of labor agents and lent money to migrants to move their families only after they had been on the job "believing that you will get a better type of man when he is willing to pay his own way."[17]

Kennedy also suggests that there was often more rumor than fact to their presence. Almost as frequent as letters about labor agents were letters indicating that migrants had been victims of fraudulent practices of those passing as labor agents.

MOBILE, ALABAMA: DECEMBER 4, 1916

> Dear Sir: While reading Sunday's Defender, I read where you are coming South looking for labor. I see you want intelligent industrious men to work in factories so I thought I would write and get a little information about it. There are a lot of idle men here that are very anxious to come North. Every day they are fooled about go and see the man. Plenty of men have quit their jobs with the expectation of going but when they go the man that is to take them can't be found. Last week there was a preacher giving lectures on going. Took up collection and when the men got to the depot he could not be found.[18]

Passes and prepaid tickets distributed by labor agents were only necessary during the initial stages of the migration. Afterward, the movement became self-generating, and those desirous of leaving the South had to pay their own fares.[19] Nonetheless, the early activities of labor agents served not only to transport numbers of workers from South to North but also to plant the seeds of awareness of opportunities in those who remained behind. As one migrant wrote to the press, "I want to get some information about getting out up there I did learn that they had a man here Agent for to send people up there I have never seen him yet and I want you to tell me how to get up there."[20]

Family and Friends

Information provided by a trusted informant, such as family member or friend, is the keystone of communication lines. According to Scott, "Personal appeals in the form of letters have a recognized weight in influencing action."[21] Perceived as having nothing to gain by providing false impressions, their accounts of life and opportunity in receiving areas are persuasive. As Marta Tienda observes, "family members who migrated at an earlier time may be influential in attracting new migrants to an area and might also be available to cushion the potentially disorganizing consequences of immigrant adjustment."[22]

In the Great Migration, this situation is found to be true. Once begun by agents, migration streams developed on their own. "The arrival of each new migrant in the North created a new contact with potential migrants, and personal communication made the labor agents superfluous."[23] Letters from migrants to relatives and friends were said to generate the "moving fever," particularly when the letter "contained money" and "offered concrete evidence of success in the North."[24] Some suggested that nine out of every ten migrants went because of the appeal through letters of friends or relatives. "A woman from Hattiesburg [Mississippi] is credited with having sent back a letter which enticed away over 200 persons."[25] Some areas emptied out so thoroughly that one woman complained, "Ain't enough people I know left to give me a decent funeral."[26] A carpenter in Chicago wrote to his family in Mississippi, "I was promoted on the first of the month. I should have been here 20 years ago. I just began to feel like a man. My children are going to the same school with the whites and I don't have to umble to no one. I have registered, will vote the next election and there isn't any 'yes sir' and 'no sir'— its all yea and no and Sam and Bill." Wrote another laborer to friends in Alabama, "People are coming here every day and are finding employment. Nothing here but money and it is not hard to get."[27] From Cleveland came word from a migrant to his friend, "I am well and is doing fine plenty to eat and drink and is making good money." And writing to his family in Gulfport, Mississippi, a migrant reported, "I'm tickled to death over this place. Sorry I was not up here years ago."[28]

Some communities would send a small, advance group to test the waters. For a week or more a period of anxious anticipation and "watchful waiting" would follow. Finally, a card would arrive bearing the report, "Home ain't nothing like this." Discussions of opportunities in the North became a frequent recreation in the South. "In Hattiesburg, Mississippi, it was stated that for a while there was no subject of discussion but the migration." According to William Tuttle, "a common evening pastime was visiting the depot to ask the Chicago porters on the Gulf and Ship Island Railroad numerous questions about the city."[29] The information was then passed throughout the black community about "Chicago's climate, the public schools, voting, and jobs." According to the Urban League, "Friends in the North to give assurance on the question of the weather, would mention the fact that they were writing with their coats off."

Letters from the North were often read in churches, and according to Scott, "fresh news on the exodus was given out."[30] Out of these discussions, clubs were formed to facilitate the migration. Leaders whose purpose it was "to notify Chicago industries, newspapers, and placement agencies that a certain number of black people were available for employment and to request train tickets" were to arrange financing. The groups "ranged in size from two or three families to more than 1,000 persons."[31] The following suggests one such arrangement:

MOBILE, ALABAMA APRIL 21, 1917

Dear Sirs: We have a club of 108 good men wants work we are willing to go north or west but we are not abel to pay rail road fare now if you can help us get work and get to it please answer at once. Hope to hear from you.[32]

Letters expressed all the hopes and fears of those unfamiliar with "the promised land." Wrote one from Florida, "So many has left the South for the North and seems as they are all gone to one place." Wrote another, "It seem quite improbable that oppertunities for good wage earning positions such as factory work and too a chance for advancement would be given to the workers of our race."[33] Allan H. Spear concludes, "Personal letters brought news of the excitement of city life, of decent treatment by whites, and of high wages. They provided assurance that the North was not just a chimera." Family and friends "influenced thousands . . . who might otherwise have indefinitely postponed their decision."[34] Comments Charles Tilly, "For people moving without a guarantee of a job the presence of friends and relatives matters a great deal more than such things as the housing supply or availability of public assistance."[35]

Service Organizations

Service organizations represent the third line of communication. Voluntary associations, it has been noted, "operate as an adaptive mechanism in situations of rapid change undergone by urban migrants" and "to strengthen the consciousness of a groups' culture of origin."[36] The Urban League may be viewed as one such organization for the Great Migration.[37] The Chicago Urban League was established in 1917 during the "period of heaviest migration of [blacks] to the city."[38] According to the Chicago Commission on Race Relations, "the numerous problems consequent upon this influx guided the development of the League's major and most pressing activities." It is estimated that between 1917 and 1919, as many as 55,000 sought jobs and dwellings from the organization.[39] Its Industrial Department alone, during 1920, "placed more than 15,000 migrants in positions, made industrial investigations in sixteen plants, and provided lectures for working men in plants and for foremen over black workers. It also investigated worker complaints, selected and fitted men for positions, secured positions for blacks where blacks had never worked before, and assisted in other ways the adjustment of blacks in industry."[40] That migrants were aware of League activities and consulted them before journeying North is evident from many letters. The following is typical:

CHICAGO URBAN LEAGUE
BROOK HAVEN, MISSISSIPPI, 4/24/17

Sirs: I was reading in the defender that theare was good openings for Men in Smalle towns near Chicago would like to know if they are seeking loborers or mechanics I am going to come north in a few days and would rather try to have me a position in view would you kindly advise me along this line as I am not particular about locateing in the city all I desire is a good position where I can earn a good liveing I am experienced in plumbing and all kinds of metal roofing and compositeon roofing an ans [answer] from you on this subject would certainly be appreciated find enclosed addressed envelop for reply I want you early reply as I want to leave here not later than May 8th I remain respectfully yours,
    P.S. will say that I am a Man of family dont thing that I am picking my job as any position in any kind of shop would be appreciated have had 12 years experience in pipe fitting.[41]

In general, however, the League was more important as a resource in northern than in southern cities. The excitement that was generated by the other lines of communication caused some, paying their own railroad fares, to leave for the North without a promise of a job or indeed without any concrete plans. Many of these would head for the office of the *Chicago Defender* upon their arrival, and someone there would send them on to the offices of the Urban League.

Again, the League collected information on jobs and housing, provided clothing for those inadequately prepared for the northern climate, and granted any other social services as could be handled. In these years before the New Deal, when social welfare activities were left in the hands of state and local agencies and when the private assumption of responsibility was in fact much greater than the public, it provided a needed service for incoming migrants. Its participation in the mobilization process as a refuge for those who could not turn to family and friends made it an important link in the migration chain. It is likely that it had a "multiplier effect" on the migration, helping to establish newcomers without personal networks, who could, in turn, after their settlement, encourage family and friends to follow.

The Ethnic Press

Ethnic presses in particular attempt to satisfy "a new and pressing need for information" generated by migration.[42] An explosion of reading and writing even among populations illiterate in their language of origin, has been frequently noted.[43]

Journalism, for the exploited and the oppressed, has often proved to be a powerful and protective weapon. "Neither colonizers nor master races have been able to snuff out the spark of independence that finds expression in the printed word."[44] The black press in America is one such vehicle. In 1941 Willis Weatherford and Charles Johnson commented:

> Negro papers are first of all race papers. They are first and foremost interested in the advancement of the race. A large percentage of the editorials are concerned with justice to the race, with equal privileges, with facts of race progress, or with complaint against conditions as they are. Of course, there occur from time to time well written editorials on topics of general interest, such as world peace, better political adjustment, or the progress of civilization; but it still remains true that most of the editorials are distinctly racial. The articles in these papers are usually propaganda—that is, they follow the line of the editorials. A great many are genuinely inflammatory.[45]

Although a black press existed even before the end of the Civil War, it became a useful weapon for the black community at the turn of the century. An important step was the founding of the *Boston Guardian* by William Monroe Trotter in 1901. Trotter "rejected the conventional etiquette of cloaking protest in the niceties of circumspection and genteel language."[46] In 1905, Robert Abbott's *Chicago Defender* was born. Abbott, who began with $.25, a kitchen table, and a half dozen pencils, developed what eventually became a nationally distributed newspaper. The *Defender* ushered in the "role as an organ of racial propaganda" featuring bold, provocative headlines and, at the same time, an emphasis on corruption and scandal. Typical was an early headline which read, "100 Negroes Murdered Weekly in United States by White Americans."[47]

The paper also attempted to report on every lynching in the South and every case of burning and pillage. In one issue, it described in graphic detail the severed head of a lynched black man that had been "thrown into a crowd of Negroes on the principle Negro street."[48] According to federal investigator R. H. Leavell, "a photograph of what purports to be the head as it lies on the deserted street is published under the telling caption, 'Not Belgium—America!' Leavell characterizes the *Defender* as "extreme" and suggests it was "all the more effective, because there is a natural tendency to minimize such justification as may exist."[49]

Some have speculated that the more lurid tales from southern communities not even on the map were manufactured by the *Defender*'s editors, not so much because of the fantastic nature of the tales as because of the unlikelihood of the paper's access to such information.[50]

Several southern cities, in retaliation, attempted to prevent its circulation by confiscation. There are reports that in some communities the *Defender* had to be dropped off in rural sections and brought into the cities in the middle of the night. Other reports suggest that when circulation was prohibited, blacks had to rely upon subscription copies delivered through the mail.[51]

Despite numerous attempts to halt its distribution, the *Defender* was circulated. Stated federal investigator T. J. Woofter, the Chicago paper "makes its lurid appeal to the lowly class of Negroes. In some sections it has probably been more effective in carrying off Negroes than all the labor agents put together."[52] During the period under study, the *Defender* was said to have sold more than 150,000 copies an issue. Frederick Detweiler, who has studied the black press extensively, concludes that a more realistic estimate of readership is 1,000 readers to every 100 copies sold.[53] A correspondent of the *Defender* wrote: "White people are paying more attention to the race in order to keep them in the South, but the *Chicago Defender* has emblazoned upon their minds 'Bound for the Promised Land.'" Copies were passed around until they were worn out. One prominent southerner asserted that "negroes grab the *Defender* like a hungry mule grabs fodder. It was the *Defender*'s "pronounced racial utterances, its criticisms of the South," and "its policy of retaliation" that increased its circulation tenfold between 1916 and 1918. "I beg of you, my brothers, to leave that benighted land," wrote the *Defender* in one of its editorials. "And your leaders will tell you the South is the best place for you. Turn a deaf ear to the scoundrel, and let him stay," it advised on another occasion.[54]

Yet, the *Defender* did more than simply editorialize about the benefits of leaving. It published advertisements of employers, and those seeking work were instructed to apply to those companies—information not available in southern presses, white or black:

> Wanted: Men for laborers and semi-skilled occupations. Address or apply to the employment department. Westinghouse Electric & Manufacturing Co.[55]

These ads stressed opportunities for young, able-bodied males, "able to take charge of their positions." It was these announcements to which migrants responded:

BATON ROUGE, LA. APRIL 26, 1917

> Dear Sir: I saw your advertisement in the Chicago Defender. I am planning to move North this summer. I am one of the R. F. D. Mail Carriers of Baton Rouge. As you are in the business of securing jobs for the newcomers, I thought possibly you could give some information concerning a transfer or a vacancy, in the government service, such as city carrier, Janitor, or something similar that requires an ordinary common school education.[56]

The paper filled its pages "with photographs, cartoons and even poems" and emphasized "in the most convincing ways the great advantages which were awaiting [those] who would go North." It also, in the words of investigator Leavell, "promoted discontent with treatment received locally at the hands of whites in the courts, in the schools, in political life, and in the distribution of public improvements."[57]

One of the most curious events of the Great Migration was manufactured by the *Defender*. "'Millions to Leave the South' was the paper's banner headline on January 6, 1917. Northern Invasion Will Start in Spring— Bound for the Promised Land." Abbott reasoned that, "the setting of a definition time was a stimulus" to migration. May 15th, 1917, was to be the date of "The Great Northern Drive" (a drive accompanied by reduced fares and special accommodations). Abbott was right. Hundreds of letters were received both by the *Defender* and by social agencies, informing "them of many Negroes who were preparing to come."[58] The following is typical:

NEW ORLEANS, LA. MAY 2, 1917

> Dear Sir: Please Sir will you kindly tell me what is meant by the great Northern Drive to take place May the 15th on tuesday. It is a rumor all over town to be ready for the 15th of May to go in the drive. the Defender first spoke of the drive the 10th of February. My husband is in the north already preparing for our family but hearing that the excursion will be $6.00 from here north on the 15 and having a large family, I could profit by it

if it is really true. Do please write me at once and say is there an excursion to leave the south. Nearly the whole of the south is getting ready for the drive or excursion as it is termed. Please write at once. We are sick to get out of the solid South.[59]

There was, however, no great northern drive, no special excursion rates. The *Defender* was forced to declare "that there were no special trains designated to leave the southern stations on May 15th, and that this date had been set simply because it was 'a good time to leave for the north, so as to become acclimated.'" But the forces had already been set in motion; arrangements to leave the South had been made. And so thousands left anyway, paying the regular fares from savings and the sale of property and belongings. The exodus was, in fact, so great that the *Defender* later proudly declared, "'The Flight Out of Egypt,' the 'Black Diaspora,' had begun."[60]

The *Defender* was respected. In Gulfport, Mississippi, it was stated, a man was regarded as "intelligent" if he read the *Defender*, and in Laurel, Mississippi, it was said that "old men who had never known how to read, bought the paper simply because it was regarded as precious."[61]

For a while, it seemed that the more violent the reactions of white southerners to the *Defender*, the greater its appeal to the black community.[62] "To the persistent rumor in southern papers that blacks would freeze to death in the North," the *Defender* argued, "If you can freeze to death in the North and be free, why freeze to death in the South and be a slave, where your mother, sister, and daughter are raped . . . where your father, brother, and son are . . . hung to a pole (and) riddled with bullets."[63] Such editorials both angered and worried whites. "Letters arrived at the *Defender*'s office threatening to kill 'some of your good Bur heads' unless the newspaper started advising blacks 'to be real niggers instead of fools.'" In Madison County, Mississippi, a resolution was adopted "claiming that the *Defender* was German propaganda designed to revive sectional issues."[64] The Governor of Arkansas "announced his intention of asking the Postmaster General to exclude the paper from the mails." One letter writer to the *Defender* suggested, in fact, that his mail to the newspaper would be confiscated.

Now what I want you to doe for me is this will you please give this letter to the Chicago Defender printers and I will bee oblige to you. I wood of back this letter to the Chicago Defender but they never wood of receve it from here.[65]

These attacks served to increase the status of the *Defender*. As one letter writer expressed it, "Allow me to congratulate you on your wonderful paper it is a help to a lot of the people of our race it shows us the difference between north and south." Sadness was even expressed by those whose copies were not delivered. "I feal so sad in hart," a girl in Macon, Georgia, wrote to a friend in Chicago, "my definder diden come yesterday I don't no why it company to me to read it."[66]

Clearly the *Defender* was instrumental in prompting "thousands of blacks to venture North." The 1919 Chicago Commission on Race Relations stated, "Many migrants in Chicago attributed their presence in the North to the *Defender*'s encouraging pictures of relief from at home with which they became increasingly dissatisfied as they read."[67] As Kennedy concludes in her 1930 study:

> [From] 1916 to 1918 the Negro press was constantly urging colored people to leave the land of oppression and discrimination and fly to the freedom and equality which awaited them in the North. Probably the most influential of the Negro newspapers was the *Chicago Defender*, published in the North yet read widely in the South. This paper is said to have increased its circulation from 10,000 to 93,000 during the years of the war migration. . . . By constantly making the Negroes conscious of their "wrongs" and holding up before them the golden opportunities of the North and the example of their fellowmen, this newspaper and others like it crystallized the more underlying economic and social causes of discontent into immediate motives for migration.[68]

Yet, the real contribution of the press was not merely to lead but to provide expression for the nascent desires developing within the black community. Speaking of the role of the newspaper editor, Alex Edelstein and Joseph Contris state:

> The successful editor, by one means or another, attempts to feel the pulse of his community, to note changes in its structure and to observe shifts in its sources of power and influence. Under the impact of social change in the economic, social and political structure, the traditional roles tend to be modified and new roles emerge. The editor, as an individual, and the press as a social institution are faced with the continuing need to respond to change. Failures in perception might and do alienate the editor from the community and reduce his potential for leadership.[69]

The black press represented an important vehicle for the articulation of the goals of migration. Ethnic presses in general may be said to be the final, reinforcing link in the migration chain.

Lines of communication are crucial to understanding how information about opportunities in advanced economic centers is conveyed to those in outlying, remote areas. They reveal three aspects of the mobilization process. They suggest, first, that links develop in successive stages. Without labor agents, it is probable that the massive migration from the South would not have occurred. As labor migration research has suggested, mobilization is, at the beginning, external to individual experience.[70] Migrant movement between work and "home" is directed by "supra-market institutions beyond the control of an individual or even a group of migrants."[71]

Second, labor agents define the initial character of the migration. They are selective of populations, establishing standards of age, health, and gender. Piore notes of nineteenth-century American immigration:

> Throughout the period, there was an active recruitment system: In Europe, that system was controlled by the steamship companies and, possibly, the railroads. But they were, in turn responsive to the demands of labor agents, who met arriving immigrants at the port city or at major railroad centers in the interior. The labor agents catered in their turn to employers and were responsive to their demands. . . . Hence, it seems more plausible to attribute the shift in the character of the migration to the changing character of labor demand.[72]

Such practices, it is argued, relate more to the labor requirements of employers than to what has been perceived as the predisposition of certain types to migrate. Again Piore states, "Commentators at the time tended to attribute the shift (in the character of migration) to the nature of the new migration. . . . Even if one could trace the pattern of circular migration to the motivation of the migrants, however, it would not constitute a satisfactory explanation for the shift because the migrations were not spontaneous."[73]

Third, direct communication between the migrant and host societies are key ingredients in the mobilization process. Not only does this communication make migrants aware of opportunities and provide a vision of a better life but it also encourages them in new modes of thought. Black migrants from the South deliberately and consciously cast off southern caste traditions in journeying North. They had, through migration, learned to want the same accommodations.

Who Migrated

With contact established and communication made between North and South, it would seem that this is one of the easiest questions to answer about the Great Migration. Yet, contemporary accounts provide conflicting evidence:

It is not the riffraff of the race, the worthless Negroes, who are leaving in such large numbers. There are, to be sure, many poor Negroes among them who have little more than the clothes on their backs, but others have property and good positions which they are sacrificing in order to get away at the first opportunity. The entire Negro population of the South seems to be deeply affected.[74]

Past researchers have neglected the question of who left because the answers, beyond gross generalizations, have been thought to be as numerous as the migrants themselves.[75] Migrants are thought to represent an undifferentiated mass. Of the Great Migration it is said, for example, "People (particularly blacks) left rural areas to take jobs in towns and cities of the South and North."[76] It has also been stated, "The areas from which the majority of the migrants came were predominantly rural."[77] Little documentation follows such assertions beyond observations such as "To the poorly-paid Southern farm hands the wages paid by Northern industries—and paid in cold cash by the week instead of in store credit once a year—seemed fabulous sums."[78] Such observations obscure more than they reveal.

Jorge Balan, Harley Browning, and Elizabeth Jelin suggest that adequate accounts of what actually occurs in the course of migration from one place to another are uncommon, whether in developed or developing countries. The authors point out that the first step ought to be investigation of the evidence.[79] Portes suggests that one characteristic of labor migrations is that the migrants are drawn from a specific sector of the population.[80]

Discovering who migrated is central to this discussion, and a series of questions are raised: Should we assume that migrants were rural peasants because the rural population was large? Was this the most likely group to leave the South at that time? Was there a direct route from southern farm to northern city? If not, did the migrants journey first to southern city and then to northern city? If they first went to southern cities, how did they fare in competition with black skilled and semiskilled artisans who had at one time been widely evident in the South? What happened to these artisans? Examination of these questions bears on our understanding of the entire migration process.

There is logic in the popular assessment that a majority of the migrants came from rural areas of the South. First, in 1910, nearly 80% of the southern black population lived in rural areas. Second, the boll weevil invasion and flooding in the South forced hundreds of thousands of families out of agriculture. Third, the net population losses were greatest in agricultural regions. However, such an assessment ignores both the composition of the southern black population and the complex pattern of black migration within the South before the Great Migration.

Southern Black Workers: A Demographic Profile

Migratory patterns within the South reveal much about the composition of the southern black population. Although popular views picture most blacks as immobile before World War I, there was in fact much movement within the South soon after emancipation. Of particular interest is the movement of farm laborers. Dissatisfied with the low remuneration for their work, they set in motion between 1890 and 1910, three migration streams. In search of industrial employment, one stream advanced upon the towns, where they subsequently glutted the labor market and reduced the small earnings of those already in such jobs. Another stream migrated west to Texas and Oklahoma, where regular seasonal wages were higher. A final stream migrated to the newly opened iron and coal mines in Alabama, Georgia, and Tennessee.[81]

Although these movements were relatively small, they resulted in urbanizing 22% of the black population in the South by 1910.[82] And at least six years before the start of the Great Migration, nearly 2 million blacks lived in southern cities, which gained even more blacks after 1910.[83] Table 2.1 shows that the gains of southern cities during the first decade of the Great Migration (588) exceed those of the northeast and north central regions combined (167 and 247 respectively).

Overall populations of southern cities were increasing at an even faster

Table 2.1
Estimates of Black Intercensal Net Migration for Urban and
Rural Portions of Regions, 1910–1920
(in thousands; minus sign denotes net out-migration)

REGION	NORTH		SOUTH	WEST
	NORTHEAST	NORTH CENTRAL		
Black Population				
Urban	167	247	588	18
Rural	3	−17	−1,013	8

SOURCE: Daniel O. Price, *Changing Characteristics—Negro Population*, (Washington, D.C.: Department of Commerce, 1965).

rate than their northern counterparts. But overshadowing the comparative gains of these cities, is the assumption, though never tested, that those who moved from rural to urban areas of the South were the same people who later journeyed north. There were in southern cities after 1910 at least three groups of likely candidates for migration: old urban residents, those residing in cities before 1890; recent urban residents, those arriving between 1890 and 1910 and newcomers, rural laborers thrown off the land by the boll weevil. The question is, "which of these went North?" Lyonel C. Florant highlights the problem in pointing out:

> True, large numbers of southern negroes moved (from rural areas) to nearby towns and cities, but whether or not these same individuals comprised the majority of those who later arrived in northern cities has not been subject to verification.[84]

Florant thinks there were two segments of migrants: first those who moved from southern farms to southern cities, and second, those who moved from southern to northern cities.

This idea is difficult to confirm because the census did not include information on migrants beyond state of birth, sex, and age until 1940. It is possible, however, to make reasonable assessment of the actual steps leading to migration from the numerous documentary accounts.

Composite Image of the Great Migration Participant

If one were to piece together a composite image of the typical migrant from fragmentary but consistent surveys and accounts, one would have portrayed a black male between the ages of twenty-five and thirty-four, resident of a medium-sized southern city who had worked between five and ten years at one or two industrial enterprises, usually as an unskilled laborer. These men were said to be drawn "from favored and vigorous elements of the general population." Many were married and had children. When surveyed, a migrant frequently cited the following reasons for going North. First, he wished to better his economic circumstances. Some said simply, "to increase wages." Second, he wanted better educational opportunities for his children. And third, he desired greater freedom of movement.

Many migrants were hard at work at the start of the Great Migration and had to quit their jobs to move North. It was not simply the promise of higher wages that drew them to the land of opportunity. Many feared that their present position in the South would not last. There were too many laborers and too few jobs to ensure that black men, even at low wages, could remain employed while white men were made idle. A number of migrants had already experienced in their working lives layoffs motivated by racial as well as economic circumstances, and they reasoned that these occasions would increase.

The decision to leave the South was made not by a single worker but by the family unit, often involving extended family members. There were several reasons for this. First, it was very expensive to travel from the South to the North, and arrangements for financing the trip depended upon the support of family and friends. Florette Henri estimates that the regular passenger fare was $.020 per mile in 1915, and $.024 in 1918. From New Orleans to Chicago was 1,126 railroad miles; from New Orleans to Detroit, 1,096 miles; from Mobile to Cleveland, 1,046 miles. Thus, in 1918, it would have cost $22.52 per adult from New Orleans to Chicago, or over $90 for a family of six. A relatively short trip of 600 miles, Norfolk to Pittsburgh, would have cost a family of six $48.[85] It was not an easy thing for anyone to get to "The Promised Land."

Tickets to the North were purchased by selling all that was owned. Labor agents, as suggested, abandoned voucher systems early on because of employer complaints. Agents were also prevented from recruiting in some areas by high fees and official harassment. Paying for the journey with savings was the only reliable method available. When funds were insufficient, family members pooled their resources and sent a single member. It was hoped that in time enough money could be saved to take the entire family North. Abraham Epstein's study of five hundred migrants in Pittsburgh, for example, suggests that 80% of them paid for the trip through the use of savings and the sale of property and household goods. The Chicago Race Commission in its 1919 report estimated that 75% of their sample did the same.

Second, with the migrant absent from the family, his wife and other family members had to support themselves until the migrant made good. Many women took jobs, particularly as domestics, to support the family. They also sold household items and moved in with other family members to keep down costs. In some families, both parents went North and grandparents or some other family member cared for the children. Third, family branches or friends in the North had to be relied upon to help with finding a job and providing initial shelter. Many migrants did, of course, board trains in the South and arrive in a northern city without a job or knowledge of how to get one. But a majority arrived with a name and address of someone, often previously contacted, who would be used to cushion the shock of the move.

Previous Work Experience

Information on the previous work experience of migrants provides the most direct support for the composite image. Epstein's study suggests that the agricultural sector was only 26%, with 5% of these individuals owning their own farms.[86] Seventy-four percent of the migrants in his study were nonagricultural laborers (see Table 2.2). The Chicago Commission on Race report suggests that only about one in four were engaged in agricultural employment.[87] A Department of Labor survey found that about half came from southern towns, with experience in lumbering, railroading, and iron and steel foundries.[88] A large number of nonagricultural experiences were also reported in the letters of the Scott collection.[89] George Haynes, head of the Negro Employment Division of the Department of Labor, who made an extensive study of the migration in 1919, described migrants as "industrial, unskilled workers many of whom were men with families or other dependents." Haynes found that, "the men went first to earn money and look over the ground. Dissatisfied with low wages, treatment and other conditions of their southern communities, many of these people accepted offers of work."

In a less comprehensive manner, the *New York Age* reported in an article in August 1916 that thirty-five Negroes were taken to Chicago by Morris and Company and given employment in their stockyards. According to

Table 2.2
Occupations of Migrants in Pittsburgh as Compared with
Statements of Occupations in South

Occupations	In Pittsburgh	%	In South	%
Common Laborer	468	95	286	54
Skilled or Semiskilled	20	4	59	11
Saw Mill Workers & Miners	0	0	45	9
Farmers	0	0	136	26
(Ran Own Farm	0	0	33	5)
Other Occupations	5	1	0	0
Total	493	100	529*	100

ADAPTED FROM: Abraham Epstein, *The Negro Migrant in Pittsburgh* (Pittsburgh: University of Pittsburgh Press, 1919).

*Differences in total may be owing to those with overlapping occupations.

the article, the men had previously been employed in the packing houses in Alabama. In another front-page piece one week later, the paper stated, "Another industrial opportunity for the Negro artisan is opened here in one of the largest establishments in this town and one of the largest machinery plants in the country. Skilled men, familiar with work in pattern shops, machine shops and foundry will be employed from $2.75 to $4 per day." While in still another story, it maintained investigation by the Urban League had found that a company in Holyoke, Massachusetts, "offers one of the best opportunities yet opened for the Negro artisan. The company proposes to employ eventually at least two hundred colored men, if qualified workers can be found."[90] Haynes believed that skilled artisans shared the dissatisfaction of the others and left with the rank and file on whom they largely depended for patronage. It is likely that the term *artisan* used in these reports exaggerates the level of the workers' skills. However, it may also be reasoned with some certainty that these workers did possess some skill. The companies were interested in employing "qualified workers."

Other contemporary reports mention "skilled" workers among the migrant population. In a 1923 report, prepared by a commissioner of the Department of Labor, an attempt was made to assess the proportion of skilled workers included in the ranks of migrants in several large industrial areas. Payroll data were secured from 273 employers of black labor in fifteen states. The employers listed with the department had 42,371 black workers in 1922 and 60,421 in 1923. Table 2.3 shows that the proportion skilled among that group is one-quarter of the population in both 1922 and 1923.[91] Similarly, a 1923 report of 122 migrant workers in Waterbury, Connecticut, suggests that the skilled represented about 30% of the work force.[92]

From the perspective of the South, researchers frequently mention the problem of the loss of experienced labor. Commenting after the start of the migration, federal investigator W. T. B. Williams stated, "In a number of industries production has slowed down, owing to the necessity of breaking in new men to take the places of experienced men, as in the lumber mills all over the South, in the mines, on the docks, and, as is likely to prove in the cotton oil mills."[93] Reports from Alabama suggest a familiar finding:

> The Negroes most sought after in the Birmingham district have been the coal miners. There has been a constant demand in the mines of Kentucky, West Virginia, Pennsylvania, and Virginia for the experienced miners here. Several months' time is required for turning a raw recruit into a skilled miner. The places of those who left could be filled only by the "boll weevil" negroes from the black belt.[94]

Table 2.3

Number of Skilled and Unskilled Migrants in Selected States* by
Number and Percentage, 1922 and 1923

| | April 30, 1922 | | April 30, 1923 | |
Classification	No.	%	No.	%
Skilled	10,794	25	14,951	25
Unskilled	31,577	75	45,470	75
Total	42,371	100	60,421	100

SOURCE: U.S. Department of Labor, "1923 Report of Migrants in 15 States," *Monthly Labor Review* (January 1924).

*273 employers surveyed from California, Connecticut, Delaware, Illinois, Indiana, Kansas, Maryland, Massachusetts, Michigan, New Jersey, New York, Ohio, Oklahoma, and Wisconsin.

The substitutions were helpful. Observed federal investigator Williams, "there were found so many willing substitutes that industries were able to keep steadily at work." There were numerous small-scale reports of this sort. Estimating from those where percent skilled were studied, it is reasonable to conclude that about one-quarter of all migrants were representatives of the black artisan class. These were the old urban residents. Using census summaries, Table 2.4 further indicates dramatic shifts in the proportion of southern black workers who were skilled and semiskilled between 1910 and 1920. Alabama, South Carolina, and Georgia, the heart of the old plantation system, have particularly high rates of skilled and semiskilled workers in 1910. By 1920, these proportions have dwindled considerably. It should be noted that the relative declines are most evident in those states where the greatest out-migration occurred. The interpretation advanced is that the relative decline in the proportion of skilled workers simultaneous to increasing industrialization is owing to the concomitant effect of displacement and out-migration. Lorenzo Green and Carter Woodson support such a position when they suggest that in the case of those possessing skills, "the South pushed its artisans out, the North pulled them in."[95]

Urban Residence

The number of skilled workers among the migrating population is also important because it refutes the idea that migrants left rural areas for the

Table 2.4
Proportion of Black Males in Skilled and Unskilled
Manufacturing and Mechanical Trade Positions, 1910 and 1920
in Major Southern States

State	Year	
	1910	1920
Alabama*	(32,604)	(56,384)
% unskilled	64%	92%
% skilled and semiskilled	36%	8%
Arkansas	(15,718)	(22,658)
% unskilled	77%	76%
% skilled and semiskilled	23%	24%
Florida	(25,492)	(34,688)
% unskilled	70%	70%
% skilled and semiskilled	30%	30%
Georgia*	(39,345)	(60,752)
% unskilled	48%	65%
% skilled and semiskilled	52%	35%
Kentucky	(17,715)	(18,308)
% unskilled	61%	61%
% skilled and semiskilled	39%	39%
Louisiana	(38,138)	(47,655)
% unskilled	72%	73%
% skilled and semiskilled	28%	27%
Mississippi	(25,702)	(33,140)
% unskilled	74%	72%
% skilled and semiskilled	26%	28%
North Carolina*	(31,891)	(46,133)
% unskilled	67%	70%
% skilled and semiskilled	33%	30%
Oklahoma	(6,233)	(8,081)
% unskilled	80%	76%
% skilled and semiskilled	20%	24%
South Carolina*	(34,952)	(32,587)
% unskilled	46%	62%
% skilled and semiskilled	54%	38%

Tennessee*	(21,939)	(33,623)
% unskilled	63%	75%
% skilled and		
semiskilled	37%	25%
Texas	(27,027)	(41,794)
% unskilled	81%	75%
% skilled and		
semiskilled	19%	25%
Virginia	(39,737)	(52,109)
% unskilled	68%	64%
% skilled and		
semiskilled	33%	36%
West Virginia	(4,207)	(4,932)
% unskilled	68%	64%
% skilled and		
semiskilled	32%	36%
Total (U.S.)	(360,700)	(486,012)
% unskilled	65%	72%
% skilled and		
semiskilled	35%	28%

SOURCE: U.S. Census of Population, 1910 and 1920.
* These states taken together account for 76% of migration population.

North. For the most part, artisans practiced their trades in southern cities.[96] But artisans, as shown, represented only one-quarter of the migrating population. It is more difficult to determine how many of the rest were rural or urban or some combination of the two. There were few direct means of gauging the number of migrants who were unskilled laborers and, like artisans, prior residents of southern cities, that is, recent urban residents. One indirect way of measuring the urban component is to examine population turnover in southern cities. In Table 2.5, the absolute numerical increases in the black population of major cities are delineated as well as the percent change of the black population as a percent of the whole. The relatively small increases in the urban black population together with an absence of change in their relative proportions suggests, at least potentially, that rural and urban populations could have traded places in southern cities. Emmett Scott hints at this when he explains, "It is next to impossible to estimate the numbers leaving the South even on the basis of the numbers leaving the cities. It is conservatively stated, for example, that Birmingham, Alabama, lost 38,000 negroes. Yet within a period of 3 months the negro population has assumed its usual proportions again."[97] As Charles Johnson writes, "closing first upon the little towns of the South, then upon the cities near the towns, and, with an unfailing consistency, sooner or later, they boarded a *Special* train bound for the North, to close in upon these cities which lured them."[98]

Literacy

To suggest that most migrants spent some time in southern towns and cities does not, however, specify the duration of that residence. Rural laborers may have worked in southern cities only long enough to finance the trip North. This doubt may be addressed by examining literacy. Because of the greater availability of schools in urban areas and the near absence of them in rural ones,[99] literacy indicates residence for some time in an urban area.

Stanley Lieberson's work on literacy and the selectivity of black migration bears on this point.[100] Lieberson wanted to discover whether the large-scale movement out of the South of the black population in 1910–1920 had a negative impact on the literacy rates of blacks in the North. That is, would literacy rates in the North have been higher if there had been no black out-migration from the South?[101] He found for the period of the Great Migration, opposite to what had been found in the past, that the rate of literacy was actually slightly higher than would have been predicted had there been no out-migration. This finding suggests that there was, during the Great Migration, a significant out-migration of literate blacks (see Table 2.6). It should be emphasized that the selectivity is particularly evident within the younger age cohorts and is stronger for

Table 2.5
Percentage of the Southern Population Living in Urban
and Rural Areas, 1900–1920
(in thousands)

Race	1900	(% of Total)	1910	(% of Total)	1920	(% of Total)
Black						
Urban	19.2 (1,365)	(6)	22.1 (1,954)	(7)	25.3 (2,251)	(7)
Rural	80.8 (5,727)	(27)	77.9 (6,895)	(23)	79.7 (6,661)	(20)
White						
Urban	21.8 (3,052)	(14)	23.2 (4,761)	(16)	29.0 (6,993)	(21)
Rural	78.2 (10,967)	(52)	76.8 (15,786)	(54)	71.0 (17,089)	(52)
Total	(21,111)		(29,396)		(32,994)	

SOURCE: Daniel O. Price, *Changing Characteristics—Negro Population* (Washington, D.C.: Department of Commerce, 1965).

men than for women.[102] These characteristics are consistent with the recruitment criteria of northern employers and labor agents and of standards suggested by the advertisements in the black press. The importance
of the literacy finding lies not in a general assessment that urban workers
are literate. Indeed, literacy is not a criteria for nonagricultural employment in the South at this time. Rather, the point is that high rates of literacy among this migrating population suggest that a majority were neither
rural laborers nor newcomers to southern cities. Concludes Lieberson:

Table 2.6
Selective Black Migration from the South Net Migration
Rates from the South, Blacks Groups by Age, Sex,
and Literacy, 1890–1920

Decade and Initial Age	Net Migration Rate			
	Male		Female	
	Illiterate	Literate	Illiterate	Literate
1890–1900				
15–24	−.01770	−.06530	−.01139	−.07191
25–34	−.01079	−.02228	−.00781	−.02023
35–44	.00941	.03483	−.00504	.02866
45–54	.00317	.01012	−.00566	.05037
55+	.00225	.02669	.00061	.16043
1900–1910				
15–24	−.01355	−.06520	−.01019	−.05679
25–34	−.00465	−.01169	−.00655	−.00591
35–44	.01082	.04272	−.00295	.01838
45–54	.00619	.01179	−.00336	.03499
55+	−.00219	.02426	−.00531	.08007
1910–1920				
15–24	−.03410	−.16668	−.02225	−.12395
25–34	−.02702	−.10043	−.01655	−.06579
35–44	−.01023	−.01738	−.01415	−.05237
45–54	−.00651	−.02741	−.01512	−.06039
55+	−.00657	−.02423	−.00796	−.06072

SOURCE: Stanley Lieberson, "Selective Black Migration from the South: A Historical
View," in *The Democracy of Racial and Ethnic Groups*, edited by Frank D. Bean
and W. Parker Frisbie (New York: Academic Press, 1949).

The great pull of southern blacks exerted by the conditions in World War I and its aftermath, as well as the South's unwitting push owing to the dismal outlook for blacks, was particularly powerful among the better educated young adults of the South.[103]

From the foregoing, it is evident that a much more selective segment of the black population left the South than previously has been assumed. It was not, as Kennedy claimed, "the Negro peasant who turned cityward."[104]

In answer to the question "Who migrated?," then, it is suggested that instead of the simple movement of the southern rural peasantry to northern cities, there occurred a complex movement of rural blacks to southern cities and a significant movement of skilled, semiskilled, and unskilled laborers and their families to northern cities. To paraphrase Charles Tilly's conclusion of the migration of the 1940s, "Anyone who keeps echoing the old idea of nonwhite migration to cities as simply an invasion of bewildered country folk is now, at best, behind the times."[105]

Moreover, the assessment that this first migration was made up significantly of nonagricultural laborers calls into question much of the explanation for the nonassimilation of black migrants in the North. Horace Hamilton, for example, writes, "The migration of the Negro population from rural to urban communities, from southern states to the metropolitan centers of the nation, has been and will continue for many years to be a major cause of human misery, social maladjustment, and interracial misunderstanding." The suggestion is, as he later states, that "the decline in agricultural employment made it almost inevitable that large numbers of Negroes would change occupations and places of residence more or less simultaneously."[106] In other words, the rural background of southern migrants led to their "misery and social maladjustment." This point is echoed by Wilson Record, who states "social disorganization, inherent in the uprooting of a rural and quasi-literate people, would have occurred even in favorable economic conditions."[107] Thus, "a rural and quasi-literate people" would have experienced a slow pace of assimilation regardless of economic conditions—a conclusion that explains if not condones their exploitation. However, nonagricultural laborers who in going North did not change occupations, reinforces an unsettling specter of the artificial fragmentation of the working class. As labor migration theorists have suggested, through invidious racial distinctions in the words of Castells, "a major trump card for the bourgeoisie in the struggle against the working class" is produced.[108]

Migration and the Women Who Serve

The Great Migration has been called the "great watershed" of black American experience. Yet one of its most striking features, that it made little difference in the working lives of black women, is rarely addressed in the literature. In part, the neglect is reflective of the general disregard of women and women's work in society. The low status and meager compensation of black women in particular masked the pivotal role they played in the maintenance of themselves and their families. This neglect is also characteristic of the way in which migration is studied. It has, in much of the social science literature, a male theme. Works are called, *Men in a Developing Society, Black Men, White Cities*; tables are calculated for men only and women, when discussed at all, are relegated to a note that mentions their special situations that deserve, but rarely receive, some future investigation.

Studies on the Great Migration, in particular, focus on "dramatic events," labor agents, northern industries, and the recruitment of black men. The mundane but necessary efforts of women seem to fade in contrast. In fact, one is left with the impression that the women simply waited for the men to make enough to carry them and the children North. At best, such works, by default, imply a relatively passive and secondary role for women, placing them on the periphery of the dynamic of migration. The explanation for the inattention to the role of women in general and black women in particular lies not only in the objective reality of their low status but in the fact that the basis of their contribution has been "casual," usually domestic, labor—labor not generally recognized as either real or meaningful. Black women, forced into the marketplace, were employed in the most hidden of occupations. Though they were making contributions that literally put food on the table, the "naturalness" of the work masked its importance.

Thus, from the end of slavery to the beginning of the Second World War, a significant number of black women were trapped in the demeaning yet demanding labor of domestic service. It was work, wrote W. E. B. DuBois, "that brought a despised race to a despised calling."[109] Unlike white women, "whose entry into the factories in the early nineteenth century coincided with industrialism, black women were excluded from virtually all areas of employment except domestic service."[110]

Domestics work long hours, longer than those in industrial employment, receive the lowest wages, and work in isolated settings. It is work that is unstandardized and unorganized, requires no formal training, and from which employees may be fired for lack of cause and without notice. "Often," state Ella Baker and Marvel Cook, a domestic's "day's slavery is rewarded with a single dollar bill or whatever her unscrupulous employer pleases to pay. More often, the clock is set back for an hour or more. Too often, she is sent away without any pay at all."[111]

In many southern communities, it was claimed that conditions for these workers were as bad, if not worse, than during the days of slavery.[112] One married worker stated that she was "compelled by contract to sleep in the house where she worked and allowed to go home only once in two weeks for an afternoon visit. Her duties included cleaning, cooking, caring for three small children and always being on call for any member of the family between midnight and morning." She was "the slave, body and soul of this family," a position for which she received ten dollars a month.[113] But women had no other choice. Going North required their necessary financial contribution and sacrifice. As Jacqueline Jones points out:

> Domestic service recapitulated the mistress-slave relationship in the midst of the late nineteenth-century industrializing America. As paid labor became increasingly associated with the time-oriented production of goods, the black nurse, maid and cook remained something of a labor force anachronism in a national if not regional (southern) context.[114]

In small towns and cities throughout the South, married women were employed on a regular basis as cooks, maids, and laundresses. Some were able to do these tasks on a part-time or contractual basis, but most were forced to spend long hours away from home, bending over someone else's sink, washing someone else's clothes, and caring for someone else's children. Ironically, service was considered easier in the South; domestics could live at home and exercise greater control over work routines. These were said to be reflections of interaction patterns begun in slavery and indications of the premodern orientations of black women workers.

Yet, in the context of the goals of migration, it is clear that black women used domestic service in a rational way. It was used first of all as a method of maintaining and sustaining the family in the initial separation of them from the male migrant worker. "When a laboring man got paid off," quotes Scott, "he bought himself a suit of overalls and a paper valise and disappeared."[115] Women ran the households and were forced "to make do," as one expressed it, until the migrant was settled and remittances were sent. Often, in addition to employment, they sacrificed furniture, household items, anything of value to maintain the family. What was left over was saved for the journey North. These tasks were not easy. As one commented in a letter, "so many women here are wanting to go. They are all working women and we can't get work here so much now, the white women tell us we just want to make money to go North and we do."[116]

Making money to go North was a consuming activity and a second major contribution made by women. Whatever could be held back was saved for the journey. As Emmett Scott points out, "young married women refused to wait any longer than the time required to save 'railroad fare.'"[117]

It was not only married women who were involved in such negotiations. Rosalyn Baxandall, Linda Gordon, and Susan Reverby cite the example of a mother attempting to negotiate for herself and her daughters.

JACKSONVILLE, FLA. APRIL 29, 1917

My dear Sir:
I take grate pleazer in writing you. as I found in your Chicago Defender this morning where you are secure job for men as I realey diden no if you can get a good job for me as an A woman and A widowe with two girls and would like to no if you can get one for me and the girls. We will do any kind of work and I would like to hear from you at once not any of us has any husbands.[118]

One familiar method of transportation for a woman was to sign a low-wage domestic labor contract that would pay costs in exchange for service over a specified period. A fee equal to one or two months' wages to be paid to the labor agent who made the arrangement was also required. Gilbert Osofsky cites a typical labor contract:

In consideration of my expenses being paid from Richmond to _____ and a situation provided for me, I agree to give _____ services after arrival as _____ to party or persons paying my expenses. And I further agree that all my personal effects may be subject to their order until I have fulfilled that contract, forfeiting all claims to said personal effects after sixty days after this date should I fail to comply with this agreement.[119]

These agreements paid the transportation costs for a single worker.[120] However, such contracts bound women to employment in the North. They were hardly free wage labor, their very belongings could be claimed by their employers in case of default.

Women as well as men directly contributed to the maintenance and transport of the migrant and the rest of his family from the South to the

North. Their crucial participation, often ignored because of the stigma attached to the work they were forced to perform, adds another dimension to the question of who migrated.

Conclusion

From the preceding discussion, a compelling case has been made for the mass exodus. The migration of black workers from the South represented a carefully orchestrated mobilization of over 400,000 people—a specific sector of the population who had been displaced and made disadvantaged by job competition. Urban skilled and unskilled labor migrants, many of whom were literate, were persuaded to give up all they had to move North. Families were forced to make great sacrifices to "save the fare." Women as well as men had to make contributions. Yet, migrants did not leave the South on their own, simply to raise wages and improve conditions. They were in some ways minor actors in a play that starred forces greater than what Charles Johnson has called "an almost uncanny unanimity of triumphant approval to this urge to migration."[121]

The question that remains unexplained in this scenario, then, is why. What were the structural transformations underway in the South that made it expedient to let go hundreds of thousands of cheap and experienced workers? And why would the North want this resource now, when presumably it had not wanted it before? It is to these topics that the next two chapters will be addressed.

CHAPTER THREE

The South before the Great War

Economy, Labor, and the Struggle for Power

Boll weevil got the cotton
Cut worm in the corn
Debil in the white man
We's going on.
—quoted in Seth M. Scheiner,
    *Negro Mecca: A History of the Negro in
    New York City, 1865–1920*

MOVING BEYOND THE LABOR unrest at the early stages of industrialization is the most difficult task of any developing society. In the South, the problem was complicated by the factor of race, which, superimposed on the structure of class, created loyalties and conflicts that were as deeply ingrained as they were contradictory. The period between the end of the Civil War and the industrial takeoff in the 1880s had been a time used by employers to find the measure of labor, white and black. The problem was that there were vast pools of workers often randomly placed who were indistinguishable save by race. Employers had to devise a way to prevent unhappy clusters of people from coming together in southern cities and demanding a larger share of what could become a booming industrial economy. They had on their side a tradition of white supremacy that tainted any attempt at biracial cooperation. And they feared, on the other, the clumsy efforts during Reconstruction and more successful ones in the Populist revolt that threatened to ignite what Reinhard Bendix has termed the "revolutionary potential" of the early phase of development.[1]

The turn of the century was a critical moment in southern economic history. Because of the newfound stability of Redemption, northern investors had provided enough capital to industrialize, and new factories were springing up across the region. The boll weevil and floods destroyed both the profitability of cotton and the harm of its single-crop dependency. But issues of composition, compensation, and competition of labor within the new order had yet to be resolved.

Black workers were caught in this economic struggle without any capital of their own. After centuries of agrarian dominance, the new industrial order brought decline rather than improvement in the training of black labor. In the cities, blacks were in a fierce competition for the lowest wage; and although literacy itself was likely to become a minimum requirement for even the most unskilled job, blacks were increasingly denied educational opportunity for their children. These deleterious conditions served to spawn the mass migration of black nonagricultural workers. They were literally pushed out of the South. Ironically, by leaving, they helped to further the cause of southern economic development. Industrialization at its early stages produces fewer jobs. The migration of blacks served as a useful safety valve because it reduced the labor surplus. Industrialization at its early stages destroys the privileged position of artisans. Slavery had created black monopolies in many trades, and black artisans left in large numbers during the Great Migration. Workers in the early stages of industrialization demand political recognition. White workers sought and were given a kind of political participation but one made weak by their agreement to use the ballot to support only one issue, the disenfranchisement of blacks.

The New Economy of the South

The South began to industrialize in the 1880s, some fifty years after its neighbors to the North. Its path to industrialization was slow and halting even though many believed that Northern industrial diversity, as contrasted with an economically homogeneous South, had largely contributed to the failure of the Confederacy. By 1920, over half of the entire population (57%) was still engaged in agriculture, a figure that compares to the North of 1850. Most industries in the South were low-wage and low value-creating enterprises that used large supplies of unskilled labor.[2] Only rarely did these manufacturers produce finished goods for the ultimate consumer. Observed the *Manufacturers' Record*, "Much of the manufacturing of the South is still largely a case of production of materials that are used elsewhere as materials in manufacture."[3]

The South was also an area drawn in sharply etched relief. At the end of the Civil War, it was the poorest region in the land. By 1880, its share of wealth in the nation was about 11%. This figure translated into an annual per capita income of $376 in the South as compared with $1,086 per capita in the rest of the country. The national average per capita was $870.[4] Yet, the area had the richest reserves of any region in the United States; 96% of the bauxite, 93% of the phosphate rock, 69% of the natural gas, and 63% of the petroleum.[5]

The comparison between "the South's poverty and the North's wealth was more than a regional disparity in a living standard."[6] According to Woodward, it was more instructive to view their differences in terms of contrasts between nations in Europe at that time. "In 1880 the estimated per capita wealth of Russia was approximately 27 percent of that of Germany. In the same year per capita wealth in the South was almost exactly 27 percent of that in the northeastern states of New England, New York, New Jersey, and Pennsylvania."[7]

The contrasts presented between an agricultural South and the industrial North were so stark that an image of the South as an underdeveloped country is appropriate. In a distribution of the percentage of workers engaged in manufacturing, a simple measure of industrial progress, it is evident that the rates for the South are well behind those for the North in 1880. (See Table 3.1). States like Alabama, Georgia, and Mississippi were four to five times less industrialized than the state of Vermont; ten times less than states like Massachusetts and Rhode Island. While the proportions in manufacturing doubled in some southern states between 1880 and 1900, the initial levels were so low that comparisons with the North remained dismal.

Part of the overall explanation for the slow pace of industrialization in the South is found in the continued profitability of its major regional industry, cotton. As Table 3.2 suggests, even with yearly fluctuations in price per pound, the acreage devoted to cotton increased steadily from 1880 to 1920. At the end of the Civil War it had at first appeared that cotton supremacy was at an end. The burning of the fields, the lack of capital, and the freeing of the slaves were devastating blows to an area ravaged by war. But cotton, which had been king not only of the southern economy but of the American export market as well, recovered.[8] It had to do so at first, however, without the backing of northern capital because of the perceived instability of the region. The South on its own, because worldwide demand for cotton remained stable, created an internal financing system and feebly nursed itself back to health.

The reorganization of labor was the first and single most important step toward the cotton recovery. One result of emancipation had been that black workers were free to contract their labor and "with relatively short

Table 3.1

Persons Engaged in Manufacturing and Mechanical Pursuits
as Percentage of Total Gainfully Employed
by Selective Regions, 1880–1900

North East	1880	1900
Rhode Island	55.4	52.2
Massachussets	50.2	46.2
Connecticut	46.8	45.3
New Hampshire	39.8	42.1
New Jersey	38.6	39.4
Pennsylvania	30.8	32.6
Maine	28.4	29.9
Ohio	23.6	27.7
Vermont	20.3	25.2

South	1880	1900
Alabama	4.2	7.8
Arkansas	4.2	6.7
Florida	8.1	14.5
Georgia	5.8	9.6
Kentucky	11.2	12.9
Louisiana	8.1	9.7
Mississippi	3.0	4.7
North Carolina	6.5	12.1
South Carolina	4.8	9.9
Tennessee	7.6	9.5
Texas	5.6	7.4
Virginia	11.6	14.1
West Virginia	12.6	14.2

SOURCE: Statistical Abstract of the United States (Washington, D.C.: Government Printing Office, 1932).

supplies to have power to insist on alternative arrangements" to the old plantation system. The preferred alternative was the partition of the antebellum plantation into smaller tenancies, each operated by a single family and divided into farms rented to freedmen, "either for a fixed rent or, more typically, for a share of the crop."[9] According to Leon Litwak, under this system "the black laborer was provided the feeling if not the actual status of a family farm."[10] For the landowners, the substitution of tenant farming for plantation labor made little difference, and they willingly acquiesced to the change.[11] Observes Henry Grady, "the planters are still lords of acres, though not of slaves."[12] The speed and success of the transformation is evident from census records. By 1880, only 9% of the agricultural land in crops could be considered plantations. The blow caused by the loss of slave labor was thwarted.

Thwarting the blow caused by the loss of financing was achieved in another manner. Southern banks and cotton brokers were "paralyzed" by the war and the failure of the southern banking system to reestablish itself quickly left many cotton producers without capital.[13] "The resulting 'credit shortage' kept many factors from reestablishing their businesses and sharply curtailed the operations of those who did attempt to do so," argue Roger Ransom and Richard Sutch.[14]

Further limiting the extension of credit in the South was the National Banking Act, legislation enacted during the Civil War, that significantly altered banking practice throughout the country. Basically, the act "established a minimum requirement of $50,000 in paid-in capital before a bank could obtain a national charter."[15] Congress further reduced the viability of state-chartered banks by creating a 10% tax for them. With insufficient capital, very few national banks were established and state institutions were also limited in number. John Hicks discovered, for example, that "one hundred and twenty-three counties in the state of Georgia were without any banking facilities whatever."[16] In their stead, a number of "private" banks appeared in southern cities. Ransom and Sutch point out that although these "new banks served the interests of the commercial establishments in the cities, they were not well adapted to deal directly with agriculture."[17] Further, the tradition of lending farmers the money in advance of the crop made it too high a risk for these marginal operations. Rural banks, unchartered businesses even more fledgling than the urban ones, developed to take up the slack. Quite frequently, the term "bank" itself was a misnomer for a lending operation run from a general store. However, according to Ransom and Sutch, the rural merchant in this period, filling the void left by other interests, became the major financier of cotton. In the absence of other direct financing, he kept the industry alive.[18]

The rural merchant helped to make cotton manufacture an important ingredient in the economic recovery of the South, but at a high price. The system established was costly in terms of exorbitant interest rates that influenced production, expansion, and profit. Farmers were exploited for short-term gain rather than controlled for long-term stability. As Hicks explains:

> Cotton almost served the purpose of money, for it was always marketable, it was comparatively imperishable, it could not be consumed by the producer and it was comparatively easy to handle. The merchant, therefore, wished his customers to raise cotton, and he objected strenuously if they proposed to raise other articles instead.[19]

Table 3.2
Demand for Cotton
Cotton Acreage, Production, and Price, 1880–1920

Year	Acreage Harvested (1,000 acres)	Production (1,000 bales)	Price Per Pound (cents)
1880	15,921	6,606	9.93
1881	16,483	5,456	10.66
1882	15,638	6,949	9.12
1883	16,295	5,713	9.13
1884	16,849	5,682	9.19
1885	17,922	6,576	8.39
1886	18,370	6,505	8.06
1887	18,793	7,047	8.55
1888	19,520	6,938	8.50
1889	20,191	7,473	8.55
1890	20,937	8,653	8.59
1891	21,503	9,035	7.24
1892	18,869	6,700	8.34
1893	20,256	7,493	7.00
1894	21,886	9,091	4.59
1895	19,839	7,162	7.62
1896	23,230	8,533	6.66
1897	25,131	10,899	6.68
1898	24,715	11,278	5.73
1899	24,663	9,346	6.98
1900	24,886	10,124	9.15
1901	27,050	9,508	7.03
1902	27,561	10,630	7.60
1903	27,762	9,851	10.49
1904	30,077	13,438	8.98
1905	27,753	10,576	10.78
1906	31,404	13,274	9.58
1907	30,729	11,106	10.36
1908	31,091	13,241	9.01
1909	30,555	10,005	13.52
1910	31,508	11,609	13.96
1911	34,916	15,694	9.65
1912	32,557	13,703	11.50
1913	35,206	14,153	12.47
1914	35,615	16,112	7.35
1915	29,951	11,172	11.22
1916	33,071	11,448	11.22
1917	32,245	11,284	27.09
1918	35,038	12,018	28.88
1919	32,906	11,141	35.34
1920	34,408	13,429	15.89

SOURCE: U.S. Bureau of the Census, *Historical Statistics of the United States, Colonial Times to 1970*, Bicentennial Edition (Washington, D.C.: U.S. Government Printing Office, 1975), pp. 517–18.

The merchant in effect forced the farmer into excessive production by refusing credit to those who sought to diversify crops. For a while, higher than usual prices masked the instability of the system. However, when prices began to decline and supplies and interest rates remained at premium levels, the only way out became increased production. By 1880, "the farms of the Cotton South were devoting over 50 percent of their acreage to cotton."[20]

This concentration also suppressed all other forms of manufacture by draining southern savings and sustaining the largely unskilled and illiterate labor force. In terms of economic growth, the continued emphasis on cotton production impoverished the South and made its work force less competitive than its northern and western counterparts. In political terms, however, it did serve to put off the problem of controlling black and white labor in a profitable manner. Cotton maintained the castes and classes of the South practically at their antebellum levels. A "let sleeping dogs lie" attitude prevented economic diversification even in the face of powerful arguments that a single-crop dependency was harmful.

Cotton suppressed, but did not prevent, development. For one thing, the South had an abundance of raw materials; and the North, having used up its cheaply extracted ones, had begun an extensive search for new resources. As suggested initially, depletion of natural resources is a crucial prerequisite for any labor migration. By the 1880s, there began to appear in southern newspapers and journals an explosion of articles about raw-material extraction and manufacture.[21] Unable to finance production through indigenous capital, manufacturers made massive appeals to outside interests.

Ironically, cotton manufacture was the first industry to take off. Between 1880 and 1890 a new manufacturing domain was created in the Piedmont area of the Carolinas and Georgia. *"From the Fields to the Factories"* was the slogan. During this time, "southern cotton mills increased in number from 160 to 400; spindles from 500,000 to over 4 million, mill operatives from 16,000 to over 97,000."[22] The cheaper labor of the South crippled the once prosperous New England mills and set the stage for further development.

One new industry was a by-product of cotton, the cottonseed-oil mill. Cottonseed oil was both a cheap substitute for lard and olive oil and a major ingredient of margarine. Although the discovery of its usefulness had been made before the Civil War, its manufacture was left untouched until this period of investment interest. Unlike the cotton textile industry, centered in the Carolinas and Georgia, the cottonseed-oil mills were scattered throughout the cotton states.[23]

Iron and coal industries also experienced tremendous growth during this time. Concentrated in Birmingham and Chattanooga, they brought employment and new wealth to a region that, in the 1880s, had stagnated under an industry that was "feebly organized, dispersed, and antiquated." With modernization, "the production of southern pig iron increased from less than 400,000 tons in 1880 to four times that amount ten years later."[24]

The bituminous coal industry was bolstered during this time by the development of new methods of exploration. In 1880, the output had been a mere six million tons, but had increased to "twenty-six million in 1890 and to twice that amount ten years later."[25] West Virginia and parts of Alabama were the centers of this industry, but it was also found in Tennessee, Virginia, and Kentucky.

Southern timber extraction also doubled between 1880 and 1890, making the South the number-one source of lumber in the nation. In North Carolina and later in Virginia and Tennessee, furniture-making industries featuring high-quality products, low labor costs, and proximity to raw materials, prospered.

Tobacco, no less than the other industries, expanded its production and greatly increased its profits in the 1880s. North Carolina, Virginia, and Kentucky were industrial centers of plug and smoking tobacco. Florida and Louisiana led in the manufacture of fine cigars.

Throughout the region, then, new industries were emerging and old ones were being greatly expanded. The South was experiencing an industrial revolution. Ironically, it was financed by northern investors who had at the end of the war been unwilling to support the cotton recovery. Their willingness to invest in the South grew over time. As early as 1860, New York financier Hamilton Fish remarked that "the South would be splendid colonies to the North."[26] By the 1870s and 1880s, northwestern lumber depletions had produced speculation by northern investors in the rich southern reserves of timber. In 1888, it was noted that northeasterners controlled the best yellow pine and cypress lands and were to reap the benefits from the rising timber industry. Southern railroad development also attracted northern capital. Between 1880 and 1881, $150 million in northern and foreign capital had been invested in southern railroads. "By the 1890s, the consolidation of these railroad companies had placed more than half of the railroad mileage in the South in the hands of a dozen large companies and their affiliates."[27]

Northern capital also became prominent in southern mineral industries. Stated an 1884 report from Birmingham, Alabama, "The Mineral Land Company of Alabama was organized here today with W. H. Woods, president, and E. Randolf, and others, all of New York, directors. The company owns all land formerly the property of Selma, Rome and Dalton Railroad Company, comprising 450,000 acres, much of which contains valuable coal and iron mines."[28]

There was an even greater interest in encouraging northeastern investments at the turn of the century. C. Vann Woodward states, "as the old century drew to a close and the new century progressed through the first decade, the penetration of the South by northeastern capital continued at an accelerated pace."[29] Northern control over the entire railroad system was completed by 1903. The southern iron and steel industry between 1893 and 1913 repeated the pattern followed by the railroads. "By 1909, the new southern mineral province of bauxite became the property of the Mellon Aluminum monopoly. Cotton production was the last of the southern industries," observes Woodward, "to conform to the pattern of colonialism." The industry was forced into change because, unlike lumber, "its chief products had to be shipped North for final processing before going to the consumer." Thus, both the financial support from the North and the dependence upon northern processing, ceded control of the South's most prominent industry.[30] It was a transformation with symbolic as well as economic and political implications.

The South's lack of ownership and control of its own industries created a dependent relationship throughout its economic system. Consumer goods, whose prices continued to rise, were manufactured or assembled in the North and sent South for sale. Decisions on development and expansion were made in corporate boardrooms thousands of miles from the center of production. Wrote one disgruntled New England laborer, "Our capitalists are going into your country because they see a chance to make money there, but you must not think that they will give your people the benefit of the money they make."[31] Even indigenous capital chose to invest in profitable, large national companies as opposed to more risky regional industries. In short, wealth flowed from the South to the North.

But industrialization and development alone did not transform the South. The area was also jolted into change by the coming of the boll weevil,[32] which had an immediate impact. Unknown in the United States before 1892, within two years it had spread to half a dozen counties in southern Texas (see Map 3.1). Thereafter, year by year the boll weevil infestation slowly advanced eastward across the region. Between 1910 and 1917, the heaviest infestation was in Alabama, Georgia, and Mississippi (see Map 3.1). Not surprisingly, it is these states which account for the heaviest out-migration from the South. An insect had finally accomplished what agriculturalists had been urging for years; southern farmers reduced their concentration upon cotton and shifted into other crops.

3.1 MAP OF THE BOLL WEEVIL INVASION

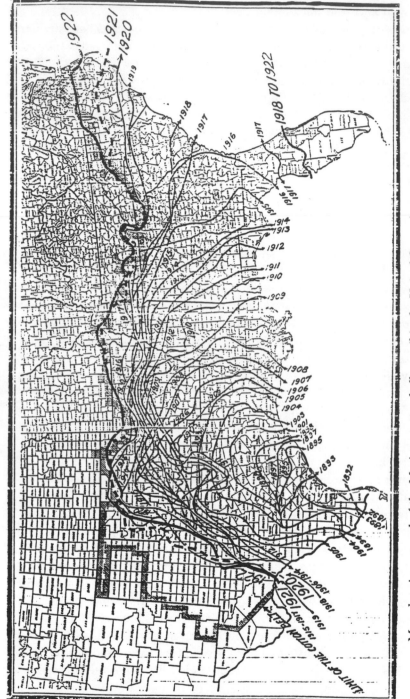

Map showing spread of the Mexican cotton boll weevil in the United States from 1892 to 1922, inclusive.

NOTE: The outer limit of the cotton belt advances or recedes slightly from year to year, and as shown on the map is not entirely accurate for 1922, as shown by the fact that in a few places the boll weevil line is a little in advance of the indicated limit of cotton culture.

SOURCE: U.S. Department of Agriculture, Farmer's Bulletin, #1329 (June, 1923).

In the path of the boll weevil, millions of acres of cotton were destroyed. Thousands of landlords were forced to dismiss their tenants and to close the commissaries from which came the daily rations. Some planters in Alabama and Mississippi advised their tenants to leave and even assisted them.[33] In the Sea Islands, South Carolina, cotton production dropped from 1,688 bales in 1918, one year before the invasion, to 167 in 1919, when the area was overrun by the pest.[34] Banks and merchants, who in the past had given mortgages for crops before they were produced, refused to extend credit when cotton was no longer to be available as a security. Consequently, a great number of tenants were left without productive work, money, or credit. "Boll weevil got half the crop," went one familiar song, "White man's got the rest." So thousands of rural laborers, black and white, were forced to go to southern cities in search of work, and the precarious labor balance threatened to erupt into a full-scale crisis.

Yet, the boll weevil's importance for migration related not to its manufacture of a rural "peasant" who drifted into northern cities but to its creation of one who helped to flood the more uncertain market of the South. R. H. Leavell's 1917 assessment of migration from Mississippi bears on this point. Leavell found not a single but several movements of labor occurring simultaneously, from farm to southern city, and from southern to northern city. Further, Leavell was skeptical of the notion of the fabled Mississippi sharecropper relocating in the North. He observed, "It is clear that the mere fact of a Negro's having moved out of his former home is no evidence that he moved to a northern city. It was town Negroes who left the region."[35]

By 1910, the South had ended its sole reliance on cotton and had achieved a level of industrial diversification. Yet, a changing economy in the region was not producing the standard of living consistent with the new order promised in the booster campaigns. Table 3.3 captures some of the shortcomings. Between 1860 and 1920, there had been a large increase in the value of manufacturers; but these levels as a percentage of the total had not reached in 1910 what they had been in 1860.

According to Woodward, after years of intensive effort, the South remained largely a raw material economy, with the attendant penalties of low wages, lack of opportunity, and poverty.[36] Its citizens could visualize the rewards of an advanced industrial economy but not taste its fruits. They produced the cloth but could not afford to wear it; they made the furniture but could not place it in their houses. "The new economy brought gasoline, automobiles, mechanical refrigerators, alcoholic beverages, insurance policies, foodstuffs and a hundred and one other articles endeared to the southern public through advertising. Yet the burden of

Table 3.3

Levels of Manufacturing in the South, 1860–1920

Year	Value of Manufactures	% of Total of U.S.
1860	$ 193,500,000	13.3
1870	277,700,000	6.6
1880	338,800,000	6.2
1890	706,800,000	7.5
1900	1,184,400,000	9.1
1910	2,637,100,000	12.1
1920	$8,375,400,000	13.4

SOURCE: *Statistical Abstract of the United States* (Washington, D.C.: Government Printing Office, 1932), p. 845.

these purchases on a poor people was devastating."[37] That the plight of the black worker was greater than that of the white, may not, however, be located purely in the new economy. To a large extent, both blacks and poor whites suffered the same deprivations of class. To black workers, however, was added the deprivation of their lower caste. They were entered into an economic competition with their arms and legs bound. It is to this topic that the next sections will be devoted.

Conditions of Black Labor in the South

Sharecropping and debt peonage usually dominate any discussion of black labor in the South between 1880 and 1916. However, as shown in chapter 2, it was not the agricultural laborer who went North in large numbers. The purpose of this section is to explore the special circumstances of the nonagricultural laborer that led to his displacement and migration.

Black southern nonagricultural workers are often ignored in the literature. Resident in southern cities, a minority of the black population, they are thought to be too insignificant to justify more than a few well-chosen sentences. Historian John Cell is one who has not neglected this group and attributes to their growing urban presence the necessity of the relatively late development of the legal system of segregation. According to Cell, Jim Crow was introduced not for the black "peasant" but for the proletariat. He describes these workers as, "bankers, undertakers, insurance salesmen, teachers, barbers, carpenters, masons—often their own bosses, city blacks were better educated, better organized politically, and more 'uppity' than those in the country."[38] It was these individuals who were readily mobilized, willing and often financially able to make the journey North.

To understand why urban workers, some of whom held relatively good jobs, migrated, it is necessary to chronicle the changes in the conditions of labor that enveloped the South after the industrial takeoff. The South began its slow path to recovery in the early 1880s with black workers dominating the lower ranks of the job hierarchy. Suggests Cell, "maintaining the large supply and low cost of labor had been the primary function of the South's political economy."[39] Blacks were mired in low paying, irregular, and low status positions swelling the ranks of the unskilled. They were, for example, especially plentiful in the tobacco factories, where they monopolized the production of chewing tobacco. They were also employed in "tanneries, cotton seed oil companies and in the rolling mills throughout the South. They were in demand as day laborers for hazardous occupations in the railroad yards, on the docks and in well digging and sewer building."[40] They did the dirty work of southern society, and most lived on the edge of poverty.

To say that things got worse for these urban workers after the turn of the century seems impossible, but their problems were three-fold. First, even before the boll weevil invasion, poor whites living in rural areas, "moved by isolation, poverty and harsh living conditions," began streaming into cities.[41] They came into immediate competition with black workers, and both groups were forced to undercut each other in terms of wages or starve. Second, the labor glut itself caused jobs to be redefined and thereby destroyed the advantage black workers had had by doing caste labor. Third, with the coming of the boll weevil, hundreds of thousands of rural blacks poured into cities and into competition with everyone already there.

Black urban workers, already disadvantaged by their low wages, were thus being undercut by an even cheaper rural reserve; and the labor glut created unemployment. In 1900, unemployment among blacks was about 13%. The situation grew worse as the decade wore on.[42] Writes Emmett Scott:

> A host of idle persons thrown suddenly on the labor market could have no other effect than to create an excess in the cities to which they flocked, make laborers easily replaceable, and consequently reduce wages.[43]

A southern paper in commenting on the unemployment declared, "there is nothing for this excess population to do. These people must live on the workers, making the workers poorer."[44]

The fierce competition over a limited number of jobs resulted in further antagonism and, for black workers, frequent displacement.[45] Complaints over their loss of employment were commonplace. Woodson cites the following:

> The husband in this family is 57 years old and has worked 11 years as a car builder's helper. His weekly wages is $14.40. The work is hazardous and he sees no chance of promotion. He stays there because it is steady and dislikes both the low wages and the danger. He was not in the strike which they had a few years ago because he was afraid that he would lose his job. The wife says, "The whites done taken all of our men's jobs; they are street workers, scavengers, dump fillers, and everything. All white men got the jobs around the city hall that colored use to have."[46]

Skilled blacks were the first group to face displacement. At the end of the Civil War, they had outnumbered whites by five to one. White workers had been slowly easing them out of these positions ever since. By 1890, black monopolies in most crafts had disappeared. By the turn of the century, the very presence of blacks in the crafts was also threatened. An appeal from New Orleans is typical of this group.

> Dear Sir: I am a water pipe corker and has worked foreman on subservice drainage and sewer in this city for ten (10) years. I am now out of work and want to leave this city.[47]

Many white southerners delighted in this change. "It is possible now," wrote an observer in 1904, "to live in New Orleans as free from any dependence on the services of Negroes as one could be in New York or Boston."[48] Although in 1879 the city directory had "listed 3,460 blacks as carpenters, cigarmakers, painters, blacksmiths and tailors, not 10 percent of that number were employed in the same trades in 1904. Yet the black population had gained more than 50 percent."[49]

The plight of the black artisan was something of an anomaly. Note Greene and Woodson, "Paradoxically enough, the struggle in the South was the reverse of that in the North. In the latter sector the whites were securely entrenched in the trades and the Negroes were trying to get in. In the South, however, blacks were strategically situated in the trades at the beginning of this period and the whites were trying to get them out."[50] Industrialization brought to the South destroyed the privileged position of the black artisan.

Examination of the experience of carpenters is instructive. In 1900, 80% of the black carpenters in the United States were in southern states.[51] In the North, employment for blacks was heavily concentrated in domestic and personal service, with only a fraction in the manufacturing and me-

Table 3.4

Woodson on Carpenters

Number of Black Carpenters by States in the South and

Selected North, for the Census Years 1900–1920

State	1900	1910	1920	
Alabama	1,807	2,601	2,552	Decline
Arkansas	569	1,120	1,250	Increase
Florida	1,150	2,181	2,052	Decline
Georgia	3,385	4,537	4,952	Increase
Kentucky	701	813	599	Decline
Louisiana	1,711	2,811	2,843	Increase
Mississippi	1,497	2,258	2,173	Decline
North Carolina	1,500	1,979	2,127	Increase
Oklahoma	35	448		
South Carolina	2,695	3,171		
Tennessee	1,308	1,685		
Texas	769	1,255		
Virginia	1,619	1,950		
West Virginia	76	110		

SOURCE: Carter G. Woodson, *The Negro in Our History* (Washington, D.C.: Association for the Study of Negro Life and History, 1932), p. 21.

chanical trades.[52] Woodson provides in Table 3.4, information on the distribution of carpenters in twenty-five states including eleven southern states.[53]

It is evident from this table that in both 1900 and 1910, opportunities for employment as carpenters are much greater for black workers in the South than in the North. Between 1910 and 1920, a changing pattern is evidenced. In the South, where manufacturing and mechanical trade positions in general and carpentry positions in particular are on the increase, positions for black workers are actually on the decline in five out of nine states.[54] Black workers, it appears, are not only unable to pass their skills on to their sons, they are in some cases unable to retain those formerly held. In the North, where opportunities in carpentry for black workers were practically nil in 1900 and 1910, dramatic increases are seen between 1910 and 1920. It must be noted that the states with the largest increases, New York, Michigan, and Illinois also received the heaviest inmigration.[55]

The decline in the fortunes of the rest of the black urban population followed close upon that of the artisans. A migrant writing from Houston in April 1917 highlights the major concerns of nonagricultural workers:

HOUSTON, TEX.: APRIL 19, 1917

> Dear Sir: I am a constant reader of the "Chicago Defender" and in your
> last issue I saw a want ad that appealed to me. I am a Negro, age 37, and
> am a core maker by trade having had about 10 years experience at the busi-
> ness, and hold good references from several shops, in which I have been
> employed. I have worked at various shops and I have always been able
> to make good. It is hard for a black man to hold a job here, as prejudice
> is very strong. I have never been discharged on account of dissatisfaction
> with my work, but I have been "let out" on account of my color.[56]

The displacement of black labor was sometimes achieved by "dramatic
processes." In Mississippi, for example, "seven blacks were murdered,
seven wounded, and one flogged because they held jobs as firemen on
a division of the Illinois Central Railroad." In Louisiana, "white merchants and landowners were urged to give preference to white laborers
over black laborers. A steamboat company there went so far as to replace
all of its black crewmen with whites."[57] In other cases, laws were
established prohibiting blacks from following their trades, such as a law
"depriving blacks of the right to cut white persons hair."[58]

Frequently, white workers demanded jobs formerly monopolized by
blacks because labor-saving machinery had been introduced. The tobacco
industry, until 1885, was largely manufactured by antebellum methods.
In the decade following, "the making of cigarettes, smoking tobacco, and
chewing tobacco was so thoroughly mechanized" that by 1900 it could
be said of what had been a handicraft industry that "everything from the
stemming of the leaf to the payment of wages is done by machinery."[59]
With these technological changes, a new occupational democracy began
to invade southern consciousness and replace the previous scorn for certain types of "nigger work."[60] Indeed, with the acceptance of whites as
barbers, waiters, and streetcleaners, calls of "back to the cotton fields—
city jobs are for white folks" were often heard.[61]

By 1910, it was clear that an industrializing South was not a mecca of
employment opportunity for black workers. Unemployment among them
had reached 20%. As Table 3.5 shows, those engaged in manufacturing
and mechanical pursuits, a census category roughly parallel to the industrial sector of the labor force, represented only 9% of the work force, or
roughly half a million people. Over 60% of the black population in 1910
was still engaged in agriculture, most of that in cotton, 18% in domestic
and personal service, and 11% in all other occupations combined.

Conditions for the new industrial workers, particularly the half a million blacks, were deplorable. Because of the abundance of labor, the
wages earned by all operatives were, in fact, from 30% to 40% lower than
those paid in the rest of the country. Moreover, there were no restrictions

Table 3.5

Labor Distribution of the Black Population 10 years of Age
and Over in the South: 1890, 1900, 1910 by Number
(in thousands) and Percentage

	1890		1900		1910	
Agriculture	1,703	(62)	2,062	(61)	2,847	(62)
Manufacturing	137	(5)	209	(6)	413	(9)
Transportation	110	(4)	142	(4)	184	(4)
Domestic	769	(28)	924	(27)	827	(18)
Other	27	(1)	67	(2)	321	(7)
Total	2,746		3,404		4,592	

SOURCE: U.S. Department of Commerce, Bureau of the Census, "The Social and Economic
Status of the Black Population in the United States: An Historical View, 1790–
1978," *Current Population Reports*, Special Studies Series P–23, no. 80 (1978), p. 73.

upon hours of work, age or sex of operatives, or hazard in the work environment.[62] There was also no job security, a result, in part, of a regional
history of unsuccessful labor organization.[63]

Mississippi provides a particularly good example of the complexity of
the employment situation for black workers. A state "with a larger percentage of blacks than any other in the Union," one that "lost a large
number of its working population," and yet one of the least industrialized
states of the South. Even with its anomalies, the migration from Mississippi was highly selective. Sawmill workers were in demand from Laurel
and Hattiesburg; dock workers, from Gulfport and Biloxi. The southern
half of the state in general, with its rich reserves and greater resources,
contributed much more significantly to the exodus than the poorer and
more isolated regions of the north and east. The labor loss quickly ef-
fected key industries and prompted some like the editor of the *Biloxi Her-
ald* to express genuine regret over the decline in what he called "the most
valuable labor supply in the state."[64]

The South's loss of its artisan class and its oversupply of unskilled and
inexperienced labor is, in part, what made it an attractive area for investment. "There was progress," wrote Pete Daniel, "if measured by smoke-
stacks, spindles and editorials." Yet, he continues, "poor blacks and
whites continued to be ground on a treadmill."[65] The replacement of
urban blacks with what was called "boll weevil Negroes" had at least one
salutary effect. An unskilled and divided work force is very difficult to
organize. This fact was not lost on southern boosters who stressed that
the area contained a "large body of strong, hearty, active, docile and eas-

ily contented Negro laborers" and claimed as well "the same virtues for the hardy native Anglo-Saxon stock."[66]

The average worker, regardless of color, suffered in the new order. He found, like many modern workers in the Third World, that the introduction of large, external corporations may actually be a very unstable base for employment and upward mobility. In few industries did wages rise significantly, and in many they remained the same or declined. In the tobacco industry, for example, cigar makers made 26 cents an hour in 1890 and 25 cents in 1900. Bricklayers' wages rose in the South Atlantic states from 35 to 37 cents an hour, while falling from 45 to 43 cents in the South Central states. Carpenters in these states got 26 cents an hour in 1890 and 27 cents in 1900.[67] Yet, production during this period soared. And, for the worker, costs continued to rise.

Low wages and high costs had to be supplemented by the employment of women and children. Of the over 1 million male children between the ages of ten and fifteen gainfully employed in the United States in 1900, the South, excluding Maryland and Delaware, accounted for nearly 60% (715,339); and it was as high (276,111) for the over 487,000 girls at work. The number of children between ten and fifteen gainfully employed was about three times as great among blacks as among native whites.[68] In 1910, 56% of the black females in the South were employed as compared to only 45% in the North and West. Among white women, the percentages were less than half that, with 17% employed in the South and 20% elsewhere.

Added to the meager wages and necessary employment of family members were long work weeks. Even in the all-white cotton mills, the average work week was seventy hours. Until 1906, the lowest minimum in any southern state was sixty-six hours a week, a seventy-five-hour week was not uncommon, and the average week in North Carolina in 1906 was sixty-nine.[69] Those at the bottom of southern society could hardly look upon the New South as an advance.

Black workers, in particular, experienced all of the disquieting aspects of the new economy. Low wages, high costs, high unemployment, and constant competition represented the fruits of their labor. The South for the first time was brought into the industrial contest with the North, and its shortcomings were made all the more evident by comparison.

That such economic conditions may be translated into motivations for migration is clear from the testimony of migrants:

PENSACOLA, FLORIDA 4/29/17

Dear Sir: In reading the Chicago Defender I saw yore want add for foundary ware house and yard men I do truly ask you to pleas give me some instruction How i can get there I am a working man I am not sport or a gamble or class with them if i know it But I am study every day working man of family wife and one child 9 years old but this is hard time in the South now and I have not the means to come.[70]

"Wages is so little we can't get out we want to leave the South and work," wrote one.[71] For another, "twenty years experience in yellow pine lumber," was an insufficient incentive to stay in the South and he was "willing to do any thing else that pays."[72] A man who had been employed as a porter, packer, and assistant shipping clerk complained, "I cant live on the pay." An experienced machinist helper, who was also "fireing boiler" and "steamfitter," from Greenville, South Carolina, was "willing to do laboring if you can not get me one off those jobs above that I can do."[73]

The impact of southern development was three-fold. First, it brought an isolated and backward South into the orbit of economic relations with the North, thus transforming everything from work itself to consumer demands for disposable items. Second, it transferred not only wealth but control of manufacture from South to North, thereby creating dependent and unequal exchange for the region. Third, it produced great expectations about the progress of a region as it was simultaneously displacing and impoverishing large sectors of its population. It is these very forces that theorists cite as important stimulants to international labor migrations.

Thus, the South of 1910 was underdeveloped. It was an agrarian society that had lost its source of wealth and an industrial economy only beginning to expand. Southern labor had many of the same problems as peripheral workers from developing regions today. In constant competition for a limited number of low paying, hazardous jobs, workers struggled for their very subsistence. Blacks, in particular, found themselves falling farther and farther behind in a land that was beginning to prosper. From the first boll weevil appearance in 1892 to the first trainload in 1916, migrants had incentive to flee the land of oppression. Even so, the mass migration was still some six years away.

The Struggle for Political Power

Between 1890 and 1910, a majority of black adults in southern states lost the right to vote. Political disenfranchisement had its roots in the new economy. Before capital could be invested, the area had to be made safe. Curiously, it was not foreign domination that brought political stability to the South and initiated the northern penetration of the economy but the withdrawal of federal troops. The unstable Reconstruction governments, considered "positively harmful to important northern interests" were forced out by Redeemers who promised "money invested here is as safe from the rude hand of mob violence as it is in the best United States bond."[74] While popular images picture Reconstruction governments as "barbaric rule" filled with corruption, ruinous taxation and high public debt, it has been shown that many of the unworkable strategies were tied to rather lofty ideals.[75] The achievement of Redemption for the South was realized in part by the fact that these governments had heavily taxed the South's citizens to pay for road construction, levees, dams, public buildings, and most importantly, a free public school system.[76] The progressive legislation introduced during Reconstruction became unpopular because it was costly. More dangerous than the public services provided to all citizens were the various measures introduced in state legislatures in support of labor tenants. Southern employers found the idea of the legal protection of workers repugnant. The *Manufacturers' Record*, for example, proclaimed "'long hours of labor and moderate wages' the rule of the South." Fears were also expressed about a social environment that was only maintained by the presence of federal troops.[77] Southern economic development awaited a change of leadership that would wrestle power from the hands of Reconstruction governments. Like foreign investment of the present day, governments that are favorable to outside interests and able to keep the peace, are mandatory. Change was accomplished most dramatically by the terrorism and intimidation of organizations like the Ku Klux Klan, and more effectively by the famous Compromise of 1877.[78]

The South had frequently been an important subject in presidential election years, and 1876 was no exception. Democrat Samuel Tilden, former governor of New York, faced Ohio-born Rutherford B. Hayes. The campaign was bitter and the election close. On election night, Tilden had a quarter of a million popular-vote plurality, but only 184 electoral votes, one short of the number required. Hayes had 166 electoral votes. Three southern states—South Carolina, Florida, and Louisiana—held between them 19 disputed electoral votes; a sufficient margin of victory for either side. Both sides in these states claimed the votes. Congress was supposed to decide the issue. According to Woodward, "The question was, who was to count the votes? Neither the Constitution, nor the laws and rules nor precedent and custom offered an acceptable solution. The strongly Democratic House of Representatives and a staunchly Republican Senate were completely at odds on methods proposed."[79]

The Republicans, who needed not just one but all of the contested ballots, set out upon a strategy to reinforce their position as a party of business and to disengage themselves from the "black burden" of the southern wing of their party. During Reconstruction, the Republican party had remained in power by their enfranchisement of and companionship with the black vote. However, in 1876, with the South as the key to victory, the party began to "reinterpret the southern problem and to view as anachronistic their policy of appealing for the votes of a propertyless electorate of manumitted slaves with a platform of radical equalitarianism."[80] As Woodward suggests, "The Republicans deserted them and undertook to protect the capitalist and manufacturer of the North."[81]

Although it may not be persuasively argued that the Republican party in general and northern business in particular directly precipitated the fall from power of blacks, it may be suggested that they willingly accepted the southern view that the price of a stable economic environment was the elimination of blacks from the political process.[82] Northern businessmen spearheaded bargaining sessions aimed at winning over to their side a new South full of capitalists rather than planters. An argument was constructed that Reconstruction governments were "bleak periods" in legislative history to support the view that most blacks were not ready for full political participation. Expansion into overseas markets in the Philippines and throughout southeast Asia also created a new northern "understanding" of race relations. Most simply, black men had become the white man's burden. As the magazine *The Nation* expressed it, "If the stronger and cleverer race is free to impose its will upon Cuba and the Philippines, why not in Mississippi and South Carolina."[83]

The Republican party hoped to capitalize upon the South's poverty and need for capital. For some time, the southern business community had been making "desperate" appeals for money. At first, relief had been applied to from the northern business community.[84] But a panic in 1873 caused these investors to retreat and the South to remain impoverished. As a last resort, legislators turned to the federal treasury making a case based on the numerous "subsidies, grants, bonds and appropriations" given to northern enterprises during the Civil War. The South, they argued, taxed to pay for such appropriations, should receive some of their benefit. Their internal improvement bills, however, were turned down. A new strategy of "retrenchment and reform" had swept the North.[85] Northern Democrats, who at best had an uneasy alliance with their southern wing, were particularly strong in their opposition to subsidies to private enterprises, North or South.

The Republicans, long supporters of such subsidies, seized upon the southern desire for internal development as well as the demand for the removal of federal troops as the keystones of the 1877 compromise. Their overtures to the South were successful, Hayes was elected president, and a new era was inaugurated. The South got its "stability" and the capital necessary to begin full-scale industrialization. But from the end of the Civil War to this point had taken thirteen years. The Compromise of 1877 signaled not only the end of Reconstruction and the fall from power of "radicals" but also the black population. It helped to usher in a new era of both economic and race relations and required legislative support to reinforce the dynamics of both. At the state and local levels, new principles were immediately put into operation. In response to the "extravagance of the Reconstruction governments," Governor George F. Drew of Florida stated that his administration "would spend nothing unless absolutely necessary." But this concern over public debt extended no farther than unwillingness to pay for public services for the masses. Redemption governments were famous for their "exorbitant grants of land to corporations" and an absence of regulation of almost any kind. Stated one knowledgeable observer, "No country offers such tempting inducements to the capitalists for profitable investments."[86]

The establishment of the New South had also created more association and competition between the races than ever before. Employers could not hope to sustain the oppression of such similar groups without some quid pro quo. The passage of Jim Crow and voting law requirements in the South at that time represented a viable solution. Playing on the deeply ingrained habits of thought, the white populace needed little persuasion that the legal system should be used to cement black inferiority. What they had to be convinced of was to accept this substitute in lieu of a living wage. "It took a lot of ritual and Jim Crow to bolster the creed of white supremacy in the bosom of a man working for a black man's wages," stated Woodward.

But removing the right to vote was certainly an important first step. Voting is one of the most cherished rights of the American system. Wrote DuBois:

> The ballot marks the difference between the citizen and the serf. Without the ballot the colored American is powerless to contend for right and justice and civil equality; with the ballot he is all-powerful to act in defense of every lawful privilege.[87]

Between 1865 and 1885, blacks were able to vote under the guarantees of various "war amendments," including what later became the Fifteenth Amendment to the U.S. Constitution. During that time, there were elected two black U.S. senators, twenty-three members of the House of Representatives, some hundred or more members of various southern state legislatures, and over five hundred who held additional governmental positions. But beginning in the 1890s, a host of forces combined to remove the power of the ballot from the black population.

Agitation came most insistently from what William Wilson calls "a new breed of southern politicians who emerged to articulate the racist feelings and to represent the interests of the most vulnerable sectors of the white working class."[88] But they were not alone. As Cell suggests, "the entire southern power elite had an even stronger interest in keeping poor whites and blacks divided by disenfranchisement."[89] Caught in a no-win struggle, some blacks countered by allying themselves with conservative Democrats, "the most conservative and politically reactionary class of whites" against the insurgent white democracy.[90] In this union, they got little. At first, the conservative Democrats had attempted to get the black vote by placing the blame for the rise of legal segregation on lower-class whites. According to Woodward, for example, "when the first state Jim Crow laws for trains was passed in 1887, a conservative paper admitted it was done 'to please the crackers.'"[91] But they, too soon joined in the movement for disenfranchisement.

Southern states campaigned to disenfranchise blacks by perfectly legal means. Mississippi, in 1890, formulated a constitution whose specific purpose was to make the existing practice of disenfranchisement conform with the law. Other southern states followed Mississippi's lead. In 1895, South Carolina enacted laws "with the explicit purpose of eliminating the electoral privileges" of blacks. Louisiana in 1898, North Carolina in 1900, Alabama in 1901, Virginia in 1902, Georgia in 1908, and Oklahoma in 1910 successfully passed laws of similar intent.

Statutes specifying poll taxes, voter examinations, and property qualifications were variously used. In Alabama, Arkansas, Florida, Louisiana, Mississippi, North and South Carolina, Tennessee, and Virginia the payment of poll taxes was a prerequisite to voting. In Georgia, these taxes had to be paid six months before the election. Property requirements were also instituted. In Alabama, there was a requirement of ownership of forty acres of land or real personal property worth three hundred dollars on which the taxes for the preceding year had been paid. There were similar requirements in Georgia, Louisiana, and South Carolina.[92] In Louisiana, a registrant had to be able to read and write and make application for registration in his own handwriting. North and South Carolina had similar provisions. Also established were understanding and grandfather clauses that permitted one who could not read to register if he could understand and reasonably interpret the constitution when read to him, and provisions for voting to extend to those whose grandfathers had voted. The latter two provisions were used to prevent the disenfranchisement of poor whites who might otherwise have suffered the same fate as blacks.[93]

This concern to separate and distinguish between the otherwise similar circumstances of blacks and poor whites represents an important way that state policy was used to impose disadvantage on the black population. Kirk Porter points out, in terms of the Mississippi law:

> Thus, it will be seen that this constitution paved the way for wholesale exclusion of the Negroes on perfectly legal grounds. The strongest point, of course, was the discretionary power vested in election officials to decide whether or not an illiterate person understood the constitution and could give a reasonable interpretation of its meaning. The ultimate ideal, of course, was to exclude all Negroes and no whites.[94]

The strategy was effective. "Three-fourths of the Negroes of the United States," it was estimated by the *Boston Guardian* in 1919, "who own more than seven hundred dollars worth of property are deprived of the right to vote."[95]

At both the local and state levels blacks became powerless in combating unfair property tax assessments, disputes over wages and services, allocations for schools and road repair, as well as more broad-based community issues of development and change. In southern cities and towns, the nonagricultural worker, having freed himself from the traditional bonds of the rural caste system, was newly enslaved by the state apparatus. Professional and laborer alike found themselves forced to rely on the goodwill of men rather than the rule of law.

An attempt was made by DuBois to compare disenfranchisement in the South with representation in the rest of the nation. DuBois estimated that in the Middle West and Southwest, on average, about 70% of the eligible voters vote while the rest "voluntarily disenfranchise themselves." In 1920, it required about 75,000 voters to seat a representative in Congress. In the South, "with a population of 23,000,000 and a voting population of about 13,000,000 there were, in 1920, less than 2,000,000 votes cast, or less than 10 percent of the total population." The southern states, however, sent 104 representatives to the sixty-seventh Congress (with representation based on population, not on number of voters), thus requiring only 21,248 voters for each representative.[96] For those who could not vote, the only redress from such statutes was expensive, time-consuming battles in the courts, often before judges appointed by the same legislative bodies. For health and safety, a more practical solution was to keep silent. In 1898 in Wilmington, North Carolina, "shortly after the whites had won an election over a thoroughly cowed black majority, a mob of 400 men led by a former Congressman demolished a black newspaper office, set it on fire, shot up the black district, killed 11 people, wounded a large number, and chased hundreds into the woods."[97]

After an election in Atlanta won by those advocating "white supremacy," mobs "looted, plundered, lynched and murdered for four days." In Louisiana in 1900, two years after the adoption of the grandfather clause, white mobs terrorized the city of New Orleans for three days, "assaulting blacks, looting, burning and shooting."[98] It was a pattern repeated throughout the South.

In discussing these battles, "Pitchfork" Bill Tillman, the South Carolina governor, was clear in explanation. "We have done our level best," he said, "we have scratched our heads to find out how we could eliminate the last one of them [blacks]; we stuffed ballot boxes. We shot them. We are not ashamed of it."[99]

With political protection removed, segregation and vulnerability increased by both law and custom. Between 1900 and 1911, ten southern states elaborated their laws requiring separation of races in transportation facilities, all of them including laws for street railways and some for ferries and steamboats. Atlanta introduced the extreme of separate elevators, though not by dictate of law, by 1908. Between 1911 and 1914 the cities of Norfolk, Richmond, Ashland, Roanoke, Winston-Salem, Greensboro, Greenville, Augusta, and Atlanta passed ordinances segregating residential areas; and in 1913 an agitation was started in North Carolina, though never passed, for the segregation of farm lands.[100]

The disenfranchisement of black labor created, in effect, a disenfranchisement of white labor. By agreeing to vote on one issue, the black, the normal split of the white vote on other questions and, more importantly, the development of a working-class consciousness against capital and privilege was abandoned.

The South in the eighties and nineties had a craft labor movement smaller than but similar to those in northern cities.[101] Members sought to test the doctrine that the South was a repository of docile labor willing to work long hours at low wages. In 1886, the Knights of Labor had over 30,000 southern members. Locals were particularly strong in the newly industrialized cities of Birmingham, Knoxville, and Richmond. A national convention of the Knights held in 1886 met in Richmond and was attended by delegates of both races. Black workers, so often depicted as antiunion, were according to one report "flocking" to the Knights.

In the latter part of the 1880s, the Knights were involved in numerous strikes in the South. These conflicts broke out in the coal mines of Alabama and Tennessee, in the cotton mills of Georgia, and among the lumber workers of Alabama, the very heart of the industrializing region.[102] Workers had a few notable successes, such as the victory over Jay Gould and the Missouri Pacific Railroad. But like their counterparts in the North, the struggle was not just with employers. Laborers were fighting an entire state system. Their victories were far outnumbered by stunning defeats. Faced with such powerful opponents, white workers chose instead to eliminate blacks as competitors by agreeing to their exclusion from the more desirable positions. It was, for white workers of the South, not a lucrative solution, but one that provided greater guarantee of security than the vicissitudes of the labor movement.

That these solutions emerged in the face of mounting profits in the industry suggests, not the power of white labor to prevent competition with black, but the continued ability of employers to offer "white supremacy" as pay. As DuBois has commented, "The southern white laborer gets low wages measured in food, clothes, shelter, and the education of his children. But in one respect he gets high pay and that is in the shape of the subtlest form of human flattery, social superiority over masses of other human beings."[103] Further, blacks were denied the ballot, not because of the actions or support of one group of whites (poor whites for Woodward, elite for Cell) versus another, but because of the dynamics of the system that made it imperative for whites of all classes to defend the disenfranchisement of blacks. State policy helped to create a sector of the population made to bear the brunt of the hardships found in the early stages of industrialization.[104]

Thousands left during these two years because they had no other choice. Disenfranchisement meant for the millions of blacks working and living in the South a precariousness reminiscent of antebellum days. "A disenfranchised working class," said DuBois, "in modern industrial civilization is worse than helpless. It is a menace, not simply to itself, but to every other group in the community, it will be diseased, it will be criminal, it will be ignorant; it will be the plaything of mobs, and will be insulted by caste restrictions."[105] And so it was.

The transformation of the southern economy created pressures of magnitude to instill in many "the moving fever." Yet, for all the harsh conditions that were endured in these first decades of the twentieth century, perhaps the most difficult to accept was the denial of opportunities for their children. "I has been here all my life," confessed one migrant, "but would be glad to go where I can educate my children where they can be of service to themselves, and this will never be here."[106]

Education and Economic Opportunity

Education, because it had been denied in slavery, had always been precious to the black community. Wrote Booker T. Washington:

> Few people who were not right in the midst of the scenes can form any
> exact idea of the intense desire which the people of my race showed for
> education. It was a whole race trying to go to school. Few were too young,
> and none too old, to make the attempt to learn.[107]

It is said by some that education is the key to economic development,
and the expansion of a public school system the central aspect of the modernization of any country.[108] One of the reasons for the centrality of education is that industrialization is linked to an occupational structure in
which an increasing proportion of the positions, regardless of level of
skill, demand formal education as a prerequisite. The occupational prospects of a majority of people in industrialized or industrializing societies
depend on formal education. Furthermore, in societies where life-styles
and life chances are greatly dependent on occupational status, education
becomes even more crucial.[109]

One of the first acts of the reconstruction governments was the establishment of free schools. Many blacks considered education their key to
the future, and as such, a crucial responsibility of government. Education, it was envisioned, should be universal and nonsegregated. One former slave commented, "I am going to school my children if I have to eat
bread and water."[110] But the advancement promised during this period
was soon lost. With the defeat of the reconstruction governments, antagonism to many of their programs was voiced. The public school systems
faced "progressive strangulation" in refutation of the regime; and universal, nonsegregated public education was abandoned. Stripped of effective
political power, blacks found they had to concentrate on safe-guarding
segregated schools, a difficult task. States that were too impoverished to
provide one effective system found it impossible to maintain even a
makeshift unit for blacks while providing at the same time for whites. The
problem was particularly acute in rural areas, where the black population
was poorer, more isolated, and more vulnerable. Landowners in particular, fearing the effects of education on their labor supply, set about undermining public schools. Universal education was too expensive, it was argued. Taxing whites to educate black children was unfair.[111]

Still, with the financial support of northern philanthropists and aid
from individuals within the black community when public funds were

unavailable, progress was made. In 1860, it had been estimated that only 5% of the 4 million freed population was literate. By 1870, only 20% of the population was literate.[112] Yet, by 1910, those figures had been reversed and literates represented 70% of the total. Under the circumstances, tremendous gains had been made.

But in 1912, there were signs of deterioration. Until the presidential election of 1912, the federal government had been the "repository of black hopes in the South, counted on as an appeal of last resort." With the election of Woodrow Wilson, however, the first southern-born president since Andrew Johnson, "the last fragile thread was broken and blacks found themselves in a no man's land between hostile states and a hostile white majority."[113] In education, this meant increased and unchallenged inequities in expenditures.

Fears were soon realized. The United States Bureau of Education pointed out in 1916 that per capita expenditures for education in southern states were, on the average, $10.32 for whites, $2.89 for blacks. Differences were also evidenced in the payment of teachers. In Louisiana, black elementary school teachers were paid annually $292; high school teachers, $661. White teachers were paid $1,007 and $1,419 respectively.[114] There were also reports of excessive numbers of students per teacher. Alabama, for example, had 52.4 black pupils per teacher, Georgia 49, and Mississippi 53.6 as compared to the average of 32 for the entire United States.

N. C. Newbold, director of the Division of Negro Education for the state of North Carolina, estimated that between 1910 and 1920, eight southern states spent for new construction of black schools $30,000,000. During the same period, $270,547,343 was spent for new schools for white children. Blacks received, therefore, 10% of the monies expended for such purposes, a percentage far below that warranted by their proportion in the scholastic population.[115]

Differences also existed in the structures themselves. In Georgia, only 1.9% of the schools for black children were built of brick or stone, as compared to over 18% of the white schools. Schools for blacks were more likely to be held in private homes, in lodge halls, in churches, or in abandoned cabins. In 1910, 61% of the black schools in Alabama were housed in such structures, 63% in Georgia, and even higher percentages in Louisiana.[116]

Observed Booker T. Washington in an article in the *New York Age* in 1915:

> On my visits to the country schools in these and other states I have seen some very pathetic sights. In some of the so-called school buildings the roofs leak, the winds blow up through the cracks of the floor and down

through the ceilings. I have seen in many of these schools five little boys
and girls trying to study out of the same book. In some cases two children
would occupy the front seat with the book between them, with two others
peeping over their shoulders and a fifth trying to peep over the shoulders
of the four.[117]

Inadequacies were also reflected in the number of days per school year
in black schools: in Mississippi, 94 days; in Alabama, 115; in Georgia, 135.
These figures compare to 167 days in southern white schools.[118]

There was no legal recourse. In a case in North Carolina, a complainant
sought to show bias in the distribution of school funds. The court ruled
that it must be clearly proved that the method of providing funds for the
black schools was both insufficient and discriminatory.[119] Intent, in addition to "effect" had to be shown. In Kentucky, it was ruled that not of
equal facilities did not mean that the accommodations provided for each
race must be identical. In many cases, the courts merely cemented the
disadvantage.

For black parents, the inadequacies and inequities of the educational
system were all too evident. From New Orleans, one migrant told of
a step migration initiated in the hope of finding opportunity for his
children.

> I have been living here in New Orleans only seven years. I formerly lived
> in the country I sold my property and moved here I didn't think there was
> any justice for my paying school taxes and had no fit school to send my
> children to.[120]

The dream of a better chance for one's children was also expressed by
a migrant from Augusta, Georgia:

> My children I wished to be educated in a different community than here.
> Where the school facilities are better and less prejudice shown and in fact
> where advantages are better for our people in all respect.[121]

In many communities, particularly rural ones, no schools, public or private existed. In others, the segregated systems were established in such
a way that black students, able to complete only seven years in their districts, would be ineligible for high school, which required eight years.
Such provisions ensured that there had to be only one high school in
the community and that it would be all white. "No high schools, no
protection for life, and the revival of the Ku Klux Klan are the three
reasons given for the wholesale desertion of the State of Georgia by
over 5,000 families last summer" run an item in the *Chicago Defender* in
October 1921. Charts were offered to show that the whites were given as
many as three high schools in one city, while blacks were educationally

abandoned after they finished grammar school. This inequity was not unusual.

Little opportunity existed for a southern black with limited financial resources to do graduate work or to obtain professional training. The only southern schools of medicine, dentistry, and pharmacy open to blacks were located at Howard University in Washington, D.C., and Mehary College in Nashville, Tennessee.[122] There were law schools at Howard and at two Baptist institutions: Simmons University in Louisville and Virginia Union in Richmond. Anyone who desired professional training was therefore forced to attend one of these schools or to go to a northern institution that did not discriminate. Graduate training prerequisites for employment in the professions was one of the many reforms of the turn of the century. Established both to protect the public from those not qualified to practice and to limit the supply within the field, such licensing nonetheless had a detrimental effect on blacks in the South who wished to become doctors or lawyers. In law, for example, it was no longer sufficient to take courses at a local institution and pass the state bar exam, career routes which many black lawyers had pursued in the past.

The limiting of educational opportunity for blacks did serve to uphold the occupational hierarchy. Not only did it provide a constant pool of workers forced to accept whatever jobs were offered them but to keep a majority of the community oppressed. Poor whites had a vested interest in keeping blacks uneducated because of the competition for jobs and for social status. "One of the things which demarcated them as superior and increased the future potentialities of their children," wrote Myrdal in *The American Dilemma*, "was the fact that their children had an educational advantage. In publicly supported school buses, they were taken to fine consolidated schools while often black children were only given what amounts to a sham education."[123] Yet, such interests were not only vested in the poor. Southern employers having sacrificed black labor to the pool of industrial expansion were hardly anxious to support expensive proposals for the public education of black children. Indeed, the current need for large supplies of unskilled labor made such schemes counterproductive. Some reasoned that education might make blacks who remained in the South conscious of "rights" they should not know about.[124]

Conclusions

Between 1880, when the South began to industrialize, and 1908, when Georgia became the last confederate state to pass a law disenfranchising voters, black workers experienced either job displacement, obsolescence, or loss or the lowering of wages. A single threat probably would have caused many to leave; concomitant economic, political, and social threats make it surprising that anyone stayed behind.

Between 1870 and 1920, the South experienced the classic elements causing labor migration. From 1870 to 1880, it struggled with issues of political stability, the first requirement for core investment in the periphery. In 1877, it achieved what was so aptly called Redemption. Between 1880 and 1890, it experienced the desired core penetration and industrial takeoff along with some undesired and greatly feared, labor unrest. Between 1890 and 1900, it quelled labor unrest by placing the burden of industrialization on the backs of a specific segment of the population, black nonagricultural workers. State policy was used in particular to cement the disadvantaged of the group. Between 1900 and 1910 it encountered core takeover, bringing with it profit that flowed out of the South, employment for the few, and poverty for the many. Between 1910 and 1920, it adjusted to the disquieting elements of development by allowing and, at times, encouraging massive out-migration.

The patterns of development and change experienced in the South during this period could be replicated in peripheral societies throughout the world brought into the orbit of core society expansion. For black workers, migration seemed an obvious alternative. The North, by contrast, offered them a job, the ballot, and educational opportunity for their children. In the past, such contrasts have been sufficient to support the argument that the North, while not a promised land, would eventually provide advancement and progress. But what they did not know was that what they saw as the end of a terrible struggle for emancipation was only another beginning, and that progress in the North would be at their expense rather than at their behest.

CHAPTER FOUR

The North
Labor, the Economy, and the Great War

The contractors make their appearance
under the American Flag among the
half-starved mudsills in the most
wretched districts of Hungary, Italy and
Denmark, tell the stories of fabulous
wages to be gotten in America, bamboo-
zle the poor creatures, rope them in and
make contracts with them to pay their
passage across the sea upon their agreeing to terms that few can understand.
When they reach the districts of this
country to which the contractors ship
them, they find their golden dreams
turned into nightmares, as they are put
to work in mines, factories, or on railroads, at even lower wages than those
of them whom they throw out of work.[1]

MIGRATION OF BLACK workers from the South must be seen in the context of prior patterns of immigration to the United States. Black workers
did not enter into an amorphous and undefined labor market. Rather, as
mentioned previously, they entered into a delicately balanced system already sustained by low wages and vulnerable European workers. It was
the loss of this labor that precipitated the immediate search for an alternative supply from the South.

While the South between 1870 and 1916 was undergoing rapid social,
economic, and political change, the North of that period was no less volatile. Devoted to manufacturing and commerce, it became the banker and
assembler for the entire nation. As such, it constantly struggled with
labor shortages and unrest, with battles over freight rates, import tariffs,
and transport of raw materials and finished products. In 1870, the North

was a region transformed by industrialism no less disquieting than that of the South.

"Transition to industrial society," E. P. Thompson has written, "entails a severe restructuring of work habits, new disciplines, new incentives and a new human nature upon which these incentives can bite effectively."[2] In the North, there developed a "progressive disintegration" of certain traditional social relationships, technological shifts leading to the restructuring of labor, and new types of machinery and production methods. It is unlikely that any society could experience such change without disruption. But the North had, on its side, a potential tonic. Large supplies of surrogate labor from outside the system served as an antidote to lessen the shock of transition.

In 1870, there began the systematic importation of millions of European laborers—able-bodied, hard-working, and cheap. Between 1871 and 1915, over 25 million Europeans migrated to this country.[3] Between 1900 and 1914, Europeans were entering the United States at a rate of over 1 million per year.[4] With them, American manufacture was thrust irrevocably onto the world scene. One of the most important factors surrounding the massive migrations of the nineteenth and twentieth centuries was the lack of legal restriction imposed on such movement in either countries of origin or countries of destination that resulted in a circulation of labor necessary to the development of both sides and constituted one of the few modern examples of "free foreign migration."[5]

European and American Economic Development: Diverging Patterns

Explanation of this large and uninhibited movement of labor lies generally in patterns of development in both Europe and the United States, particularly in American business cycles. Historically in Europe, industrialization had resulted in a series of economic dislocations that affected both rural and urban populations and provided the major stimulus for emigration. In the countryside, improved farm technology reduced the need for labor. It also transformed the organization of rural economies, leading to a consolidation of small farms into larger and more productive estates.[6]

At the same time, demographic changes brought on by an improved food supply and better health care produced falling mortality rates and a rapid growth in population. This demographic transition, in turn, led to a mass migration of rural populations into urban areas, where they further glutted labor markets already overcrowded with workers. Labor conditions deteriorated.

Cities were already experiencing another kind of transition because of the introduction of the factory system. Factories had displaced craftsmen and artisans from their traditional occupations because machinery could be used for work that was previously done by hand. New urban industrial workers tending these machines were at the mercy of a system of labor that had made them homogeneous, substitutable, and expendable. Unemployment was high, wages were low, and workers struggled for their very subsistence. As indicated in chapter 3, such conditions are characteristic of early periods of industrialism. Once the transition from preindustrial to industrial society is made, local opportunities increase and emigration tends to decline.[7] This situation obtained throughout the industrializing nations of Europe in the nineteenth century. The industrial shift, what Simon Kuznets calls the "trial of the Industrial Revolution," did not occur simultaneously and lead to alteration in the proportions emigrating from different areas over time. In England, for example, industrialism began in the 1770s and continued in the described patterns of upheaval until the 1850s.[8] Emigration from Britain to the United States was very high during this period. Germany and France, societies undergoing similar development and change, also contributed to the immigration of this time. As Dudley Kirk comments, "Emigration followed the speed of modern economic development from its centers in northwestern Europe to the peripheries of the continent."[9] The ebb and flow of populations was not only tied to the timing of industrialization but was also tied to economic conditions in the United States. Rates of departure rose in boom times and declined in slack periods.

In the 1880s, the period under study, the heaviest emigration was from southern and eastern Europe. Immigrants from Italy, Russia, and almost every other place in between entered a labor market desperate for large supplies of cheap labor. "More numerous and less isomorphic" than their northern and western counterparts, they were greeted with far more suspicion and enmity by the citizenry as a whole.[10] They represented an ideal source of vulnerable and exploitable labor.

The "pull" to America is explained by a different pattern of development. This country had abundant resources, high in quality and exploitable with relatively small amounts of capital.[11] The United States, in the early stages of English industrialization, was a mercantile economy and a frontier. It absorbed large amounts of English labor not because of its advanced development but because of its own labor shortage.[12]

From the earlier mercantile stage, sufficient domestic capital had been derived to finance extraction. Both its wealth and its innovation allowed it to escape becoming a periphery of Europe's core. What it lacked in 1830 was a reservoir of cheap labor. At first, the shortcoming had been overcome by the creative use of technology. Early on, "American industrial production distinguished itself from its European counterparts by the establishment of a pattern of high capital intensity in its operations." By 1850, for example, there came into being "the principles and practices of quantity manufacture of standardized products characterized by interchangeable parts and the use of a growing array of machine tools and specialized jigs and fixtures."[13] The effect of this technology was to increase productivity while decreasing the need for expensive craftsmen's labor. Employers realized that a diminution of the skill required could not only increase production through a division of labor but also reduce the bargaining power of the skilled worker.

After the Civil War, American productivity continued its rapid rise. "Commodity output increased some 54% while the population increased only 24%."[14] The increase in productivity created a further shift in the character of employment. A growing proportion of the work force now offered their services for hire to those who controlled the means of production. Work processes themselves became more rationalized and routinized and required little prior industrial experience. A high volume of manufacture could be done by any laborer with only a few day's instruction. Growth was limited only by the pool of willing and able workers. Profit was limited only by their cheapness.

The labor pool and the industrial expansion went hand in hand. Technological changes that had been introduced before the Civil War were extensively applied during this period, thus further facilitating development. Explained the Immigration Commission:

> It may be said, therefore, that industrial expansion was the original reason for the employment of races of recent immigration, but that after the availability of this labor became known further industrial expansion was stimulated by the fact of this availability, the original cause thus becoming largely an effect of the conditions it had created.[15]

Labor availability also aided one of the most notable achievements of this time, the creation of a national transport system. This feat was crucial to modernization of industry not only because it furthered regional specialization but also because it enabled easy movement of products to consumers. The timing of the northern penetration of the South was tied to this desired increase in distribution, with the South's separate railroad system an important link in the chain. Overcoming regional barriers and sectional loyalties as well as wresting control from local interests was a long and protracted struggle. However, the rewards justified the efforts.

Accessibility by rail created "mass demand" for goods and made the United States the "largest consuming population in the world."[16]

The success of the American system in this period is evident in comparative industrial statistics. In 1880, American coal and pig iron production trailed Britain's and just equaled the latter's crude steel output. By 1913, "the United States had surpassed Britain, Germany and Belgium-Luxembourg combined in production of coal and steel and nearly equaled their total of pig iron."[17]

Immigrant Recruitment

In an environment of economic displacement in Europe, emigration inducements by the United States hardly needed to be extensive. Though some came because of political and religious persecution, most came simply to improve their economic lot.[18] Over time, improvements in steamship transport made passage relatively cheap and of a short, ten days' duration. In the period under study, 1870–1914, immigrants, usually males, traveled alone. Their intent was to stay from two to three years in this country and save up enough money to return home, where they would pay off a mortgage, buy a piece of land, or start a small business.

The Immigration Commission said that these new immigrants constituted

> an immigration largely of individuals, a considerable portion of whom apparently have no intention of permanently changing their residence, their only purpose in coming to America being to temporarily take advantage of the greater wages paid for industrial labor in this country.[19]

The commission characterized them as "unskilled laborers: 75% male, 83% between the ages of 14 and 45 and consequently producers rather than dependents."[20] Further, the commission indicated that 35% were illiterate and that 40% of those who had come in the last ten years had already returned. This pattern of transience was of particular importance. It differed from that of the old immigrant group, only 3% of whom had returned, and signaled the incorporation of a new type of migrant worker.[21] As suggested in chapter 1, workers who were willing to take jobs shunned by the native population are an important ingredient of modern economic development. Employers gain a decided advantage because the temporary status of such workers increases their vulnerability. Immigrants were particularly used in the "dirty work" jobs in such large-scale productive enterprises as iron and steel.[22]

Immigrant vulnerability was expressed in other ways. Most immigrants first learned of the promised land through agents of American employers in search of their labor or representatives of steamship and railroad companies. They were directed to specific jobs, firms, and locations. For example, in testimony given before Congress in 1883, P. H. McLoughlen, representative of the Chicago Trades Assembly, stated:

> We know that, notably, men working the mines in the upper lake region frequently make contracts in Europe, in Sweden, and Denmark, and import a number of laborers from there. It may be said to be, in a modified form, the Chinese Cooley system over again. . . . Those men are imported from Europe, and they work from one to two years under contracts made in Europe. . . . We cannot conceive how we can be really protected when the same manufacturer who advocates the "protection" of American labor can, in a case of a lockout, go over to Germany, or some other part of Europe, and import as many mechanics or laborers as he pleases, to compete with our American mechanics here at home.[23]

In many cases, middlemen, whose job it was to supply businesses and contractors with cheap labor, hired men directly, provided them with room and board until work was available, collected wages from the employer, and paid the men a previously agreed-upon rate.[24] Abuses in this system were legion. The agent often profited from the transport, food, and living quarters with which he provided his men at inflated prices.[25] The middleman, however, was not without value, as he was thought to protect the newly arrived from a hostile society and to provide safe harbor in a manner employers had long ago abandoned.[26] The new immigrants arrived at and remained in the larger eastern and midwestern cities. There they were concentrated in run-down areas with poor housing, where they lacked educational opportunities and faced widespread prejudice and discrimination from indigenous populations and authorities, a plight they shared with most labor migrants. At the edge of poverty, they were also the most affected by any economic downturn. During the depression of 1893, many migrants wrote home expressing what one called the "fear that the historical experiment in America might end in catastrophe."[27] The parallels between this immigrant recruitment and that of black migrants from the South are striking. It is not surprising that many sociologists predicted that their paths to assimilation would be similar.

The Use of Immigrant Labor in the United States

European immigrants played an important role in furthering economic development in the United States. Uprooted from their families and communities, they were deployed to low-wage industries such as mining and railroad construction that could not attract native workers in sufficient numbers.

Their position as temporary migrants led many to view work as instrumental—a source of income only, not something that confers status.[28] At times, the result of this attitude was disastrous. At the Carnegie South Works, for example, it was estimated that 25% of the recent immigrants were injured or killed each year. Yet, these workers rarely protested in collective ways. Their intention to leave after a short stay made protest futile.[29]

In addition, their large numbers, abject poverty, and lack of standing in the communities to which they migrated, permitted employers to cast aside prior social relations. Where previously employers had by custom and tradition been expected to enter into a responsible relationship with their workers, now they were "only too eager to be relieved of that necessity by the advent of a (new) class of labor."[30] Strategies of cheapening the cost of labor through ethnic rotation were common. Explained a clothing cutter of the tailoring industry:

> These people [Russian Jews] made a sort of combination and came down town and made an offer to several clothing houses that they would do the work cheaper than the others who were doing it; that what the Germans had received $2.50 for they would do for $1.50. The work was given to them on trial and it was found that they did the same work $1 cheaper than the Germans, and that has driven the Germans almost entirely out of the business.[31]

With the introduction of Irish workers in the textile mills of New England in the 1850s, manufacturers began to reorganize the management of labor. Worker protection at the workplace was reduced to a minimum. By the 1880s, industrial accidents were increasing at an alarming rate. Yet, ethnic differences between employer and employee seemed to weaken sympathy and understanding and, more importantly, the ability of the workers to demand protection. Had the economic changes occurred in a more homogeneous society, it is likely that the class conflict and exploitation would have been more apparent to the workers. As it was, the ethnic rotation of the employers clouded many efforts at cooperation. Relationships between employer and employee were now limited to and revolved around the "cash nexus of employment."

But European labor by itself did not transform the American economy. Structured on the development of the factory and constant technological change and sustained by the proliferation of workers and products, tremendous expansion in the system occurred between 1870 and 1900.[32] Growth produced both wealth and a host of problems. In the 1880s, a series of depressions convinced many large companies that greater control over workers as well as over markets and competition was the key to survival. In the beginning of the decade, great fortunes were lost in what was interpreted as "the uncertainties of the marketplace."[33] Companies now strove to make the organization of production more uniform. It was hoped that the more that was owned, the less variation there would be in prices and wages.

According to David Gordon, Richard Edwards, and Michael Reich, companies were aided in these efforts by three main developments. The first was the already mentioned completion of the rail network in the 1880s that standardized rate schedules and thus eliminated many geographic barriers and monopolies. In short, concentration became more possible and therefore more profitable. Second, as has been shown in the southern example, investors' experience with outside capital investment in the railroads supplied the model for a more general system of finance. As the authors note, the market for industrial securities emerged and grew rapidly during the 1880s and 1890s. And finally, "the New Jersey holding company legislation of 1889 produced the legal model facilitating corporate consolidation."[34]

This legislation was to have particular significance. Thus Edward C. Kirkland concludes, "the holding company signalized the final triumph of the corporation, for now corporations could be made to combine corporations."[35] Between 1898 and 1902, there were over "3,600 recorded mergers, twenty-five times the total number in the preceding three years and six times the number in the succeeding five years."[36] According to Daniel Nelson, between one quarter and one third of the entire U.S. manufacturing capital stock was consolidated between 1892 and 1902. By "1904 the top four percent of American concerns produced 57 percent of the total industrial output by value."[37]

The merger movement did not end all problems of competition and economic security, Gordon, Edwards, and Reid argue. For that there needed to occur greater product market monopoly and much greater intraindustry cooperation.[38] There were impediments to these needed changes. Opposing large firms in their plans for monopolistic security were small businessmen who feared that their own interests were threatened by the growing power of the new companies.[39] To voice their opposition, they became leaders in the movements for antitrust and reform legislation aimed at curbing the excesses of the large corporate and financial interests.[40] Together with middle class reformers and certain sectors of the Republican party, their efforts helped to pass the "Progressive Era" programs of the Federal Reserve System, the Federal Trade Commission, and other regulatory agencies.[41] The purpose of these agencies was to provide "supervision and regulation as to prevent any restriction of competition from being to the detriment of the public."[42] Their hope of creating countervailing power was obvious.

The great desire of small business for "more vigorous prosecution of various combinations" merely slowed but did not halt the establishment of a full corporate program.[43] "This is an age of combination," Theodore Roosevelt told Congress in his Annual Message to Congress in 1905, "and any effort to prevent combination will not only be useless, but in the end vicious, because of the contempt for law which the failure to enforce law inevitably produces."[44]

Though divided on the issue of mergers, large and small capitalists could unite on the larger issue of the need to control trade unions. Union labor was costly for small business owners, who continually made efforts to destroy the unions and maintain open shops. Even though unions, too, opposed the merger movement, small business was more fearful of them than of the larger companies.[45] As a result, the shared fear created the initial common thread that led to compromise. Antitrust was relegated to occasional regulation of corporations thought to have exceeded the boundaries of accepted practice. Thus, the victory permitted large corporations to devote their energies and resources to the still unresolved issue of control over workers.[46]

Control over workers, however, was not easily won, even with increased concentration. A report from the U.S. commissioner of labor in 1906 states that there were "2,307 strikes in 1904 as opposed to only 695 in 1885."[47] Worker control required further manipulation. It was attempted by reduction of jobs to a common, semiskilled category, thus creating greater dominance over the work process by employers and greater substitutability of workers.[48] This change in labor status represented a battle constantly waged from the turn of the century onward.

Employers had long since learned that direct confrontation between labor and management was costly. Many also believed that such action was as repugnant to workers as it was to employers. Argued Jay Gould in 1883, "I think there is no disagreement between the great mass of the employees and their employers. These societies that are gotten up magnify these things and create evils which do not exist—create troubles which ought not to exist."[49]

If these "good and honest" workers could be made to see that changes in the internal environment of the "outdated" factory were actually in their own interests, it was reasoned, then harmony and profit could prevail. The internal environment of the factory had much that needed to be changed. Although companies had come a long way since the 1860s, when "spheres of artisan influence" had made the pace of production irregular and returns to investments unpredictable, there was still much to be done. In the depressions of the 1870s and 1880s, companies had sought effective measures to reduce production costs. Suggested Gould, "The returns of capital are not high; they are going lower. Manufacturers, for instance, do not expect to make the profits that they made some years ago; they expect to make a less profit, and make it up on larger sales."[50]

What were eventually instituted were new methods of mechanization that eliminated skilled workers, reduced required skills to the barest minimum, provided greater regulation over the pace of production, and generated a spreading homogeneity in the work tasks and working conditions of industrial employees.[51] "The effect of the introduction of machinery in any trade," stated Henry George, "is to dispense with skill and to make the laborer more helpless."[52] In short, workers were controlled in the name of progress and efficiency.

The process of mechanization represented a long struggle, waged with organized labor, that culminated in what Frederick Winslow Taylor called "enforced standardization of methods, enforced adoption of the best implements and working conditions, and enforced cooperation of all the employees under management's detailed direction."[53] Testified a telegraph operator, "I claim that these investors are all capital saving machines. They do not save labor in any way at all."[54]

Between 1900 and 1920, companies had to create structures that would regulate both the labor of workers and the new kinds of machines upon which they worked. The new machines required larger establishments, and those large establishments in turn required a larger volume of production to support the capital investment.[55] Throughout U.S. manufacturing, the numbers of workers per establishment increased dramatically. According to the 1900 census of manufacturers, establishment size for selected industries increased on average over three-fold between 1860 and 1900.[56] Nelson suggests that "factories increased from roughly 1,500 workers per establishment in 1880 to a range of 20,000 to 60,000 during the 1920's."[57]

This rapid increase in factory size had a significant impact on social relations. Up through the 1860s, plant size remained small enough to sustain relatively personal relations between supervisor and supervisee. As factories expanded, however, intimate and particularistic relationships were much more difficult to maintain. Authority became less personal, and each worker became increasingly liable to the threat of dismissal and more vulnerable to the fear of replacement by a member of the reserve work force. Now almost anyone could work in the large factories, where jobs increasingly required only nominal skills.[58] Under the craft system, there had been "apprentices, journeymen, helpers, assistants, and master craftsmen, all with widely disparate job tasks and skill levels."[59] Now, more and more often there was a single class of semiskilled factory operatives who required virtually no skills in order to perform their jobs.[60]

Drawing the new "industrial wage earners" from the most vulnerable sectors of the society further aided the corporate program. In the three decades between 1870 and 1900, when large and continuing numbers of immigrants were entering the country, labor unions had to struggle mightily to organize those who could neither speak English nor speak to each other. In the bituminous coal mines of Pennsylvania and Ohio, "the importation of migrant strikebreakers became a feature of nearly every important strike."[61] Migrants were used in a strategy of "diverted aggression," where resident workers blamed them for losses in their privileged position in the labor force.[62]

Both because of the changes in the nature of work and because of the use of cheaper immigrant labor, labor unrest intensified throughout the 1880s. Labor fought back. Uncertainty within the workplace produced great activity on the part of unions themselves, including recruitment regardless of ethnicity, and caused the number of union members in the work force to increase four-fold. The nationalization of the economic structure pressed workers toward national unions. The Knights of Labor, active in the South of the 1880s, had begun in the North in 1868 as an organization of garment cutters who took in members from other trades. By 1886, it had over 700,000 members nationwide. As the Knights began to fade because of failure in critical strikes not only in the South but also in the North, the American Federation of Labor began to achieve prominence. In 1900, it had over 800,000 members.

The business community again responded. In order to retain greater control over labor, particularly in the light of increased union membership, they made use of such tactics as antilabor legislation, private police forces, and work stoppage injunctions. Their ability to harness the power of the state against labor was equally effective in the North and inhibited the union movement there.

As skills were reduced and craft workers were replaced, foremen began to assume the roles and authority formerly performed by craft workers. The first three decades after 1900 were characterized by Nelson as the "foreman's empire."[63] "The number of foremen in manufacturing increased from 90,000 in 1900 to 296,000 in 1920, an increase of more than 300 percent, whereas total manufacturing employment increased by only 96 percent over the same years."[64] Although the distinction between workers and foremen was not based on the latter's skill, as that between apprentice and craftsman had been, still the foreman in a shop played a vital part. His major task was to establish and maintain discipline. This meant, in turn, that the expertise needed to become "foreman" was based on management rather than productive skills—expertise provided in a system of instruction introduced by the industries themselves.[65] According to Gordon, Edwards, and Reich, foremen headed a "ladder of artificial divisions and distinctions made among jobs."[66]

While the foreman replaced the craft worker, he retained little of the craftsman's power. The old craft foreman had "virtually unlimited discretionary authority to hire, fire and promote workers."[67] An argument was advanced that such a system created problems in efficiency. Foremen, it was said, were likely "to make friends of the employees of his department on the basis of friendship rather than fitness" and to "sell jobs" or "hold his favorites in soft assignments."[68]

To overcome this inefficiency, hiring, firing, and promotion were removed from the foremen's authority and placed in that of newly installed, centralized personnel offices. By so doing, employers gained greater control over the entire work process and, in particular, over worker job actions. Disgruntled workers, now part of an increasingly homogeneous and substitutable work force, could be routinely dismissed.

Large-scale immigration coincided with the labor needs of industrial manufacturers. Southern and eastern European workers entered the country at the initial and most stressful period of industrial development, when the need for relatively less-skilled workers was at its peak.[69] While historians may debate whether such groups gained more than they lost in this cooperative venture, it is nonetheless clear, as Stephen Steinberg has concluded, "that America needed the immigrant at least as much as the immigrant needed America."[70]

Native Reaction to Immigrant Labor

By 1910, the foreign born made up a quarter of the nation's work force, and in many of the industries closest to the industrial center, the foreign born were a clear majority. For example, 48% of the workers in coal mines were foreign born, 67% in iron mines, 76% in clothing factories, 76% in slaughter and packing houses, and 53% in steel mills.[71] The Immigration Commission concluded in that year that the economic expansion of the previous two decades would not have been possible without the "immigrant hordes."[72]

The foreign born in 1910 were overrepresented at the lower end of the occupational hierarchy. They constituted nearly half of the laborers and over one-third of the operatives. This disparity is reflected in income figures. The Immigration Commission found that the weekly earnings of native-born whites of native-born parents was $14.37. The weekly earnings of native-born whites of foreign-born parents was $13.91. The weekly earnings of the foreign born was $11.92.[73] To the more recent arrivals, then, fell the lot of the less skilled and lower-paid occupational roles. This was the case regardless of their level of skill. Their vulnerability coupled with abundant supplies kept their wages down.

Some have viewed this finding as an indication that migrants push earlier arrivals up in the occupational hierarchy and into better income levels.[74] Such explanations assume that the labor market remains constant over time and that what changes is the ethnicity of migrants. New European immigrants, however, entered a labor market very different from previous ones. Newcomers, at the bottom of the hierarchy, constituted the majority of workers. In future, the dilemma would be to replicate this imbalance while, at the same time, maintaining at least a semblance of opportunity for the workers. As pointed out earlier, this is a major function of labor migration. By their very desire to return home, new immigrants proved useful. They came to the United States to gather income, income to be taken back to the home community and used to fulfill roles within that social structure. In this context, issues of wages, hours, conditions, or even types of work were less important than the simple act of saving money for a specific goal. The business community understood this fact and benefited from it.

Resident workers, on the other hand, continued to be unsettled both by the introduction of newcomers and by, what appeared to be, their systematic rotation. They directed more animosity toward immigrants than toward the employers. The most obvious example of this disdain was their attempt to restrict immigration, which began as early as 1850 and grew to a crescendo by 1900. Initially, the restriction movements stressed the direct economic threat that immigrant workers represented to native workers. Such appeals were most compelling to those immediately affected. Over time, the argument against the immigrant expanded to more general fears of cultural decline. To the "native" American, the immigrant was one "who maintained strange customs, spoke peculiar languages, dressed oddly, and practiced alien Catholic and Jewish religions; they had not the proper reverence for American values, symbols and heroes."[75]

It was but a short step from here to the formulation of a theory of racial superiority. Hayes suggests, "Americans had long cherished their Anglo-Saxon backgrounds, had attributed their flourishing society to superior Anglo-Saxon institutions, and had waxed enthusiastic over their 'manifest destiny,' their duty to carry their way of life to the rest of the world."[76] Under the influence of the economic crisis of the 1890s and the fear of alien threats to American society, these views hardened into "a desperate racial vindictiveness which stressed a more clearcut race superiority."[77] Newcomers from southern and eastern Europe were judged to be inherently inferior and detrimental to American society.

In 1894, a group of New Englanders, leaders in the professions and public life, formed the Immigration Restriction League for this purpose. Joining with labor officials who fought competition from cheaper immigrant workers, the league popularized the literacy test for all immigrants. Obviously, the measure was particularly intended adversely to affect recent arrivals. In 1897, Congress approved a literacy test, which President Cleveland vetoed. Taft again vetoed such legislation in 1913, and Wilson in 1915. In each case, the House failed by a slim margin to override their vetoes.[78] The business community, sustained by these supplies of cheap labor, argued strenuously to keep the doors open and restrictions down. The importance of immigrant labor to American industry was too established to allow such xenophobic schemes to advance. It was only when an alternative supply of cheap labor had been located that restrictive legislation was finally passed in 1921. Yet, immigration was cut off in 1915. What immediately restricted European immigration was neither specific legislation nor, more generally, a change in attitude but the coming of the War.

The Great War and the Decline of Immigrant Labor

Although the immediate cause of the war was the assassination of Archduke Ferdinand of Austria, extreme nationalism, which had become rampant throughout Europe since the turn of the century, and current imperialist expansion were the underlying provocation. Both led to bitter struggles between nations over territory, wealth, and human capital.

The United States desired to stay out of a war many felt represented regional conflict that had nothing to do with this country. In 1914, President Wilson issued a proclamation of neutrality. The sinking of the Lusitania in 1915 altered somewhat the sentiment, but its supporters were still in a majority. There were even segments of the population who believed that, should the United States enter the war, it should enter on the side of Germany. Thus, little consensus about the Great War existed in 1915.

The industrial might of a neutral United States, moreover, created an opportunity for the business community to establish itself as the arms dealer of the world. American munitions factories boomed even before the eventual entrance of the United States into the war on the side of Britain and France. Industrial establishments were enlarged and new ones created in response to the war demand for American manufactured goods.[79] It was not uncommon for a plant to double or treble its labor force. A typical case was one of the large packing plants in the Chicago yards that increased its workers during the war from 8,000 to 17,000.[80]

Although the war stimulated the demand for goods and therefore for labor, it, at the same time, decreased the available supply. Immigration from the nations at war immediately ceased, and there was a marked decrease in immigration from other countries. In addition, American immigrants in large numbers departed to join the fighting forces of their native lands. In 1915, immigration had been cut by one-third over the levels of the previous year. By 1918, almost as many Europeans left as came into the United States.[81]

The labor shortage became even more acute after the United States entered the war in 1917, and enlistments withdrew hundreds of thousands of men from northern industries. Blacks "who often had to fight to fight," were the largest and most accessible substitute.[82] The North's search for cheap labor in the South is not surprising. It is perhaps more surprising that the industrial North waited so long to take advantage of it. In the 1870s, when the first orchestrated search for cheap labor had been made, employers chose new European labor instead of the southern black reserves. There are three reasons for this selection. First, there was in the North a great fear of waves of black workers streaming into cities, which made employers hesitant, because of community opposition, to open the flood gates.[83] Second, the critical role that cotton played not only in the southern economy but also in the national made southern black labor indispensable.[84]

Finally, the South in the 1870s was isolated and economically undeveloped. It would have been impractical for a northern company, on its own, to travel to the South and attempt to collect a set of workers. The task would have been tedious, time consuming, and probably would have netted few workers. The South was not yet undergoing the kind of development necessary to create labor displacements needed for a migrant pool.

But by 1916, all of these restrictions had been removed. With the war and the loss of the immigrant, there was in the North a demand for labor greater than the supply. In the South, displaced nonagricultural laborers were battling with newly arrived rural folk in cities that were already overflowing with labor. And northern economic development in the South was established to the degree that the South was no longer isolated. With all of these changes occurring at virtually the same time, it is no wonder that many thought a judgment day was at hand.

Blacks and the Great War

The availability of black labor during the war was tied to the country's general uncertainty about the place the group was to occupy in the society. There was never a consensus about whether blacks should be allowed in service in the military, in any capacity. The desire of black soldiers to fight was part of the same dynamic. Many saw the war itself as a referendum on assimilation. It was the first opportunity after the start of the migration to test the American dream. But the war also produced an extensive debate within the black press about whether blacks should fight. Typically, the Reverend A. Clayton Powell, father of the United States congressman wrote:

> While we love our flag and country, we do not believe in fighting for the protection of commerce on the high seas until the powers that be give us at least some verbal assurance that the property and lives of the members of our race are going to be protected from Maine to Mississippi. . . . Let us have the courage to say to the white American people, . . . Give us the same rights which you enjoy, and then we will fight by your side with all of our might for every intentional right on land and sea.[85]

However, the more usual public response was echoed in an impassioned editorial by DuBois called "Close Ranks" urging all "to forget their special grievances."[86]

Within the rank and file of the community, the voices of support for the war held sway. Many, who could not serve in any other way, bought war bonds. And the general patriotism in the society led to the conviction on the part of some that here was an opportunity to prove to the nation not only that blacks were good and brave soldiers but also that the scientific stigma of inferiority and bestiality recently applied was inappropriate.

In 1918, at war's end, it was concluded by most that America was not going to live up to her promise for black citizens. An editorial in the journal *Messenger* (July 1919, p. 12) stated, "Lynchings, riots, segregation, disenfranchisements, discriminations are more rampant than even before the war. The colored men gave their lives, their health, their homes— their best selves to the privileged classes of America, England, France, Belgium, Japan, and Italy in this war. They are enjoying none of the profits." It was a case of another set of dreams turned into nightmares of betrayal.

When the United States entered the war, a number of black leaders had argued that a grateful nation would give recognition to the heroism of black soldiers. The nature of the gratitude was first seen in August 1917 in Houston, Texas. A basic training camp had been established there and housed both black and white soldiers. Because of its southern location, the camp instituted many of the same Jim Crow regulations that existed in the surrounding communities.[87]

Black soldiers, recentful over the restrictions, were greatly influenced by a widely circulated rumor that "a mob numbering thousands of armed white men" were advancing on the camp with the intent to attack them. Someone's shout of "The mob is coming, Get your guns" apparently set off the violence on the night of August 23. Two blacks and seventeen whites died in the battles.

A war department investigator was later to conclude that the trouble began because black soldiers attempted to "assert their rights as United States citizens and American soldiers," an ironic assertion for an event that was almost universally labeled by the white press as barbarism on the part of blacks. Within a few days of the incident, a court-martial was held for those blacks believed to be the leaders. Thirteen were found guilty and sentenced to die, forty-one were found guilty and sentenced to life imprisonment. The thirteen sentenced to die were hanged within days of the incident. According to an observer who had read the court-martial proceedings, both the prosecution and the defense agreed:

> There had been a number of instances wherein trouble had occurred be-
> tween the Negro soldiers and white men over the enforcement of the Texas
> "Jim Crow" law, which required segregation of Negroes and whites. It
> would appear that this could have been avoided by the exercise of a little
> judgement upon the part of commanding officers. 10/19

Further trials produced death sentences for fifteen more, and twelve more were sentenced to life. Six of the fifteen sentenced to die were hanged; the rest had their sentences commuted. No whites were ever charged with any crime.[88]

Although there was outrage from numerous sectors of the black community over both the severity and the inequity of the sentences, no attempts at appeasement on the part of the government were made. According to the *Messenger*, W. E. B. DuBois, who had at first expressed interest in publishing a poem by Archibald Grimke mourning the death of the soldiers, later withdrew his support suggesting that he had been "specially warned by the Department of Justice that some of our articles are considered disloyal." "I would not dare to print this just now," wrote DuBois to Grimke. Upset over the general disregard, the *Afro-American* in Baltimore proclaimed, "The Negroes of the entire country will regard the thirteen Negro soldiers of the Twenty-fourth Infantry executed as martyrs."[89]

Rather than concern, a debate increased within the military about whether such an incident confirmed the suspicion that blacks were mentally incapable of being good soldiers.

The events in Houston severely rattled but did not entirely destroy confidence in the military among blacks. In the end, 100,000 blacks did serve overseas in World War I.[90] Most were drafted after October 1917, several months after whites because the War Department did not know where to send them once they were drafted. The problem of training black soldiers while in the United States was one that had plagued the War Department even before the incident in Houston.[91] Most of the basic training camps were in the South because of the climate, and most southern communities objected strenuously to the idea of having blacks with guns, particularly northern-born ones, nearby.[92] While various schemes were proposed for their disposition, including segregated units, black soldiers were finally trained in carefully controlled, integrated settings.

Of the 100,000 who served, approximately 70,000 were listed in the various categories of military laborers, and only 30,000 saw actual combat. Many of those who worked as laborers reproduced the menial employment reserved for blacks outside of the military, making the experience neither heroic nor uncommon. Often they were placed in the worst housing, poorly fed, and deprived of adequate medical care. To add to their woes, they were staffed by southern white officers who, it was felt, knew how to handle blacks. The casualties of this war were as scarred as many of the physically wounded. "I am beginning to wonder," wrote one soldier, "whether it will ever be possible for me to see an American whiteman without wishing he were in his Satanic Majesty's private domain."[93]

Those who fought in combat units seemed to fare better than those in labor. Many took very seriously the special responsibility accorded by their being elevated above the usual menial level, as if some badge of merit had been bestowed upon them. Some were placed in various divisions of the French army and were treated by the less color-conscious French with actual respect and dignity; a treatment too often missing from the American side. In fact, black soldiers moved about freely in France and associated openly with French men and women, often to the anger of white American soldiers. Battles between Americans, white and black, were not unusual. Observed Lerone Bennett, "White officers spent so much time trying to inoculate Frenchmen with their prejudices that militant Negro leaders said white Americans fought more valiantly against the Negroes than they did against the Germans."[94]

Black soldiers also fought alongside of white Americans, many without incident and a few with acknowledged honor and decoration. But generally, the opportunity to prove themselves envisioned by black leaders had not been met in the war. Neglect, confusion, and offhand treatment were the best that was to be expected with racism always just under the surface of every encounter.

Blacks were not permitted to march in the Allied victory parade in Paris under the American flag, though black colonials marched under the banners of Britain and France. "In the Pantheon de la Guerre, where the achievements of the Allied armies are shown in a great painting, representing the history of the war, it was ordered that there should appear no face of a black American, although black colonials and Indians are represented," wrote A. M. Moore, head of the North Carolina Mutual Life Insurance Company, in 1920.[95] In fact, the army's plan for black troops after the war was to keep them under tight control and to ship them home as rapidly as possible. There was an official uneasiness about both the attitudes and the expectations of victorious black soldiers. They had learned bad habits in Europe, it was said. As one southern newspaper editorialized at war's end:

> You niggers are wondering how you are going to be treated after the war. Well I'll tell you. You are going to be treated exactly like you were before the war: this is a white man's country and we expect to rule it.[96]

There were, of course, parades and enthusiastic receptions at home for black soldiers in Buffalo, Saint Louis, and New York, where for years after people still talked with awe of the return of the 369th Division, marching up Fifth Avenue to Harlem. There was pride in many black communities over the return of the heroic soldiers. The May 1919 issue of *Crisis* proclaimed, "We Return! We Return from Fighting!" with a new spirit and a militancy that may be the reason the postal authorities held up its circulation for twenty-four hours.[97] But on the whole, although individuals boasted, the militancy and the spirit merely smoldered. And as the war wound down in Europe, the Great Migration proceeded on the home front, gaining in strength after the war.

Conclusion

The introduction of temporary migrants and the ascendancy of the corporate program had been the main ingredients of the economic transformation of 1870–1914. In their wake, the relations between workers and employers and the factory itself were all altered. Workers, who were often perplexed by the necessity of adapting to an age of machines, national markets, and giant business corporations, blamed each other for the changes.

Workers struggled in this period to retain some control over their work. They hoped to overcome their disadvantage in two ways. First, they attempted to establish a truly national union. Craft losses, wage competition and the simplification of industrial jobs brought on by more efficient equipment, and national markets made them realize that bargaining and organizing were no longer issues of purely local concern. Second, they attempted to discredit the newcomers by restrictive immigration legislation and perpetuation of notions of ethnic superiority.

In 1910, these strategies met with mixed success. Although the ideal of a national union was certainly not dead in the minds and hearts of labor leaders, the business community proved far more successful. And although restrictive legislation gained majority support in Congress, it did not become law.

By 1916, labor felt it had won a partial victory. The war had achieved what other strategies had not, it rid second- and third-generation as well as native workers of their cheap, first-generation competition. At the beginning of the war, there was optimism that wages would rise because of the combination of war demand and labor shortage. But what was unanticipated was that in going South, the North had gathered an even more formidable competitor.

The isolation and general poverty of rural areas reinforces the argument that most migrants came from southern towns.

PHOTOGRAPHER: Dorothea Lange
LOCATION: rural Mississippi
SOURCE: U.S. Department of Agriculture, negative number 17304-C

Laboring in the fields from "sun-up to sun-down" was common for rural workers. Reading employment advertisements in the *Chicago Defender*, on the other hand, was more unusual.

PHOTOGRAPHER: Dorothea Lange
LOCATION: rural Mississippi
SOURCE: U.S. Department of Agriculture, negative number 17462-E

The dress of town folk differed from that in rural areas, even among those who were idle.

PHOTOGRAPHER: Walker Evans
LOCATION: Mississippi town
SOURCE: U.S. Department of Agriculture, negative number 8061-A

Southern women living in towns more closely resembled their northern counterparts in dress.

PHOTOGRAPHER: Marion Post Wolcott
LOCATION: Mississippi town
SOURCE: U.S. Department of Agriculture, negative number 54967-E

Domestics in southern cities were often among the better dressed in the communities, in uniform or out of uniform.

PHOTOGRAPHER: Marion Post Wolcott
LOCATION: Mississippi town
SOURCE: U.S. Department of Agriculture, negative number 54985-E

A NEGRO FAMILY JUST ARRIVED IN CHICAGO FROM THE
RURAL SOUTH

"THESE ARE THEY WITH HOPE IN THEIR HEART"

The photograph at the top with its telling caption, "just arrived from the rural
South" is often printed without comment. The dress of the family is hardly
typical of the region. Moreover, it contrasts sharply with what is a more
representative photo, at the bottom, of a rural family from Florida.

PHOTOGRAPHER unknown
LOCATION: Chicago, Illinois and Newark, New Jersey
SOURCES: *Chicago Race Commission* 1919 (Chicago) *Survey* May 1918 (Newark)

COLLEGE-TRAINED MEN IN A CRACK DEPARTMENT OF THE PACKARD MOTOR CAR CO., DETROIT

THREE- AND FOUR-YEAR MEN ARE INCLUDED IN THIS GROUP FROM A WORKING FORCE OF 1,100 NEGROES

Work in the North was not easy. Although the label "college trained men" in the top photo probably exaggerates their experience, the employment of previously trained men is very likely as judged by their demeanor in both examples.

PHOTOGRAPHER unknown
LOCATION: Detroit
SOURCE: *Survey* May 1918

The Ida B. Wells housing project, federally financed, was a desired destination for lucky migrants. Built in 1938, it was, according to Cayton and Drake, "the unrealized dream of respectable lowers who wanted to make the mobility step to lower middle class." The project sponsored many self improvement clubs and had long waiting lists.

PHOTOGRAPHER: Jack Delano
LOCATION: Chicago
SOURCE: U.S. Department of Agriculture, negative number 820-D

Self governance was also an important feature of the housing project as this photograph suggests, emblematic of the desire to be as American as possible.

PHOTOGRAPHER: Jack Delano
LOCATION: Chicago
SOURCE: U.S. Department of Agriculture, negative number 665-D

Again, while not necessarily typical, this photo of recent migrants working in Chicago and living in the project reflects the diversity of the population, a point often neglected in previous analyses.

PHOTOGRAPHER: Jack Delano
LOCATION: Chicago
SOURCE: U.S. Department of Agriculture, negative number 803-D

CHAPTER FIVE

Migration and Reaction

We have many noble men,
But the South has held them back
The South was ne'er my people's
friend—
They kept him in the sack.
Yankee land, my future home,
O, how I long for thee.
Upon they bosom let me roam,
And feel that I am free.

Some good old sweet spring morn,
You'll say dat crowd dat built de South
Is sho nuff good an' gone.[1]

IN ANY MIGRATION, IT IS usual to find a disparity between the inflated hopes of the movers and the somber reality of their move. Blacks, like many of the European immigrants who had come before them, saw the American North as a "promised land"; and like their predecessors, they found unrealized dreams at the end of the journey. The host society labors, too, under false and overblown expectations of the gift of immigration, believing that migrants who fail do so by the inelasticity of their own bootstraps and that failure rests with them alone.

Many sociologists and historians have framed their studies of the Great Migration along similar lines. They argue that its importance lies in the opportunity it gave blacks to move from traditional agriculture to industrial employment. The migration is examined as if it were the first step in the difficult transformation of the black peasant into modern worker, a change akin to the passage of the black savage child into adulthood. The underlying paternalism of such analyses are often liberally couched with pervasive optimism. In time, the backward black worker will compete on an equal footing with his more modern white counterpart, but it must be understood that it will take a very long time. That the road has been hard and the journey slowed by discrimination and exploitation is repeatedly acknowledged but ultimately discounted by the more significant "evidence" of the innate characteristics of the newcomers. After all, it is argued, Negro "peasants" journeying northward lacked the educational background to advance. Unskilled and ignorant, this southern black sharecropper would not have advanced in the sophisticated and increasingly skilled city, even in the absence of discrimination and exploitation. And perhaps most insistently, a folk culture of slavery, poverty, and matriarchal tendencies left the population too weak and vulnerable to thrive in a society founded on independence, wealth, and patriarchy.

The actual migrant who went North was nearly invisible. Identified solely by his thick accent and dark skin, the content of his experience was assumed rather than revealed. "There are many false impressions," lamented one Department of Agriculture investigator. "Many white people have been amazed at the migrant's aptness," commented another.[2] Indeed, past failures to understand who actually migrated are systematically reflected in accounts of what happened to them after the fact. In this chapter, I shall examine the "great opportunity" of black workers and make assessments about the position of economic advantage into which they moved. From the start, those who went North faced hardships. With the experiences of the war, these hardships took on new meaning. Migrants found, in fact, that in the North there was another war going on; this one between themselves, employers, and white workers.

Employers' Use of Migrant Labor

For employers, the introduction of southern black laborers proved even more advantageous than most had hoped. "If it hadn't been for the negro at that time," said a former official of the Carnegie Steel Company in Pittsburgh, "we could hardly have carried on our operations."[3]

This new labor was used not merely as a surrogate for lost labor, but also to reinforce the advantage of employers over workers. By capitalizing on racial antagonisms, employers could combat and undermine most attempts at worker organization. The process took a variety of forms. In some instances, employers imported black workers to replace whites who were on strike. In others, an entire work group would be replaced by black workers as a sign to the remaining white workers to stay in line.

Subtler forms of persuasion were also used. In Saint Louis, a border city, companies such as Missouri Malleable Iron Works and Swift, Armour, Nelson, and Morris made it a policy "to keep three classes of men at work and as nearly equal numerically as possible."[4] The division was one-third foreign whites, one-third American whites, and one-third blacks. The theory was that these three groups would never unite to form a strike. A large steel plant in that city, after experiencing labor unrest, took the extreme precaution of hiring a black worker for each white worker employed from the lowest to the highest skills.[5]

Employers gained as well from the fact that they did not have to assume either the recruitment or training costs of the new workers. As shown, migrants were experienced in many of the fields for which their labor was sought and paid for the journey North themselves. It was the South that financed both the education and the training of these migrants, a now familiar pattern of a peripheral area supplying and subsidizing employment for a wealthier and more developed core.[6]

By selecting on the basis of age and health, employers also avoided many health or "lost-time" expenses connected with a population unable to do the strenuous work expected of them.[7] Migrants were given "dirty work" jobs shunned by higher-priced white labor. At times the work involved tasks that no one wanted to do at any wage. But often it was the wage rather than the activity that turned away those who had other opportunities. As Castells suggests, "these jobs were given up primarily because they were less well-paid, not because they were dirty."[8]

Further, low-paying jobs had a high concentration of black workers because blacks were unable to secure work elsewhere, not because they were less skilled.[9] Migrant Charles Denby describes his first job:

> As I looked around, all the men were dirty and greasy and smoked up. They were beyond recognition. There were only three or four whites. These were Polish. Negroes told me later they were the only ones able to stand the work. Their faces looked exactly like Negro faces. They were so matted and covered with oil and dirt that no skin showed. Hines [his friend] and I went home discussing how it was that they could say everyone was free with equal rights up North. There was no one in the foundry but Negroes.[10]

But perhaps the greatest benefit to employers was that the appearance of a population crippled by a host of interrelated problems was always stronger than the reality of one hampered by exploitation. Believed to be fundamentally stupid, docile, and apathetic, fleeing the oppression of the South, strangers in a new land whose natives viewed them with suspicion, the labor migrants became easy targets. Why are wages low? Black workers have been brought in from the South. Why have conditions in the factories deteriorated? Black workers have been brought in from the South. Why are white men idle? Black men have been brought in from the South. Their sins were so accepted, they were forced to beg for the very privilege of being exploited. Observed federal investigator Frances Tyson:

The industrial opportunity which the Negro can get is not even the same as is demanded by his more fortunate white-skinned brother. While his fellow human beings demand a larger voice in industry and business and a greater share of the product in industry, the Negro is still meekly begging for his inalienable right to participate in industry.[11]

The disadvantage of having to "beg to participate" was further aggravated by regional differences in wage levels. The wage disparity between North and South was very real. According to Charles Wesley, "unskilled foundry workers in Alabama received $2.50 for a ten-hour day. The same workers in Illinois received $3.20 per ten-hour day, to $4.25 per nine-hour day."[12] Black migrants were heavily represented in these bottom-level jobs, receiving the lowest wage and viewing it as an advance. It is not surprising, as Wesley found in Pittsburgh, "that while one plant's output was reduced by 60 percent and white workmen were released, the entire Negro force was retained."[13]

The large number of black laborers in the South desirous of going North put the newly arrived, who had jobs, at an even greater disadvantage. Again Denby chronicles:

They would pay us off right there if we looked back or stopped working. Workers passed out from the heat. The foremen rushed a stretcher over and two workers would take the man out, give him fifteen minutes to revive and then he would have to go back to work. When a man passed out, the foreman would be running out to see if the guy was conscious. He would be cursing all the time. If the worker took too long, he'd shake him. They never mentioned a wound serious enough to go to first aid.[14]

The combination of the handicaps of regional wage differences, vulnerability, and the surplus made the new laborers recruited from the South particularly valuable to employers. What began as an experiment on the part of a few was soon transformed into standard and accepted practice. Declared one, "Since 1916 the negro's relation to industry has changed from that of a labor reserve to be drawn on in emergencies to a permanent part of the labor force."[15] And, as André Gorz has more pointedly observed about immigrant labor in general, without them, "hours of work, conditions and modes of work would have to be radically improved."[16]

Employers obtained what at first appeared to be an unlimited supply of desperate, cheap, and capable workers. It is not surprising, then, that in questionnaires distributed to 137 employers in Chicago by the Chicago Commission on Race Relations, 118 stated that they were satisfied with the migrant labor. In comparing the efficiency of black and white workers, 70% stated that they considered "the Negro equally efficient."[17] This would be a surprising revelation if applied to the rural, inexperienced, and untrained population assumed to be the typical migrant. But the selection process, as has been shown, favored those with experience and training. In fact, it was significant to the commission that "ability was shown by Negro workers in widely dissimilar occupations and industries."[18] One foundry superintendent reported:

> I know of a Pullman porter who has been with the Pullman Company twenty years who turned out to be as good a helper as we had in the foundry. Take a man who has made beds for twenty years, put him to carrying melted iron in a ladle, which is a real man's job, and make good at it, and I think he's going some. We had one man who did that and did it well. He was a helper that the different foremen tried to get hold of, wanted to have him with them.[19]

Some mentioned that "because of his knowledge of English, the Negro is frequently more efficient than the foreign-speaking worker."[20] The vice-president of the Packard Company "stated that in both skilled and unskilled labor, the Negroes had been good workers and that they were 'considerably better than' the average foreigner."[21] One wool warehouse company, for example, reported that:

> Poles were satisfactory under the old method of shipping wool in carloads from a single shipper, but the new system, with shipments of hundreds of sacks tagged with the names of as many shippers, required laborers unloading the cars to separate the shipments into sections. This the Poles were unable to do, while the Negroes did the work very efficiently.[22]

A superintendent in a large packing company stated:

> Negroes do not require as much supervision as some of those racial groups who do not understand the language. We can talk to a man and tell him what to do, where to go to do the work and how to do it, we can accomplish a whole lot more than if we had to send an individual with him constantly from place to place to show him how to do it. To that extent the Negro has the advantage over the man who cannot talk the English language.[23]

In part, these invidious comparisons merely served the racist ideology of division, for favorable comparisons between blacks and immigrants went beyond simple issues of language to the complex question of political acumen and national character. According to one employer, "the Negro is no trouble maker. When he is dissatisfied, he quits." Such behavior was considered praiseworthy because it reflected an awareness of basic American traditions. Explained another, "they do not bring with them any of the communistic or socialistic spirit to be found among some immigrants from certain portions of Europe."[24] Such pronouncements were reminiscent of southern boosters' praise of Anglo-Saxon stock—hardy, hardworking, and docile—and suggest that even when migrants were perceived of as behaving admirably, the perception was for the purpose of oppressing them.

But comparison also reflected more practical considerations. An Urban League worker in Detroit reported:

> Many of the employers feel that it is cheaper to work negroes in dangerous places in their plants than it is to work foreigners because the negroes understand English. And because of the fact, the company is kept from paying large sums of money for accidents.[25]

Employers were well pleased with the experiment to import black labor. Black workers proved more than adequate as a substitute for those who left, and their employment kept the factories producing at wartime rates of profit and, as the next section will show, effectively disciplined any who opposed the latest labor reserve.

The War with White Labor

Perhaps the greatest advantage gained by employers was in regard to labor unions. Explains Castells, "the utility of immigrant labor to capital derives primarily from the fact that it can act toward it as though the labor movement did not exist, thereby moving the class struggle back several decades."[26] Historically, black participation in unions in the North had been a constant dilemma for national labor organizations. Even when their statutes denied color barriers, many locals were strictly segregated. The result was that the rate of black unionization was very low. It was racism, in the words of Castells, "diffused by the dominant ideology." Castells observes further that, "trade unions are sometimes afraid to counteract the xenophobic attitudes of part of the labor force and end up reinforcing the situation which they themselves denounce."[27] Although some black workers made efforts to organize themselves, these attempts were few.[28] Most were unwilling to "expose themselves to union local discrimination when they could avoid it by simply not joining a union."[29]

Employers capitalized on this situation. Epstein concludes in his study of Pittsburgh that "while it may be said that the true motives may not be to break up the labor movement, it was self-evident that the employers would scarcely admit that motive even if it were paramount." It seems to Epstein, moreover, that the employers used migrants against the securing of the eight-hour day, which the local unions were attempting to attain. The employment agent of one of the large industrial plants in Pittsburgh, which had undergone a big strike a few years before, pointed out:

one of the great values of the Negro migration lies in the fact that it gives me a chance to 'mix up my labor forces and to establish a balance of power,' as the Negro, he claimed is more individualistic, does not like to group and does not follow a leader, as readily as some foreigners do.[30]

Tying such neglect to "the individualistic" nature of the black worker was not warranted. As shown in chapter 3, blacks had been heavily involved in nascent attempts at unionization in the South. Epstein found that "a single local of the Hod Carriers Union, a strong labor organization, had over four hundred blacks among its six hundred members. It had proved how easy it was to organize even the newest migrants by enlisting over one hundred and fifty southern hod carriers within a single year." Such neglect, then, is more readily tied to custom, tradition, and erroneous perceptions of the black worker.[31]

The experiences of two black migrants who were painters from Georgia highlight the situation. They had applied to a Pittsburgh union for membership in 1916. Both claimed over nineteen years of experience in the trade. The union refused them. The result was that one of these men found work on his own, in a nonunion shop. He received $20 per week for eight-and-one-half-hour days, as compared with $5.50 for an eight-hour day union scale. He was working longer hours and for less pay. Both white worker and black worker lost out in this example; the white worker because of the viability of the nonunion shop, the black worker because of his low pay. That many of the skilled black workers knew of such discriminatory union practices and did not attempt to join them is probable. One migrant, on being questioned about why he did not try to join, shrugged his shoulders and said, "What's the use?"[32] Labor, however, viewed such expressions as reactionary.

Misunderstanding further complicated patterns of exclusion. In Pittsburgh, this was apparent in a report from the plasterers' union. Members stated that "the greatest objection" they had was that black "plasterers asked for a smaller scale of wages ($4.50 a day as compared for $6 for whites)." However, when questioned about why black workers did not "prefer a higher wage," it was "explained that they could not get work as no one would employ a person of color at the same wages as a white person."[33]

The relationship between black and white labor was often a stormy one. Difficulties centered around both union membership and the fact that at times blacks were imported as strikebreakers and were effectively used to break the unions. In March and April of 1917, the Industrial Workers of the World (IWW) organized a strike in a sugar refinery in Philadelphia. The company tried to man the factory with black workers, who were trucked in. They were subsequently attacked by the striking whites, and when they attempted to defend themselves, they were arrested for assault and battery. When the trouble had subsided, the union had been defeated and black workers, rather than the company, were blamed. In an oil-refining company in that same city, the policy of refusing to hire black workers had been changed "when a spontaneous strike for an eight-hour day and a higher wage involved almost 70 percent of the 4,000 foreign workers at the plant." With the introduction of black workers, the strike had been broken, and blacks became a permanent part of the work force.[34]

Although there is much discussion in the literature that "the black man is not given to striking," it is not always clear that the imported workers were aware of the true purpose of their employment. In 1901, the Latrobe Steel Company of Chicago brought in 317 black workers from Birmingham, Alabama. When these workers realized that they were to be used as scabs, they refused to work and asked to be returned to Alabama. Stating that he had a decent paying job in Birmingham, one of the steelworkers said that he had no idea that he "would be asked to take the place of any man on strike" or he "never would have left the South."[35]

There were, however, other instances where the strikebreaking activities were clear. One migrant, writing from the South in a pattern typical of many, stated that he had read of a strike in the newspaper and was inquiring about the possibility of employment because of it. There had been historical precedents to such activity. A meat cutter's union in Chicago, which had been formed in 1902, struck in June 1904. The strike lasted only ten weeks because thousands of replacements lined up each day to take the places of the strikers. In this strike as in the one several years before, white workers considered the villains of the piece to be the black workers brought in. One observer estimated that "upwards of eighteen thousand blacks served as strikebreakers, with almost fourteen hundred arriving in one trainload."[36]

It is probable that these figures are exaggerated, for it was known that many white workers also served as strikebreakers, including white women. However, the presence of a sizable proportion of blacks was sufficient to have them exclusively labeled as the enemies of white labor. Speaking of this meat cutters' strike, Sterling D. Spero and Abram L. Harris estimate that in actuality only eight hundred blacks were used out of a strike force of five thousand. But the black worker stood out in the crowd. "The presence of a dozen blacks in a force of strikebreakers appears to the strikers like a hundred," the authors maintain.[37]

The notion of damage brought on by the presence of black labor was reinforced in the press. In October 1916, the *Fort Wayne Gazette* carried an editorial which read:

> That the introduction of so much black labor contains a menace to organized labor is recognized by the officials of the American Federation of Labor and President Gompers has directed a thorough inquiry into the situation, which it is concerned may grow into the gravest problem labor unionism in the North has had to confront.[38]

Elevating the problem of black labor above those of hours, wages, conditions, and collective bargaining reflects the seriousness with which the issue was viewed. During the period of the Great Migration, blacks were successfully used as strikebreakers in the steel industry in 1919, in the Detroit metal trades strike in 1921, in the bricklayers strike in Newark in 1923, and in the fig and date packers strike in Chicago in 1926.[39]

Adding to the conflict was the fact that the use of blacks as strikebreakers was supported by much of the black leadership. Marcus Garvey counseled, "beware the white man's union." Professor Kelly Miller of Howard University declared, "For the negro wantonly to flout the generous advances of the great industries by joining the restless ranks which threaten industrial ruin would be fatuous suicide." On their part, the restless ranks "gained the impression that the negro group, in its efforts to overcome its disadvantages had allied itself with capital against the interests of white labor."[40]

No laborers gained in such battles. Still, an assessment of pervasive antiunionism within the black community represents too facile an argument. Spero and Harris point out that the strikebreaking activities of blacks should be put in proper perspective:

> When all is said and done, the number of strikes broken by black labor has been few as compared with the number broken by white labor. What is more, the Negro has seldom been the only or even the most important strikebreaking element. Employers in emergencies take whatever labor they can get and the Negro is only one of many groups involved. But the bitterness of American race prejudice has always made his presence an especially sore point and not infrequently a signal for exceptional disorder.[41]

Union exclusion, the authors concluded, "served as a moral justification for the Negro's breaking the white man's strike, and served for the white unionists as a justification to intensify his anti-black feeling."[42] When in the 1930s unions finally welcomed black membership, it was almost too late to heal the deep wounds that had been inflicted in those early years; and the power accrued in strong biracial trade unionism was never what it could have been.

There were, then, both winners and losers in the North as a result of the Great Migration. Capital benefited greatly. Seeking the largest profit out of labor, employers willingly used black workers at a scale reasonably below the standard union wage. White unionists lost. Demanding, through their organizations, standard wages, they were all too often undercut by this new and more formidable labor reserve.

The State as Mediator

As suggested initially, the state was not a disinterested party in interactions between capital, organized labor, and migrant workers. At the turn of the century, a belief emerged and gained ascendancy among a small and powerful lobby that progress would most effectively be obtained by an enlightened merger of previously warring factions. For business, it was a self-serving philosophy with the threat of risks in the present outweighed by the promise of large gains for the future. James Weinstein characterizes it as,

> a conscious and successful effort to guide and control the economic and social policies of federal, state, and municipal governments by various business groupings in their own long-range interest as they perceived it.[43]

For labor, the opportunity to work with the business community held both the promise of the much-sought-after benefit of recognition and the feared label of capitulation.

The first arena for this effort was the development of the National Civic Federation (NCF), an organization begun in 1900 with the altruistic goal of producing "better relations between capital and labor."[44] Its membership included Andrew Carnegie, Samuel Insull, and "several partners in J.P. Morgan and Company," as well as Samuel Gompers and John Mitchell of the United Mine Workers (UMW). Weinstein points out that "in its initial years—until 1905—the Federation saw its main role to be that of a direct mediator in labor disputes."[45] Although it never lost this thrust, it began in succeeding years to expand into other areas, including regulatory legislation, immigration policy, and child labor laws. What the NCF saw itself doing was prodding state governments toward uniform laws in the public interest, such as those affecting workmen's compensation and minimum-wage laws. But some members of the labor movement saw something quite different. The Manifesto of the Industrial Workers of the World, for example, stated that "the Civic Federation was the industrialist's way to conceal his daggers while hoodwinking those he would rule and exploit."[46]

Indeed, throughout its existence, the organization struggled with the difficulty of "reaching consensus between business" on the one hand and labor on the other. There were numerous occasions where the results were unsatisfactory. Immigration policy was one of the most evident areas of conflict, with business leaders espousing open borders and labor severe restrictions. Under those conditions, the NCF could only stand in the wings stating, it had "no opinions and no policy to advance on the subject."[47]

In 1913, on the other hand, with a pending railroad strike, the NCF not only acted as mediator in the particular dispute but drafted more general legislation, which was then introduced into the Senate and eventually became law. One of the purposes of this legislation was to establish specific procedures for settling strikes. What the NCF had done, in essence, was to increase the stakes, passing on the role of conciliator to the federal level, and directly involving the state on their own terms.

The product of this legislation was the U.S. Conciliation Service, a division of the Department of Labor. Not surprisingly, during the period of the Great Migration, many of the labor disputes under its jurisdiction involved migrating black workers. Often agents were dispensed to trouble spots North and South and asked to mediate between workers and employers. Having assessed the situation, agents would then communicate directly to the Department of Labor, often by telegram. The agency was continually limiting the parameters of its role vis-à-vis workers. Typically, in October 1918, in a butchers' strike in Saint Louis involving black strikebreakers, an agent informed union leaders "that it would be unwise for any employees to strike before the Government had an opportunity to adjust the difficulty, and instructed them to inform the employees that the Government would not tolerate a strike."[48]

Similarly, when two black workers complained of union discrimination by the Chicago Grain Elevators, the agent contacted, after investigation, explained "that there was nothing any one could do to prevent the organization from deciding who shall or shall not be admitted to membership."[49]

What both instances suggest is a policy of regulation within very narrow ranges of operation, as suggested by Bach, and a consistent support for the status quo. In some cases, a clear conflict of interest emerged, as when in a dispute in Pensacola, Florida, the agent wrote back:

> These men did not want to accept this agreement as their whole desire seemed to be to secure not only a closed shop, but an immediate increase in wages as well as double time for over time. However as it looked as though the situation might be prolonged, some of the men leaving for other localities, the work delayed as well, I simply demanded that the issue be brought to a close, hence the compliance of same.[50]

At issue was completion of a government contract for submarine chasers for the Navy Department. The mediator in this instance was well aware in whose favor the decision would be made and seemed to express surprise at the "excessive" union demands.

Generally, the results of this state activity were three-fold. First, it minimized the more violent reactions of organized labor to the newcomers by providing piecemeal and selective solutions to more widespread and endemic problems. Second, it persuaded businesses, in the interest of order and profit, to give in on modest wage demand proposals as a compromise that would be for their benefit in the long term. And third, it used the threat of force to cool off the most volatile of situations. Ultimately, its impact was to conciliate labor while at the same time disciplining its members with migrant workers.

Migrants at Work

Migrants were directed to specific industrial centers, industries, and jobs. Between 1910 and 1920, for example, New York experienced a 66% increase in its black population; Chicago, a 148% increase; Detroit, a 611% increase; and Philadelphia, a 59% increase. (Table 5.1). By 1920, almost 40% of the black population in the North was concentrated in these cities.

The great bulk of migrants found their way into manufacturing industries, with a 40% increase over levels established in 1910. Relatedly, their presence in domestic and personal service declined nearly 6%. However, region-wide statistics mask the real changes that were occurring in the cities. In Chicago, for example, 51% of the male black labor force was engaged in domestic and personal service in 1910, while only 28% was so engaged in 1920.[51]

In Chicago, increases were most dramatic in packing houses and in the steel industry. In packing houses, there were only 67 blacks employed in 1910 and nearly 3,000 in 1920. In steel, black representation increased from 6% in 1910 to 17% in 1920. Detroit automobile plants first hired blacks in 1916, and their numbers reached 11,000 by 1926.[52]

As previously mentioned, most who went North were hired in low-paid work regardless of their skill or experience. The majority became unskilled or semiskilled operatives. Many of those who followed skilled crafts in the South were banned from them in the North by company policy, urban regulations, or craft tradition where there was no union. As Scott suggests, "vacancies for blacks in industry were made at the bottom."[53]

Workers frequently signed wage contracts in the South before going

Table 5.1
Increases in Black Population in Major
Northern Cities, 1910–1920

Cities	1910	1920	Increase 1910 to 1920 No.	1920 %
New York, N.Y.	91,709	152,467	60,758	66.3
Chicago, Ill.	44,103	109,458	65,355	148.2
Philadelphia, Pa.	84,459	134,229	49,770	58.9
Detroit, Mi.	5,741	40,838	35,097	611.3
Cleveland, Ohio	8,448	34,451	26,003	307.8
Pittsburgh, Pa.	25,623	37,725	12,102	47.2
Cincinnati, Ohio	19,639	30,079	10,440	53.2
Indianapolis, Ind.	21,816	34,678	12,862	59.0
Newark, N.J.	9,475	16,977	7,502	79.2
Kansas City, Mo.	23,566	30,719	7,153	30.4

SOURCE: U.S. Department of Commerce, *Negroes in the United States 1920–1932* (Washington, D.C.: Government Printing Office, 1935), p. 55.

North, and in ignorance of prevailing wages, accepted lower amounts. The following is a typical wage contract for a railroad, a pattern, however, not exclusive to this industry:

> It is hereby understood that I am to work for the above named company . . . , the rate to pay to be _____. The _____ railroad agrees to furnish transportation and food to destination. I agree to work on any part of the _____Railroad where I may be assigned. I further agree to reimburse the _____Railroad for the cost of meals and other expenses incidental to my employment. I authorize the company to deduct from my wages money to pay for the above expenses. In consideration of the _____ Railroad paying my car fare, board and other expenses, I agree to remain in the service of the aforesaid company until such time as I reimburse them for the expenses of my transportation, food, etc. It is agreed upon the part of the railroad company that if I shall remain in the service for one year the _____ Railroad agrees to return to me the amount of car fare from point of shipment to _____. By continuous service for one year is meant that I shall not absent myself from duty any time during the period without the consent of my superior officer. It is understood by me that the _____ Railroad will not grant me free transportation to the point where I was employed. I am not less than 21 years or more than 45 years of age, and have no venereal disease. If my statement is found to be incorrect this contract becomes void.[54]

Those who did not sign prior wage agreements were little better off. Arriving in the North with few assets, they were hardly in a position to bargain over wages. High cost of food and lodging were sufficient incentives to force many to take the first available job. This disadvantage was reflected in comparative wage rates. The earnings of black workers were less than those of white men because they did different work.[55] In the North, there was little discrimination in wage rates for workers doing the same work. However, in plants where blacks constituted a large proportion of the work force, wages were lower than in those where they were a minority.[56] This plant-wide pattern of discrimination was found throughout northern industry, with many companies attempting to increase black workers for this reason alone.

The promise of high wages drew many families North. Some, for the first time in their lives were able to buy goods and services they had only dreamed of in the past. "Should have come here twenty years ago," commented one migrant. Another stated, "Well, Dr., with the aid of God I am making very good. I make $75 per month. I am carrying enough insurance to pay me $20 per week if I am not able to be on duty."[57] But surprisingly, a sizable proportion went North to lower wages. Epstein reports, for example, that of the over four hundred studied, 15% stated that their wages were over $3.60 in the South, while only 5% reported such wages in the North.[58]

The Chicago Race Commission cited the case of the Jones family who were "leading citizens in their southern hometown. They owned their own home and two other places of property in the same town, one of which brought in $20 a month." Trained as a boiler maker in the South, Mr. Jones found a similar position in the North at the same wages. When asked why they went, they replied: "to escape segregation and to secure improved conditions of work, although there is no difference in the wages."[59] What migrants found was low wages, poor working conditions, lack of opportunity, and a higher cost of living.

While actual wages varied by city, industry, and level of skill, the average migrant earned about $25 for a forty-eight to sixty-hour work week.[60] Bricklayers and plasterers in Chicago could make as much as $30 for a forty-hour week, and Pullman porters as much as $35. By contrast to wages, prices rose sharply throughout the migration period. A loaf of bread that cost 5 cents in 1914, cost over 11 cents in 1920. Coffee went from 30 cents a pound to 47 cents; sugar, from 38 cents for five pounds to 97 cents; and a dozen eggs from 35 cents to 68 cents. In 1919, the Bureau of Labor Statistics estimated that "$43.51 was the weekly income necessary to maintain an acceptable standard of living for a family of five."[61] Obviously, on the migrants' salary alone, most families could not achieve this standard.

Direct information on the migrant experience is difficult to attain. However, a rough comparison of incomes may be made between migrant and nonmigrant populations using a current subsample of the General Social Sciences survey. The sample was taken between 1974 and 1984, and contained men and women, black and white, and an array of age groups including those born between 1883 and 1923, and 1924 and 1944. These two cohorts may be used as a substitute for the migrating population. Respondents were asked their current income levels and the responses were dichotomized into categories of below average, average, and above.

Although these data serve as a weak approximation both for the Great Migration population and for their actual earnings, it does nonetheless provide some opportunity for a comparative assessment over time and between the races. Most importantly, a comparison may be made by race between those who remained in the South (S-S), moved South to North (S-N), and those who were born and remained in the North (N-N).

In Table 5.2 a comparison is made between education and earnings, broken down by race. This table suggests that low education and average or above income combines for a majority of only one segment of the black population, those born and reared in the North. There is a 12% difference

Table 5.2

Income Levels of Black and White Workers, Born between
1883 and 1923, with 0–12 Years of Schooling, by Region
(in percentage)

| Black Workers | Income | | | N |
	Average or above	Below		
N-N	55	45	100	40
S-N	43	57	100	107
S-S	43	57	100	230
Total				377

| White Workers | Income | | | N |
	Average or above	Below		
N-N	65	35	100	1,320
S-N	61	39	100	45
S-S	61	39	100	581
Total				1,946

SOURCE: General Social Science Survey, 1972–1984.

between their average or above income percentages and the rest. There is a more modest difference (4%), though one in the same direction, for the white population. However, it is of even more interest to note that in terms of income, moving North or remaining in the South made little difference for the rest of the black population. For migrants, the great northern payoff never materialized. As has been suggested by other documentation, the direct monetary rewards of the Great Migration were negligible.

Table 5.3 makes the same comparison using populations with high levels of educational attainment. Here, an advantage to stay in the South is suggested, with 69% of the southern black population remaining in the South earning average or above incomes. Taken together, both tables suggest that migrants (S-N), regardless of their level of education, gained little in going North (see tables 5.2 and 5.3). This finding provides the most direct confirmation of the contention made throughout that migrants were recruited as a source of cheap labor and that their personal abilities mattered little. On the other hand, for the white population similarly situated, increased education was not discounted in the North. Taken to-

Table 5.3

Income Levels of Black and White Workers, Born between 1883 and 1923, with Twelve Years of Schooling or Above, by Region

(in percentage)

Black Workers	Income			N
	Average or above	*Below*		
N-N	61	39	100	36
S-N	56	44	100	34
S-S	69	31	100	45
Total				115

White Workers	Income			N
	Average or above	*Below*		
N-N	79	21	100	1,547
S-N	80	20	100	79
S-S	80	20	100	388
Total				2,014

SOURCE: General Social Science Survey, 1972–1984.

gether, these tables lend support for the general disappointment found in the promises of the migration.

Because an argument could be advanced that the migration benefit may not be realized in the first generation, a second subsample was drawn of populations born between 1924 and 1944. These are the children and the grandchildren of the migrant era population. It is evident from Table 5.4 that the northern advantage has been lessened. There is only a 4% difference between blacks born in the South moving North and the rest. While some may argue that this could be owing, in part, to the black southern influence (i.e., population contains children of parents born in the South), a reduction is also found within the white community (1% difference). Gone, too, is the southern benefit for educated populations, as shown in Table 5.5. But, most importantly, the advance for the black population is very slight. Forty-three percent of the cohort between 1883 and 1923, with less than twelve years of education, had average incomes or above, and 44% of the later cohort. In numerical terms, they made a 1% gain. Fifty-six percent of the earlier cohort with higher education had average or above incomes, and 61% of the later cohort. Theirs was a mod-

Table 5.4

Income Levels of Black and White Workers, Born between
1924 and 1943, with 0–12 Years of Schooling, by Region
(in percentage)

Black Workers	Income Average or above	Below		N
N-N	47	53	100	47
S-N	44	56	100	69
S-S	43	57	100	134
Total				250

White Workers	Income Average or above	Below		N
N-N	69	31	100	654
S-N	70	30	100	46
S-S	68	32	100	385
Total				1,085

SOURCE: General Social Science Survey, 1972–1984.

Table 5.5

Income Levels of Black and White Workers, Born between
1924 and 1943, with Twelve Years of Schooling or Above,
by Region
(in percentage)

| Black Workers | Income | | | N |
	Average or above	Below		
N-N	66	34	100	111
S-N	61	39	100	71
S-S	61	39	100	103
Total				285

| White Workers | Income | | | N |
	Average or above	Below		
N-N	83	17	100	2,265
S-N	88	12	100	120
S-S	86	14	100	651
Total				3,036

SOURCE: General Social Science Survey, 1972–1984.

est 5% increase. Whites did consistently better, achieving a 9% improvement in the first instance and an 8% improvement in the second. Even in the second generation, the migration failed to make a significant difference in their lives.

Migrant Advancement and Promotion

After wages, the most common complaint among migrants was lack of opportunity for advancement or promotion. This was often joined with the complaint that foremen favored white workers. Migrants complained of "discrimination in the distribution of work, in recognition of efficiency, or in permitting the earning of overtime rates."[62]

In a foundry company, migrants stated that the foreman in one department deliberately established conditions discouraging to black workers. He had an even number of black and white workers employed as partners on a certain process of piecework rates, each doing half of a joint task. When a man was absent, partners would be shifted about so that a black worker would be left without a partner instead of a white man. This handicapped the single worker by slowing down the process so he could not earn a full day's pay. It was also said that the same foreman allowed white workers to accumulate a supply of material for their work, although he ordered black workers to stop this practice, thus forcing them to lose time in making frequent trips for material.[63] Such preferential treatment of white workers was costly for black workers.

It was even more costly for blacks to be denied access to promotion. From interviews with representatives of the packing companies, the Chicago Race Commission learned "that the Negro in reality has little opportunity for promotion in the yards. There were no Negro foremen over mixed gangs. The highest position a Negro was able to reach was that of subforeman over a group of Negro workmen."[64] The general superintendent of one of the packing companies admitted that he had never tried out a Negro as foreman over a mixed gang because he would not want to work under a Negro himself. Such an attitude closed the door to advancement and limited the opportunities of even the most experienced blacks.

The opportunity for advancement signaled in the breakthrough in industry had not been met. According to Spear, blacks entering at the bottom of the job hierarchy were following a path similar to that of Poles and Czechs who had entered at that point in the 1880s. In the 1920s, some Poles and Czechs had moved into supervisory and even managerial positions. Over time, it was likely that blacks would do the same. Yet, suggests Spear, there were in 1920, indications that for blacks "the ladder of advancement would have slippery rungs."[65] Unlike their predecessors, black industrial gains were tenuous and limited.

Family Contributions to Income

The low wages black workers received in the North meant that women as well as men had to work. Their being forced into the marketplace even after migration separated black women from their white counterparts, not so much in fact as in intensity. A New York survey found that over 30% of married black women worked as against only 3.4% of married white women.[66] Nearly half of all black women could expect to work most of their adult lives. Unlike white women, whose work declined sharply after age twenty, the proportion of black women employed did not drop significantly until age sixty-five. Writing in 1902, activist and educator Mary Church Terrell observed, "Black women contributed as much support to the family income as men, and when they were out of a job, the whole family suffered.[67]

As they had in the South, most black women in the North worked as domestics. The general term "domestic" includes a variety of work arrangements. In the south, a live-out system had predominated in which a domestic lived near her employers and was able to return to her own home at scheduled intervals. In the North, shortly after the migration, a live-in system predominated in which a domestic lived with her employers, receiving time off periodically, such as two Sundays a month. Over time, while live-in systems survived, a more popular arrangement became day's work, done either for a single family, over the course of a week, with a return home each night, or work done for several families over the course of the same period.

Although day's work was less well paying, it was preferred by many because it allowed them to have more time with their families. Migrant women were put in the difficult situation of having both to work and to leave the running of their households to the eldest female child or a friendly neighbor, if the children were too small. The popularity of day's work was explained succinctly by one domestic. "The living-in jobs just kept you running, never stopped. Day or night you'd be getting something for somebody. You'd serve them. It was never a minutes' peace. But when I went out days on my job, I'd get my work done and be gone. I guess that's it. This work had an end."[68] It was imperative that these women work to supplement the meager earnings of their husbands, and yet they sought in the midst of large numbers in the work force, worker substitutability, and vulnerability, to transform their labor so that they could not only fulfill their roles as wives and mothers but also gain, as this quote suggests, an element of worker control.

As work, domestic service is most appropriately located within the informal sector of the economy. It is isolated work that provides neither accident protection nor job or wage security. Usually, they performed a variety of household jobs for a single white family and were "permitted to scrub floors on bended knees, to hang precariously from window sills, or to strain and sweat over steaming tubs of heavy blankets, spreads, and furniture covers."[69] They worked as many as fourteen hours a day, frequently on an irregular schedule, worked longer than was arranged, got less than was promised, and had to accept clothing instead of cash.

A Washington survey of domestics cited a typical work situation. The woman, a native of South Carolina, was twenty-six years old and had worked as a domestic for twelve years. She had no other work experience. "Her work included the cooking, waiting, heavy cleaning, light laundry, and marketing for a family of five adults, who lived in a house of seventeen rooms and four baths. She was the only employee. Her work week totaled 79½ hours, and her usual 12½ hour day included two hours on call. She had two half days free each week and three weeks annual vacation without pay. Her wages were $8 weekly and carfare to and from work."

When paid, the typical domestic in a northern city, as the above suggests, earned between $1.50 and $2.00 a day plus a meal. Some were also provided carfare and "service plan" or "toting privileges," that is they were allowed to take left-over food home. Food supplements "kept many migrant families from starving" and compensated them to some extent for low wages. Moreover, the $2.00 earned in a single day in the North was only a little less than would have been collected in a week in the South.[70] As indicated, the average male earned about $25.00 a week. Working as a domestic, then, a black woman could, in a seven-day week, increase the family income by nearly one-half. Earning $14.00, she could help the family to approach though not exceed, the acceptable standard for a family of five.

Some of the earnings of black women were hidden. For example, many supplemented family incomes by taking in lodgers. Estimates suggest that as many as one-third of all black families in large northern cities took in lodgers.[71] According to the Urban League, about 80% of those who let rooms were families headed by a woman.[72] With housing at a premium, lodgers were necessary to make up the rent for large and costly units, often the only available housing. The optimum lodger was a distant family member or close friend from the southern community left behind. But the luxury of a lodger known to the family was not common.[73] Arrangements for lodgers varied. Some were merely supplied with a room, others took meals with the family. Regardless of the arrangement, the additional income aided the family.

Women also worked in the home on an occasional basis as laundresses and seamstresses. In 1920, over 70% of the laundresses in the country were black.[74] While some of these worked in factories on a regular schedule, a sizable proportion worked at home.[75] According to Elizabeth Pleck, "black married women could more easily reconcile this employment with running their own households."[76]

A few "lucky" women found employment in manufacturing. Between 1910 and 1920, the number of black women thus employed increased from 68,000 to 105,000, while the number engaged in domestic and personal service declined from 853,000 to 794,000.[77] The number of women engaged in manufacturing in 1910, 68,000, is something of a misnomer. Most were employed as seamstresses and in related tasks in the home.[78]

But the increase between 1910 and 1920 did represent their use, for the first time, in industrial enterprises. Many became unskilled laborers in the tobacco industry, garment trades, munitions factories, and tanneries.[79]

Their industrial employment, however, was short-lived. Employers admitted they hired black women only because of the labor shortage during the war. They favored the most marginal group of industrial workers, who were hired only when and where there was acute need. Victims of sex and race discrimination in industry, these women got the least desirable jobs at the worst pay with no chance for advancement.[80]

Society did not reward black women for the income they provided. Many social scientists blamed them for the breakup of their family, child neglect, and in cases of male unemployment, emasculation. But as this discussion suggests, without their financial contributions, migrant families would not have survived in the North.

The Plight of the Black Workers

Recounting the problems of migrant employment strikes at the heart of the thesis of this work. It has been argued that black migrants played an important role in a scenario of economic transformation that included other vulnerable ethnic groups. I argue, in addition, that black migrants played a special role in that process. Throughout the period from 1900 to 1920, employers had attempted to overcome worker opposition to homogenization, new methods of work, and new machinery by a variety of strategies, as has been shown. The introduction of black workers into the northern economy during the latter end of this period provided employers with a unique opportunity. The war demand for goods had created a booming economy. The war effort had also softened criticism of larger, monopolistic companies, and demands for their regulation had been silenced. And it caused a virtual halt to European immigration as well as a significant return migration of young men wanting to fight for their homelands.[81] The insertion of large numbers of black workers into the economy, particularly when it involved strikebreaking activity, although no different in form from the previous introduction of immigrant workers, now had a different result. It allowed a split to develop in the work force where none had existed before because of the following:

First, the newcomers were from an area, the South, dependent upon the North for development. This meant that employers had much greater control than they had ever had before on the duration and flow of a migrant work force.[82] Second, the small numbers of black workers used in northern industry before the Great Migration coupled with the historic tradition of racism, a tradition fueled in the first two decades of the century by legions of scholarly theories on racial inferiority, meant that racial antagonism was at a different order of magnitude from ethnic antagonism. Most of the old immigrants had blended into the scenery with amazing rapidity.[83] Even the native-born sons of the newer immigrants who remained moved into a distribution of jobs more closely resembling that of native whites.[84] But blacks were different. The suspicion in the society that blacks in general were less than human was, not surprisingly, translated at the level of the factory into opposition by white workers to having to work alongside them. Spero and Harris suggest that there were instances of white workers objecting so strongly to the use of blacks that they left their jobs.[85] They cite examples of 60 strikes over this issue between 1880 and 1900 alone. While they found no available figures for subsequent years, David Montgomery points out that between 1914 and 1921 there were over 23,000 strikes in the United States, with the bulk of these (11,592) occurring in the two years of the Great Migration, 1916–1918.[86] It is logical that many of these occurred because of the importation of black labor. In East Saint Louis in 1917, over 10,000 black workers were brought in to break a strike, and riots resulted. As an officer of the Illinois Central Railroad put it, "We took Negro labor out of the South until it hurt."[87]

Employers, of course, were more than cognizant of the antagonism; they helped to encourage it. When differential racial allocation threatened collective action, they would immediately integrate the work groups. Lorenzo Greene and Carter G. Woodson point out that, "Many plants fortified themselves against strikes by so intermixing Negro workers among their white laborers as to render almost impossible any such thing as concerned action."[88]

White workers were not powerless in this situation. They, in fact, de-

Table 5.6
Number of Foremen in Manufacturing[1]
by Race, 1900, 1920, 1930

	1900	1920	1930
White	88,814	292,556	290,347
Black	1,186	3,444	2,653
Total	90,000	296,000	293,000

[1]The overall decline in 1930 is owing, according to GC&R, to the growth of personnel administration that transferred supervisory functions from foremen to personnel administrators. Blacks were excluded even more significantly from this new white-collar employment.

manded and gained one significant advantage over black workers. The newcomers were excluded from upper-level, supervisory positions (see table 5.3).[89] Much commented upon in the literature, previous research has concluded two things about this disparity: First, that exclusion of blacks from supervisory positions was a matter of convention.[90] And second, that black exclusion was a manifestation of the power of white workers.[91] Although neither explanation is disputed in this research, it is maintained that black exclusion also provided several advantages for employers. It created for the otherwise disgruntled white worker a belief in the possibility of upward mobility not afforded to the black worker. This motivational element within any job hierarchy is important. People work in order that they might advance.[92] For some, the mere vision of advancement softened the harsh reality of homogenization. But for many others, the use of race-conscious promotion represented a real advantage. This was, after all, a time of explosion in the number of positions for foremen (see table 5.6).[93] Also, it meant that black workers could be used to fill the most unskilled and demanding jobs—undesirable jobs at the very bottom of the social hierarchy. These jobs are traditionally difficult to fill not only because of their lack of remuneration but because of their total lack of status. No one willingly agrees to remain at the bottom, but black workers had no choice. They had either to fill the low-paying, "dirty-work" tasks shunned by native and, increasingly, foreign labor or return to the South. As Herman D. Bloch quotes one official from a New York commission, "The Negro had one-half of a bad chance to get a job."[94] Finally, and this was perhaps the greatest advantage, black exclusion represented a structure that could be dismantled at any time. Employers had gained control, between 1900 and 1920, over hiring, firing, promotion, and work routines.[95] The foreman's last remaining responsibility was discipline within the shop. Unlike a traditional notion of "an aristocracy of labor" where higher paid workers are differentiated by "the acquisition of certain essential skills" and "by denial of access to general education thereby making training for quick replacements difficult," the differentiation in this case was without substance.[96] If white workers demanded too much, they could readily be replaced by black workers. The steel strike of 1919 is instructive of this point. The strike was organized by a broad coalition of unions representing both skilled and unskilled workers.[97] The main strategy used by steel companies to break the strike was to exploit the decisions that "separated native-born and English-speaking steelworkers, many of them skilled workers, from the thirty or more eastern European immigrant groups among steelworkers, most of them unskilled and not English-speaking."[98]

The strategy failed. The unskilled immigrant workers proved to be strong supporters of the strike.[99] The steel companies then resorted to the use of black workers. Although black employment in the steel mills had increased during the war, blacks were still excluded from the skilled workers' union, even during the union organizing drives of 1918–1919.[100] In the sixth week of the strike, the steel companies imported over thirty thousand black strikebreakers, employed them at every level of operation, and kept the plants operating. This strategy defeated the strike.

The special role played by black workers represented more than occasional strikebreaking activities, more than a reserve industrial labor pool, more than a permanent "underclass", though these were all major ingredients of their part. Much of the previous research on this topic has emphasized at least some of these issues.[101] Yet, what is often neglected is a discussion of the extent to which black exclusion was in fact a necessary ingredient in the development of the modern economic system. It was not that black workers were a backward element in a system that passed them by. Instead, the system progressed because it created artificially backward elements. As Harold Baron suggests:

> Although in the mature capitalist society both economic and political imperatives exist for a certain limiting of the exploitation of the working class as a whole, each corporation still has to operate on the basis of maximizing of profits. The fostering of a section of the working class that will have to work [at low rates] works to meet the needs of profit maximization. . . . In all the developed Western capitalist states, there exists a group of workers to fill jobs that the more politically established sectors of the working class shun.[102]

Once black workers were relegated, by custom or official policy, to positions from which there was no mobility (the forerunner of the segmented labor market), then industries could rely on a labor supply to fill the bottom jobs within the hierarchy.[103] According to Piore, even a cursory glance at industries that employ such labor suggests that competitive pressure prevents them from paying the wages required to attract "native" labor.[104] Moreover, the limits on the rate of economic expansion suggested by an absence of this cheap labor would "undoubtedly result in slower rates of economic growth and quite possibly higher rates of unemployment."[105] Many industries begin within the cheap-labor-dominated secondary sector and, as they prosper, become monopolized. In addition, Bonacich has pointed out in her theses of "middle men minorities" that monopolies buy supplies from secondary industries instead of making them themselves because these products are cheap and because they can obtain higher returns on their investments elsewhere.[106] That is, the relative cheapness of black labor permitted industries both to prosper and to hire more expensive white labor. In the 1920s, this was a trade-off willingly accepted by the racially exclusive labor unions.

Black workers represented a key element in the operation and process of the economy after the First World War. Previous employer attempts to create division among the working classes met, when the element of race was introduced, with much greater success than had past attempts. But race alone does not explain what happened to the black worker. The transformation of the economy had created a need for a worker who was not only economically vulnerable but also politically unable to defend his interests. In this context, migrant status, particularly appropriate for the black worker because of the colonial nature of the southern economy, helped to make the exploitation possible. Black workers came from outside the reward system of the North and remained apart from the social structure in which jobs were located.[107] Their costs of training had been borne outside the system. Their wage level was pegged to levels of the South rather than the North. Their political vulnerability caused their labor to fall outside the protective legislation against injury, illness, or unemployment afforded to white workers.

Ironically, citizenship would ultimately work against black workers. Their broad use in the 1920s, expressed in higher employment rates for them than for whites, was reversed in later decades. Their role has now been taken over by even more vulnerable migrant groups who, when no longer needed, may voluntarily return home or, as is proposed in the "guest worker" provisions of the Simpson and Mazzoli legislation, be returned.

The acceptance of the permanence of black labor, even after the Depression, never translated into advantage for the group. The black worker has never been fully incorporated into American society. He has been used for a variety of tasks, but from each he finds little chance for opportunity. Perhaps the most telling indication of this dilemma is found in comparative income statistics. In 1900, it is estimated, black family income was almost 57% of that of white families. In 1950, some thirty years after the Great Migration, ten years after the Great Depression, and a few years after the Second World War migration, it was at approximately the same level.[108] It remains so today.[109]

Conclusion

The expectation that southern blacks would benefit from migration never translated into actual experience. They did not begin at the bottom, as earlier immigrant groups had done, and work their way up. On the average, they advanced very little relative to the dominant population. Previous explanations of the inability of large segments of the black population to experience upward mobility have relied first on an assessment that black workers had the wrong work experience. Unskilled workers arrived in an increasingly skilled city and therefore were out of favor in the labor market. Yet, this research suggests that homogenization, not differentiation, characterized much industrial employment. For the most part, jobs in manufacturing were reduced more rather than less to a routine. Blacks were excluded from supervisory positions, not because of lack of skill, but because of advantages that accrued to both employers and white workers from black exclusion. A second explanation suggests that blacks as the last immigrants were on the bottom and awaited a new, more vulnerable migrant group to cause their movement upward within the hierarchy of jobs. From present experience, it seems more appropriate to conclude that migrant labor, particularly when recruited for low-level jobs, no longer advances up or down a job hierarchy but instead is used and discarded. That is, employers seek a constant supply of cheap, vulnerable, and wherever possible, exportable labor to fill jobs at the bottom. A third explanation, the most compelling of the three, points out that employers benefit from the racism endemic to this society and that it is this racism that ultimately explains the subordinate status of blacks. Yet, racism alone accounts neither for the differential experiences of black workers from the Great Migration to the Great Depression nor for the underutilization of black labor of the present day.

Black workers entered a game where all the rules had changed. They entered factories no longer controlled by labor. They entered a manufacturing economy shifting from industrial to monopolistic concentrations. They were excluded from employment by political as well as economic pressure. They were despised by the very society that profited from them. This was their gain from the "unprecedented economic opportunity." This was freedom in the promised land.

CHAPTER SIX

Migrants in the North

The Political and Social Wars

It is certainly not the old, law abiding
negro population, the friends of the
white man, that has been committing
these crimes . . . that [has] incited white
men to a general war against negroes. It
must be the new negro population
brought in by the war.

Editorial, *New York Times*, July 23, 1919

THE WELCOME TO "TIRED" and "poor masses yearning to breathe
free" has never been extended without reservation to newcomers to
American shores, even in times of acute labor shortages. Rather, there
is a widely held presentiment that immigrants must prove themselves
worthy to receive the gift of naturalization. Immigrants, on their side,
take up the challenge willingly, anxious to prove themselves in the new
and strange land of opportunity. In the Great Migration, black migrants
accepted the role of apprentice citizen, though they and their ancestors
had been in the country for many years. But their movement North was
greeted with more than the usual hostility because a rapidly changing society was caught in a frantic search for scapegoats. Blacks were not alone
in being signaled out for concern. The Red scares, treason trials, and
Palmer raids after the war all centered on a common and desperate witch-
hunt. But the large influx of dark-skinned and strangely accented
newcomers certainly brought a special concern. In the 1919 riots in the
nation's capital, the *Washington Times* headlined its accounts with the
language of conquest, "Armed posses" and "lynching."[1] It was hardly
the welcome anticipated in migrant letters.

The Political War in the North

"In states like New York where we are beginning to learn the meaning and use of the ballot," wrote Carter G. Woodson in 1924, "we are building a firm and unshakable basis of permanent freedom while every advance in the South unprotected by political power is based on chance and changing personalities."[2]

The painful experience of disenfranchisement in the South and the belief in the power of the ballot led many migrants to register to vote upon their very arrival in the North. Having received for so long such a small share for their public tax dollar, they now sought representation. In the second ward of Chicago, for example, which had the highest proportion of blacks in the city, it was estimated that "72 percent of the eligible voters were registered in 1920 as compared with 66 percent for the city as a whole."[3] A high percentage of the black voters were new migrants from the South. Harold Gosnell, in examining place of birth information on almost ten thousand registered black voters in Chicago, found that nearly "one-half of them were born in the East South Central states and that half of these had come North in the last five years, 85% within the last fifteen."[4]

Many of the migrants had brought with them bitter memories of political exclusion in the South. Some had witnessed firsthand the violence and intimidation used against black voters; others had merely been told of them. Such experiences led most to dissociate themselves from the Democratic party. A laborer from Alabama told an investigator that, "he could never vote for a Democrat as long as he kept his memory." The Democrats he knew in Alabama were the "imps of Satan." A woman from Georgia, who had lived in the city for seventeen years, "did not like the attitude of the colored people in voting for the other party candidate." She thought that "anyone who lived in the South should forever hate the Democratic party, not because all Democrats are bad, but because the party keeps its foot on the black man." An elderly man, who had lived in the city for six years, said that "he had cast his first ballot in the presidential election of 1880 in a Tennessee village and voted regularly there until disqualified by the grandfather clause." He stated that "he had always voted the straight Republican ticket and always will." He thought that the "colored people" who voted for a Democratic candidate would be "putting their heads in the lion's mouth."[5]

Loyalty to the Republican party, however, did not advance or enhance the interests of black migrants particularly in their desire to eliminate oppression. There were several reasons for this. First, their status as immigrants initially cut them off from the indigenous working class, and their status as blacks solidified that division. Thus, unlike immigrants who had come before, they could not build an ethnic bloc in the midst of a working-class movement. Indeed, in their attempts to win political power, issues of race continually overshadowed those of class. Second, once removed from the arena of class struggle, they were written off by both parties for all but the most symbolic of actions. Third, their residential segregation, while assuring at least token political representation, also exacerbated their powerlessness. In big-city politics, they were rewarded with the meager political prizes of a barren and isolated reservation.

The direction that black political participation took reflected these limitations. Migrants had a genuine interest in voting that was attached to the black population's unfailing belief in the democratic principles of the American system. It was unnecessary for any party organization to recruit this constituency. It was ready and eager to become involved. That was the product of high expectations of citizenship. Writing in 1920, A. M. Moore, expressed the hopes of a people that exceeded the rhetoric that one might associate with his class position.

> The Negro asks the white man to extend the ballot to properly qualified persons as a guarantee of their full protection. He does not desire to rule but he does desire to share in the government of his country, and he would not be a worth while citizen if he did not.[6]

His words were similar in meaning to those of a migrant who stated simply, "I registered to vote, first thing." These expectations went beyond examples of direct and personal gain toward more general desires to create a power base to secure protective legislation from Congress. DuBois calculated, for example, that black voters would represent the balance of power in no less than nine states and thereby could be an instrumental force in the election of a number of United States senators. For the black community there was promise of political power unprecedented in the North.[7]

The initial step, it was felt, was the election of black candidates. Such representatives were thought to be important because the symbolic as well as actual power of the race was increased when a member was elected to an important political position. Such beliefs were held even when, as was often the case, the actual candidate was selected by a white political machine. This was not as self-defeating as it might at first seem. The concentration of blacks in some northern urban districts did give to black officials, once elected, "a measure of independence from white bosses and their financial resources." Such residual power was not taken lightly. Stated the *Chicago Defender*:

Unless we are diligent in fighting our own cause, we cannot expect to leave the job to somebody else. We believe that these successes and victories are but the first steps to real power and a voice unfettered by jobs held at the mercy or whim of some white political leader, but held because the man in office has a mandate from the voters of his race and of his home district to be there.[8]

By their very concentration, blacks were potentially influential. In 1919, Carl Sandburg observed, "The black belt of Chicago is probably the strongest effective unit of political power, good or bad, in America."[9] But black power as an independent force was really only effective when there was a divided white electorate and blacks could tip the balance of power. In the early years of the migration, blacks attempted to sustain this advantage. In Chicago, in particular, they won key victories. But there, as in much of the North, ultimately they lost the war.

During the period of the migration, "Chicago's black vote" was "twice decisive in mayoralty" contests and had elected two black aldermen to the city council. But there were few spoils from those victories. The pattern was established in the mayoralty race of 1915. In the 1915 primaries, the predominately black Second Ward, a ward that had been only 25% black five years before, cast over 8,000 votes for Republican candidate William Hale Thompson, while his opponent received fewer than 2,000 votes. "Thompson's city-wide plurality was only 2,508; and it was apparent that this popularity among the black voters of the Second Ward provided the margin of victory." Because of a Democratic split in the general election, Thompson was "swept into office with an impressive majority."[10]

During the course of the election, Thompson had made a number of enemies. His support for neutrality in the war won him the ire of veterans' groups and the American Legion and National Security League "branded him pro-German and a traitor." Chicago's Catholics accused him of being an antipapist because of his statement that a Catholic mayor would corrupt the public school system. Women, only recently franchised, voted against him in large numbers because of his perceived ties to previous corrupt administrations. His brief closing of saloons on Sundays in 1915, created large protests among saloonkeepers, distillers, and brewers. Both his opponents and the press labeled him "indolent, ignorant of public issues, inefficient and incompetent as an administrator."[11]

For the black population, however, Thompson represented something rare and enticing; a politician who actively sought their votes. Elected alderman of the Second Ward in 1900, when the district was still predominately white, he had sponsored "Chicago's first municipal playground, which was probably the first of the nation of blacks," an achievement which brought him notoriety within the community. "Grandson of a drafter of Chicago's first charter and son of a Civil War hero," he used his present wealth and family fortune as tools in the construction of a finely crafted coalition. He was, stated Ira Katznelson, "a skillful exploiter of ethnic politics in his city."[12]

Although he left office in 1904, Thompson continued to be remembered in the black belt and to exercise influence there. By 1915, his political friends in the community "included the *Chicago Defender*, several fraternal and military organizations," and other leading black citizens.[13]

Thompson's past efforts on behalf of the black community were amply rewarded, as the 1915 primary and election show. He publicly articulated and sympathized with issues of particular concern within the community. "I'll give you people jobs," he would often promise. "And if any of you want to shoot craps go ahead and do it. When I'm Mayor the police will have something better to do than break up a friendly crap game."[14]

In the general context of political and social neglect, the success of Thompson's approach is not surprising. Add to this a flamboyant personality and a migrant community filled with frustration and a longing to participate and the ingredients of a mass mobilization of voters are produced. And, according to Tuttle, "Thompson was a showman. He nearly always wooed his black audiences by denouncing his political foes as 'crackers' and by praising heroes of the black race."[15] "To deny equal opportunity to the Negro in this land is out of harmony with American history, untrue to sacred history, untrue to the sacred principles of liberty and equal rights," he stated.[16] Thompson called himself the "defender of the weak, the champion of the people."[17] For example, "while practically all white politicians were mute, 'Big Bill,'" as he was known, "castigated the film 'The Birth of a Nation' as an abomination and an insult to millions of American citizens" and banned its showing. In addition, suggests Tuttle "the fact that several Chicago newspapers, particularly the *Tribune*, seemed to denounce him and the black people in the same breath, reinforced his popularity."[18]

It would be a mistake, however, to view Thompson as a real champion of black concerns. He was an accomplished politician. His success among blacks was duplicated with other constituencies and his supporters were as loud in his defense as his detractors were in his denunciation. Furthermore, "the Thompson-black alliance was partly fortuitous."[19] According to Spear, "As heir to a faction of the Republican party, Thompson naturally gained the support of many of the black politicians who were in its camp. Also, he was able to make an immediate appeal to migrants who had already been conditioned by their southern experience to support the Republican party." Thompson, however, exploited the advantage and won the decided support of the black electorate.[20]

Once in office, Thompson immediately appointed two black assistant corporation counsels and a black investigator in the law department. "I'll give you people the best opportunities you've ever had if you elect me," he had promised an audience in 1915. On this issue, he kept his word.[21]

In the mayor's race of 1919, Thompson continued to be identified as anti-Catholic because of his statements in the 1915 campaign. In Chicago, a city that was about half-Protestant, half-Catholic and had experienced numerous religious conflicts and rivalries, such statements were remembered.[22]

When Thompson ran in the February primary, he was strongly opposed by Catholic groups, proponents of good government, and certain women's groups. During his term in office, he had won over few of his former enemies. But he still had significant backing from others within his own party, and the black electorate voted in large numbers. The Second Ward cast 12,143 votes for Thompson, while the combined totals of his two Republican rivals was only slightly over 1,700. Thompson won the primary. The general election was a tougher contest. According to Tuttle, "All of Chicago's daily newspapers fought against his re-election."[23] The campaign was bitter. "Thompson was labeled as a 'nigger lover' who kissed black babies, and his black cohorts were blamed for the decline of South Side real estate values, for putting white men out of jobs, and for the deterioration of the South Side schools." But the opposition to Thompson was not united. Instead, the Democratic machine candidate had to share votes with both reform and labor candidates.[24] On election day, the turnout was heavy with nearly 700,000 Chicagoans going to the polls. The *New York Times* called it, "the wildest mayoralty campaign in Chicago's history."[25] Although Thompson's opponents polled over 62% of the vote, Thompson had gained a plurality. "His unprecedented margin in 1915 of 150,000 votes had slipped in 1919 to only 21,622. A Democratic spokesman promptly imputed his slim triumph to fraud in the black belt." Others insisted that "the black vote alone had elected Thompson."[26] In the Second Ward, Thompson polled over 15,000 votes to less than 3,500 for his Democrat opponent. Obviously, the black vote alone could not and did not reelect Thompson, but it did more than provide his plurality. The *Chicago Daily Journal* proclaimed in its headlines the next day: "Negroes Elect BIG BILL."[27]

The black community was proud of the achievement. "Reveling in the Democratic recognition of black political potency, the *Defender* proclaimed: 'If this was intended as a criticism of our action, we cheerfully accept it.' The *Defender*, moreover, congratulated itself for its role in the triumph, rationalizing that since all the daily newspapers had opposed Thompson and the *Defender* alone had zealously advocated his re-election. It boasted: 'Modesty prevents us from claiming that "The World's Greatest Weekly" wields more political influence than all the Chicago dailies combined, but results are what counts.'"[28]

Alliance with Thompson brought little to the mass of the black electorate because Thompson tended to substitute patronage jobs for any improvement in city services let alone sharing in political decision-making.[29] In fact, in 1920, with the campaign over and a difficult summer of racial tensions just past, Thompson wrote to Theodore Bilbo, governor of Mississippi "to inquire if it would be possible to send some of Chicago's surplus of Mississippi migrants back home."[30] This would have been a fine reward indeed for his loyal supporters.

A number of black politicians, however, did rise to prominence during this era partly as a result of Thompson's influence. Oscar DePriest, who had made a fortune in real estate and was elected as the first black alderman in 1904, was made floor leader in the City Council by Thompson in 1915. DePriest's time in office was full of controversy. Black politicians in general, because of their high visibility, had to answer to more than their constituents. DePriest was under constant public scrutiny. The Municipal Voters' League, for example, censured DePriest after his first term stating that not only had he voted against almost every reform measure proposed but "no alderman in Chicago's history [has] piled up a more notorious record in so short a time."[31]

In 1917, DePriest was, in fact, indicted for accepting payoffs from gambling lords and for bribery of police officers. Though later acquitted, "he had not yet been cleared at the time of the 1917 municipal election and so decided not to seek reelection."[32]

Regardless of his guilt or innocence, it is clear that black politicians at the bottom of the machine hierarchy were much more likely to be given up as sacrificial lambs to a reform-minded public than white politicians at the top.

Reformers had other ideas about the source of the corruption. The Municipal Voters' League published several pieces about Louis B. Anderson, DePriest's successor, calling him to task for his "bad record," especially for his failure to support ordinances "regulating dry cabarets" and "prohibiting owners and drivers of taxicabs from using them for immoral purposes. Quite as bad as his predecessor, the League concluded."[33]

The editors of the journal *Messenger* were even more harsh in their criticism. They observed with some bitterness:

> The intellectually decrepit Negro leaders have seemed to have had some vague, religious reliance upon the "goodness" of all white Republicans, and they have not been able to appreciate the fact that they have been mere pawns upon the political chess boards for conniving, wire-pulling unscrupulous Republican tricksters.[34]

In New York City in 1918, a similar tale of political corruption and black powerless leadership was unfolded, though on this occasion the personal aggrandizement is less in evidence. Black assemblyman E. A. Johnson, a Republican, introduced a bill "to permit children 12 years and older to work." Johnson told the press that the bill was needed because of "the recent exodus of Negroes from the South and the likelihood of idle Negro children getting into mischief in the streets of New York." Opposing him in his efforts were both "educators and union leaders," but behind him were local canneries seeking an alternative source of cheap labor.[35] Pawns or merely machine politicians, leaders gained little for the community as a whole.

These experiences reveal the dilemma of black political activity in the North. Having been totally disenfranchised in the South, this new opportunity not only to vote but, on occasion, to tip the balance among equally divided white populations represented an opportunity to effect political change. Yet, the advance itself favored the few over the many, providing rewards for selected individuals rather than significant services for the community as a whole. Said A. Philip Randolph, "The fact that the Republican Party, every four years, gives 10,000,000 Negroes a registrar of the treasury, a collector of revenue, sealed the mouths and closed the eyes of his leaders to the fact that the rank and file have no voice in government."[36]

It is perhaps in the nature of urban political machines that their largess is distributed in this manner. The Chicago Commission on Race Relations concluded:

> Political action on the part of blacks had failed to protect them against mob violence, against bombings, and against vice resorts and that it had failed to provide for all homes that were fit to live in, clean streets and alleys, sufficient recreational facilities, adequate school accommodations, and the necessary public welfare services.[37]

For the black community, northern enfranchisement was at best only a modest advance over southern disenfranchisement.

Blacks also paid a price for their increasing political importance. There developed a feeling of resentment in Chicago that the Great Migration had produced a "Negro menace."[38] When blacks responded in collective ways to their exploitation and lack of minimal services, the possibility arose that whites would react in a similarly race-conscious manner. It took significant amounts of aplomb and expertise to win concessions from a system structured on their impoverishment. More often than not they failed. Katznelson concludes about black political participation:

> The new political linkages the black migrants fashioned in the North were undoubtedly more successful (from the perspective of the group) than those they had left behind in the South. Yet the migrants' aspirations were not collectively realized. Their political relationships established in the critical period of migration were far from satisfactory. New, more indirect, but almost equally powerless quasi-colonial patterns of racial dominance and social control replaced the southern colonial system.[39]

The Social War in the North

While all migrant groups have faced problems of low wages, poor conditions, and the high cost of living in core areas, the sudden, large, and constant introduction of black migrants brought out hostility at levels previously unknown. Explained a Department of Agriculture investigator:

> Other races have come to the city bringing all their foreign customs, superstitions, and varying modes of living, and although they have come to this industrial center in large numbers, their coming has not been attended by outbursts of hatred and demonstrations in public places. They have been accepted—not always as a desirable element—but at least as something to be tolerated.[40]

Before the Great Migration, blacks had been scattered throughout many northern cities with few really discernible patterns of residential segregation. The appearance of a new black neighbor often caused little reaction. But as the population began to grow, a panic developed. Whites began fleeing, James Weldon Johnson commented, "as from a plague." The City of San Francisco actually sent experts to the Midwest to study techniques and strategies of exclusion. "The very best people—bankers, realtors, editors, merchants, and community leaders—led the black exclusion movement."[41] According to Bennett, "real estate interests and property owner's associations led a campaign of fear based on myths of inferiority, property value decline and rapid neighborhood turnover which resulted in blacks being charged higher rents than whites for the same accommodations."[42] Ray Stannard Baker reported that in Indianapolis, landlords got $25 a month "for flimsy one-story frame row houses that would have rented to whites for $18." Chicago surveys in 1909 and 1919 showed blacks paying 100% more. According to Henri, the situation prevailed in every major northern city except Washington.[43] And with each successive decade, the patterns of segregation and concentration grew stronger. How different was this from the pattern of Jewish concentration on New York's Lower East Side, where, according to Steinberg, the peak of 73% in the 1880s was reduced to a mere 23% by the 1920s. Over a similar time span, black concentration grew stronger.

Migrants could hardly be considered to have chosen these neighborhoods. Housing was, more often than not, dilapidated and uninhabitable. In Pittsburgh, "about half of all migrant families lived in one-room apartments and only a little better than 10 percent in three rooms." A health officer in Newark reported that, "these houses are rented out as housekeeping apartments irrespective of the fact that there are no facilities for such purposes. Kitchen ranges, lavatories, baths and toilets are either altogether absent or inadequate." On a single day in Chicago in 1917, real estate brokers had "over 600 black families apply for housing, with only 53 units available." A profitable practice for landlords was to divide larger units, without alteration, and with no decrease in rent. Not surprisingly, this caused differential overcrowding in many black communities. In Cleveland, for example, "the population density of the black district was thirty-five to forty persons per acre, contrasted with a citywide density of twenty-one." In other cities, black neighborhoods had densities several times that of white areas.[44] "With the additional separation in churches, schools, railways, streetcars and other public places, even hospitals and cemeteries," wrote George Haynes, "there is developing a racial cleavage from cradle to grave."[45]

Poverty, segregation, and overcrowding compounded problems of poor health. Philadelphia, Pittsburgh, and Cleveland had outbreaks of smallpox that were thought to be attributable directly to migrants and their life-styles. Tuberculosis was common, as were pneumonia and venereal diseases. According to contemporary observers, the causes of most of these diseases were environmental. It was not only the crowded living conditions and poor quality of housing that affected the health of the population but the working conditions as well. Migrants had to do hard work for long hours with insufficient food, clothing, and rest. Confinement and lack of ventilation on the job served to increase their susceptibility. In Newark, for example, it was reported that "fumes from munition factories made many temporarily ill" and forced some to seek employment elsewhere at reduced wages.[46]

Baker noted that more than twice as many blacks as whites in Philadelphia required hospital care. He found that "sickness was more prevalent among blacks than among Germans, Irish or native Americans and believed that it was the chief cause of black poverty."[47] In addition, in most hospitals blacks met with discriminatory treatment, further exacerbating their conditions. As a result, the black death rate was consistently higher than the white. In 1910, the white death rate was 14.5 per 1,000; the non-white, 21.7. In 1920 the white rate was 12.6; the nonwhite, 17.7. In Pittsburgh between 1915 and 1917, black deaths nearly doubled, although the black population increased by only 45%.[48]

Children were even worse off than their parents. According to Henri, a "startling" number died before the age of ten. More than one-quarter of these children never reached their first birthday, an infant death rate twice that of white infants. Between 1915 and 1919, 150 black babies died among each 1,000 born, compared to 92.8 white babies per 1,000.[49]

Infant mortality was highest in the summer months in the overcrowded black areas where, as Mary White Ovington pointed out, "the babies die like flies." Observed Henri, "They died of convulsions due to unidentified diseases, of the 'summer complaint' they got from contaminated food and milk, or whooping cough, tuberculosis, and pneumonia, and of rickets from improper diet and lack of sunshine."[50] The high death rate among blacks in comparison with the foreign-born population is most indicative of the degree and extent of hardship faced by the southern migrants.

Blacks were overrepresented not only in rates of ill-health and mortality but crime as well. From August 1916 to August 1917, there was an increase of black prisoners from "9 per cent of the total to 57 per cent." During the same period, white prisoners decreased by more than 50%. The Committee on Urban Conditions Among Negroes concluded that "the large number is due to the large Negro migration from the South, including many who have bad records in their former homes; to lack of proper housing and recreation; to ignorance of northern customs and laws; and to a cumbersome probation system." But they further observed that "most were locked up on minor charges."[51]

Related to this practice was the high rate of dismissal of such cases. It suggests the degree of suspicion with which migrants were regarded by the agents of the host society. For example, most who were picked up for vagrancy were found to be migrants, newly arrived, in search of a job and a place to stay.[52]

Many were arrested for such minor offenses as gambling, being drunk and disorderly, or violating minor city ordinances. Some cases would probably have been dismissed with a fine, but migrants had no money. And it should be remembered, as suggested by the Census Bureau, that "an offense committed by a Negro is perhaps more likely to be punished than the same offense committed by a white man."[53] Any misstep on the part of migrants was magnified into general assessments of racial criminal tendencies and reported upon with great frequency in the white press.

Antagonism spread along with poverty, disease, and suffering and exploded into violent conflict in East Saint Louis in 1917 and into numerous race riots in what came to be called the "Red Summer" of 1919. The East Saint Louis riot was the only riot to result directly from fear by white working men of black economic advances. It began when the labor force of an aluminum plant went on strike, and the company hired black workers. A labor union delegation called on the mayor and asked that further migration of blacks to East Saint Louis be stopped. As the men were leaving City Hall, they heard that a Negro had accidentally shot a white man during a holdup. In a few minutes, rumor had replaced fact; the shooting was intentional—a white woman had been insulted—white girls were shot. By this time, three thousand people had gathered and were demanding "vengeance." Mobs roamed the streets harassing, threatening, and beating blacks. Local police stood by and did nothing. The mayor, fearful of antagonizing his white constituency, refused to ask for reinforcements.[54]

Finally, the National Guard was brought in to restore order. But when they were withdrawn by the governor, the violence started up again. The press fanned the fires of discontent by continuing to emphasize the incidents of black crimes. "White pickets and black workers at the aluminum company skirmished and, on July 1, some whites drove through the main black neighborhood firing into homes. Black residents armed themselves. When a police car drove down the street, it was riddled with gunshot."[55]

The next day a black man was shot on the main street, and a new riot was under way. The area became a "bloody half mile" for three or four hours:

> Streetcars were stopped, and blacks, without regard to age or sex, were pulled off and stoned, clubbed and kicked, and mob leaders calmly shot and killed blacks who were lying in blood on the street. As victims were placed in ambulances, the crowds cheered and applauded.[56]

Other rioters set fire to black homes, and by midnight the black section was in flames and "refugees fled half naked" through the streets searching for safety. There were forty-eight dead, hundreds injured, and more than three hundred buildings destroyed. Wrote one eyewitness:

> It was a distressing sight to see block after block where peaceful homes had been located burned to the ground. The innocent suffered with the guilty. Thrifty black folk, who were doing their bit by raising vegetables, were murdered. I saw the ruins of their homes, into which had gone the labor and savings of years. The little thrift gardens had escaped the flames

and the orderly rows where seeds had been planted gave the plots the appearance of miniature graveyards.[57]

The riots of 1919, though often less violent, were more widespread. For one whole day, the nation's capital was in the hands of a black "mob." For thirteen days, blacks and whites clashed, burned, and traded shots in Omaha, Knoxville, Norfolk, and other cities.

It was the climax of a chain of events that began with the "indifference and hostility of a new administration in Washington and was sustained through the turbulence of the Great Migration and the humiliations of World War I." It was as if a day of reckoning were at hand. With blacks segregated into the most deteriorated sections of the city, forced to pay high prices for inferior housing, and discriminated against in the workplace, it was inevitable that before long grievances would come together into widespread community unrest. In the summer of 1919, there were riots in twenty-six cities.[58]

On July 27, a racial incident on a beach in Chicago erupted into a four-day disturbance that swept uncontrolled through parts of the city and left 38 persons dead, 537 injured, and 1,000 rendered homeless and destitute.[59] Blacks faced a serious housing situation in Chicago. There was little new construction in the city during the war, and it was physically impossible for a doubled black population to live in the space occupied in 1915. Blacks spread out of established areas into neighborhoods nearby that had been exclusively white. In the "invaded" neighborhoods, bombs were thrown by gangs of white youths at the houses of blacks who had moved in and of real estate agents, white and black, who sold or rented property to the newcomers. The police were generally unwilling or unable to arrest those responsible for the crimes.[60] From July 1, 1917, to July 27, 1919, the day the riot began, twenty-four such bombs were thrown.

On that particular afternoon in July, a seventeen-year-old youth was swimming at a beach, by custom, strictly divided between the races. He drifted into the part used by whites. At that time a group of blacks attempted to enter the water from the white side of the beach. There began a series of attacks and retreats; counterattacks, and stone throwing. The youth, "who had remained in the water during the fracas, found a railroad tie and clung to it, stones meanwhile frequently striking the water near him." A white child moved towards him. As the boy neared, "the black youth let go of the tie, took a few strokes and went down." Later, the coroner's jury would render a verdict that "he had drowned because fear of stone-throwing kept him from shore." The coroner's report stated that there was "a superficial abrasion on the decedent's body," but this could not have caused death. Within the black community the belief was strong that "he had been hit by one of the stones and drowned as a result."[61]

The tragedy quieted the crowd. For an hour both whites and blacks searched for the boy to no avail. A report circulated that "a police officer refused to arrest the murderer," a white man identified by several black witnesses. "The blacks in the crowd began to amass. At a crucial point the accused policeman arrested a black man on a white man's complaint. Blacks mobbed the white officer, and the riot was under way."[62]

For the most part, the riot was confined to the south side of the city, where 90% of the black population lived. Crowds formed and whites who came into contact with them were beaten. But sections where blacks had recently invaded were also subject to violence, and blacks in these areas suffered at the hands of white gangs. Most of the one thousand families made homeless were black.[63] John Hope Franklin concludes of the Chicago riot, "It was the nations worst race war and shocked even the most indifferent persons into a realization that interracial conflicts in the United States had reached a serious stage."[64]

In Washington, D.C., a combination of increasing population and racial suspicion fueled a massive eruption. For weeks before the actual riot, the press had carried "lurid tales of black rapists."[65] "In July, four women allegedly were assaulted" in the District. The press produced sensational "accounts of these attacks, imputing them all, without substantial evidence, to blacks." Racial tension rose as a result of the coverage, and whites, especially military personnel stationed near the Capitol, prepared to retaliate. "On Saturday, July 19, the *Washington Post* ran headlines telling of another sexual assault. The next night Washington exploded. It began with a minor dispute on Pennsylvania Avenue in the midst of their city." Thereafter, "roaming bands of soldiers, sailors, and marines began to molest any black person in sight, hauling them off streetcars and out of restaurants, chasing them up alleys, and beating them mercilessly on street corners." White mobs ran through the streets unrestrained and "violence reigned for three days. Blacks retaliated on the fourth day when the whites threatened to burn their homes." Federal troops had to be called in, and with the aid of them and a heavy rain, the violence finally subsided on July 22. Six blacks were left dead and hundreds injured.[66]

Conclusion

All of the disturbances in 1919 were at least indirectly attributable to labor competition. The sudden introduction of so many southern workers into northern industrial centers created numerous tensions. Uncertainty and fear mingled with feelings of hatred and mistrust to yield highly volatile circumstances. The riots were inevitable.

The number of problems found with the black community served to fuel a judgment of inferiority. An assessment was produced that chronic overcrowding of households, job instability, crime, and violence were all traits characteristic of the race itself. This process of misinterpretation of cause and effect seems endemic to labor migrations. Michael Burawoy points out that in present-day South Africa, for example, although both government and industry create elaborate mechanisms including reserves and identity cards to regulate black labor, systems that produce great benefit for them, the ideological explanation for such structures is that the Africans must have them to sustain their tribal traditions. These rationalizations go beyond a scheme of "blaming the victim" to suggesting that victims demand systems that produce their own exploitation.[67] And so we find in the case of the Great Migration scholars attributing such conditions to the peculiar proclivities of the race.

Further, the physical isolation of black migrants made even easier the tasks of solidifying their "systematic political repression" and "eliminating their ability to defend themselves," characteristics inherent in migrant status but less readily attributable to this population of citizens.[68] Thus, the same racist and xenophobic appeals used in England and France at a later period to "avert the impact of the contradictions of capital" were applied with equal success at this earlier time to an indigenous group.[69]

Black workers had been brought North into an economy that accommodated them only at the lowest level. They took jobs—that native workers would not do—and paid a heavy price in their health and in the fact that the nature of the jobs provided no room for advancement. Further, they were exploited by all sectors of the society with which they came into contact, from landlords to large companies. They lived in the worst housing. They had the worst jobs. Even one migrant's boastful claim, "they had the privilege of dying a 'natural' death there" required a little qualification.[70]

CHAPTER SEVEN

Migration as a Benefit to the Migrant

Whenever I uttered a word of three or more syllables a group of voices would yell for me to repeat it. I used the phrase "social responsibility" and they yelled: "What's that word you say, boy?" "Social responsibility," I said.
"What?"
"Social . . ."
"Louder."
". . . responsibility."
"More!"
"Respon-"
"Repeat!"
"-sibility"
The room filled with the uproar of laughter until, no doubt distracted by having to gulp down my blood, I made a mistake and yelled a phrase I had often seen denounced in newspaper editorials, heard debated in private.
"Social . . ."
"What?" they yelled.
". . . equality-"
The laughter hung smoke-like in the sudden stillness. I opened my eyes puzzled. Sounds of displeasure filled the room.[1]

MIGRANTS PLAY a relatively minor part in the spectrum of labor migration. To be sure, they decide when, how, and even if they will leave, but the structural forces that make migration possible in the first place are mainly beyond their control. Still, the examination of migrant incorporation "as individuals and as a group," to use the phrase of Gunnar Myrdal, into the host society is a subject worthy of investigation.[2] Few have taken the time to ask what happens to migrants once settled, as if its micro-perspective were beyond the scope of the macrostructures of labor migration theory. As suggested initially, what research does exist has found variously that migrants may benefit from assimilation, return migration, and immigrant enclaves. In this chapter, each will be examined in light of the Great Migration.

Assimilation

Ideally, assimilation is "a long-run policy of cultural and sometimes racial unity [which] permits minorities to absorb the dominant patterns in their own way and at their own speed, and it envisages reciprocal assimilation, a blending of the diverse group, not a one-way adjustment."[3] In a democratic and multiethnic society like the United States, assimilation was once thought to be inevitable. Writes Paul Metzger:

> The incorporation of America's ethnic and racial groups into the mainstream culture is virtually inevitable. . . . Successful assimilation, moreover, has been viewed as synonymous with equality of opportunity and upward mobility for the members of minority groups; "opportunity," in this system, is the opportunity to discard one's ethnicity and to partake fully in the "American way of life." In this sense, assimilation is viewed as the embodiment of the democratic ethos.[4]

Newcomers, sometimes gradually, sometimes rapidly, depending on their similarity to the existing population, were said to melt into the fabric of society. This melting pot analogy, in addressing both cherished beliefs and observable patterns, was particularly dear to the social science literature. However, in the late 1950s, almost two generations after the first black migrants had made their way to northern cities, doubt replaced much of the optimism, and concern was increasingly expressed that perhaps some groups were unassimilatable. The problem was particularly acute for a black population highly concentrated in major urban centers, mired in the lowest paid jobs, the worst housing, and not advancing as other immigrants had done.

One explanation for the diverging perspectives on the degree of assimilation for all groups may be tied to the definition of the concept itself. Milton Gordon has argued that some confusion is attached to the fact that assimilation is "not a single phenomenon, but several related but analytically distinct processes."[5] For Gordon there are three types of assimilation: cultural, structural, and marital. Cultural assimilation refers to behavioral acculturation and "involves the acquisition by a minority group of the cultural characteristics of the dominant group."[6] Structural assimilation, which is further divided into primary and secondary levels, refers "to patterns of social interaction among individuals of different ethnic backgrounds." At the primary level, it involves interaction that is "warm, intimate and personal within associations, clubs and friendship networks." At the secondary level, it involves interaction in places of employment and recreation. Marital assimilation refers to "intermarriage among different ethnic groups."[7] Variation between ethnic groups occurs, then, among both types of assimilation and among rates of acceptance.

For the purposes of this discussion, structural assimilation at the secondary level will be examined. This decision is based on the assumption, widely held, that assimilation may occur in a series of stages and that structural assimilation at the secondary level represents a logical beginning point, with marital assimilation the highest stage.

Robert Park was one of the first sociologists to attempt to trace the patterns of assimilation. As initially discussed by him, intergroup contact is at first characterized by incidental contact and conflict. For example, new immigrants may be universally regarded with suspicion and antagonism because of language and cultural differences, competition in employment and housing, and psychological predispositions to regard that which is different as bad. Over time, as immigrants are settled and the worst fears are not realized, the response of the host society may change from one of conflict to uneasy accommodation. Distance is still maintained between the newcomers and their hosts, particularly in areas of intimate contact, but the right of immigrants to be there is no longer universally questioned. Time and frequency of incidental contact, it could be argued, usher in the stage of structural assimilation where migrants are at least individually accepted and are judged in the aggregate to be a part of the host society.

Both Park's introduction of the theory of assimilation and Milton Gordon's later elaboration of it suggest that the time between stages leading toward incorporation is not fixed. Some groups travel more rapidly through the stages than others. Gordon argues further that some groups may never reach primary structural assimilation or marital assimilation, being instead part of a pluralist structure that "retains their separate sociological structures."[8] In the matter of race, Gordon states, "There is no good reason to believe that White Protestant America has ever extended a firm and cordial invitation to its minorities to dance. . . . With the racial minorities, there was not even the pretense of an invitation."[9]

There is much evidence, nonetheless, that the black migrant in traveling North had high expectations of peaceful "interaction in places of employment and recreation." Though later generations would abandon this optimism, in the 1920s it was rare to find the community writing about anything else. At the time of the Great Migration, the editors of the "radical" journal *Messenger* went so far as to claim, "society is the beneficiary of race miscegenation."[10] While few others would go to this extreme, a modicum of assimilation was a common goal. Nothing mattered so much as the desire to become a part of the whole. Editorials in the black press and guest columns in the white press repeatedly emphasized this theme. Professor John Wesley Gilbert, of Payne College in Georgia, observed in a statement of the "fair price" for participation in the war, "Black men are ready to give their lives, as American soldiers in this world war to make the world safe for democracy but they want to feel their own lives and liberties are safe in the democracy here at home."[11] At a conference held in Blue Ridge, North Carolina, in 1917 (an assembly that advocated "a vision of a new South in which the Negro shall live happily,") it was resolved by a number of experts in the field of race relations:

> We hold as fundamental that for the Negro, as well as for all other human beings, home ownership is the basis of security, stability of citizenship, full-statured civic responsibility, law and order, and social progress.[12]

In this simple statement, an agenda for structural assimilation is established. Yet, it is unnecessary to delineate the inequities in housing, education, and employment initially faced by the southern black migrant upon his arrival in the North and perpetuated in successive decades. Observed Karl Taeuber and Alma Taeuber in 1965:

> Unlike the European immigrant before him, the Negro encountered nearly impenetrable barriers both to occupational and economic advancement and to residential movement outside the Negro areas. European immigrants or their children or grandchildren were often able to overcome prejudice and discrimination, and for most immigrant groups the handicaps of ethnic background diminished over time.[13]

Not so for the black migrant, the authors conclude.

The failure of black migrants to assimilate has, in recent years, been the subject of intense discussion and debate. The most prevalent set of explanations center on the matter of race, variously pointing to forced migration, the legacy of slavery, and the endemic character of "the etiquette of race relations."[14] Such explanations, while forceful, do little to build a general theory of race contact. A second set of explanations center on periods of economic development and conclude that, in general, some times are better than others to migrate and that blacks, in particular, migrated at the wrong time. These explanations represent an advance over the first set in that they provide a context within which a number of other migrant groups also may be studied. By way of elaboration, Wilson points out,

> The shift from goods producing to service producing industries, the increasing segmentation of the labor market, the growing use of

industrial technology, and the relocation of industries out of the central city (are changes) that, in themselves, have little to do with race. . . . The new barriers have racial significance only in their consequences, not in their origins.[15]

Yet, in the particular case of the black experience, such theories leave unexplained why the 300,000 black workers residing in northern cities in the expansive period of the 1890s, many of whom were children of freedmen, advanced very little in a society that was opening wide its doors to immigrant populations. The perspective assumes there was a better time for black migration but begs the question of when that time would have been.

Without abandoning the importance of either racism or timing, it is evident from the study of the Great Migration that assimilation as a societal response is slowed by two important factors. The first is recency. In his comparative study, *A Piece of the Pie*, Lieberson argues that "the cessation of migration" provides "long-run advantages to those members of the group already in the nation."[16] One could argue, by extension, that ethnic antagonism is at its height during immigration when the host society is most anxious to establish barriers between itself and the newcomers. Migrants, during these periods, suffer the greatest discrimination and exclusion.

As Lieberson points out, antagonism toward southern, central, and eastern Europeans in this country began to decline only when their immigration was cut off by law in the 1920s.[17] It could be argued, similarly, that for blacks in the North the most intensive period of discrimination occurred between 1910 and 1950, with each successive decade, save for that of the Depression, experiencing an even larger influx. Black migration from the South, after reaching its peak between 1940 and 1950, began to decline in the 1960s—precisely the time when societal support for nondiscriminatory legislation at the national, state, and local levels rose.

The decline in immigration cycles, then, creates a facilitating environment for the structural assimilation of newcomers. Moreover, it is not, as some have argued, that second and third generations simply become more "like" the native population and therefore more acceptable but that the society is more willing to remove barriers to their success.

Second, newcomers experience intense discrimination the greater their numbers in the context of their use. This idea relates not to the frequently cited endemic character of size itself but to the uses to which labor-importing societies put large immigrant flows. The strategies outlined in chapter 1 are only effective when the migrant population is of sufficient size to undercut and discipline the existing labor force. Immigrant flows

smaller in number, on the other hand, are often allowed to develop specialized economic niches that may both sustain and protect them from
the ire of the host society. Differences in the rate of assimilation among
not only black but also Mexican and Puerto Rican populations may, in
part, be explained by this factor. Further, it is a more powerful explanation for differences between American black and West Indian populations
than the cultural perspective suggested by many, most notably Nathan
Glazer and Daniel Patrick Moynihan.[18]

Thus, the forty-year immigration cycle of large numbers of southern
blacks made it unlikely that even structural assimilation would occur rapidly. In the 1950s, as immigration waned in the North, some things
changed more slowly than others. There was improvement in educational
attainment levels and in occupational distributions but almost no change
in the more primary levels of residential segregation. Certain forms of discrimination, it would appear, are more deeply ingrained and difficult to
break, even when changes in other sectors are being made.

Still, this diversity would represent a relatively optimistic view of the
incorporation of blacks as a group into society sometime in the future
were it not for the fact that legislative improvements during the decline
of immigration bifurcated the black community, introducing not only an
impenetrable barrier between top- and bottom-level jobs, but between
those who held them. Like a game of musical chairs, all those who were
seated when the music stopped, including some blacks, were rewarded.
Most of these left standing, including a sizable proportion of the black
population, will probably never be rewarded or accommodated. This is
the real importance of Wilson's "declining significance of race" thesis, a
point also discussed in Sidney Wilhelm's earlier work, *Who Needs the
Negro.*[19] For those blacks who were seated, to continue the analogy, racial
discrimination in comparison to past practice, could be significantly reduced. It is, in fact, no longer meaningful to divide merely by color because there are a number of whites who are also left standing. This does
not mean that racism is at an end. Blacks who gain admittance to top-level
jobs are certainly discriminated against in terms of hiring, salaries, and
promotion in comparison with whites at the same level. However, they
do not suffer in either extent or degree as those at the bottom suffer
through their class disadvantage. Moreover, with each successive generation of labor migrants after the Great Migration, the pattern is etched
more forcefully into the human tapestry of immigrant experience.

All of these points suggest that migrants, depending on the size and
recency of their immigration, may be said to experience structural assimilation at progressively faster or slower speeds and that blacks in particular, because of both the size and the duration of their migration, did not

gain the hoped-for incorporation into American society. Of greater potential for large-scale modern migration is the second positive alternative, return migration.

Return Migration

Returning to place of origin is the dream of many migrants, particularly those who succeed in the host society. It is a logical option because of the migrant's familiarity with its language, culture, and custom and because wage disparities between sending and receiving areas provide migrants with a distinct advantage. As stated in chapter 4, many of the "new immigrants" from southern, central, and eastern Europe traveled to America at the turn of the century without their families and left when able to buy a piece of land or start a small business in their homeland. Return migrants, when they are able to take with them the trappings of the core in terms of appliances, clothing, and other disposable items, are especially valued upon their homecoming.

This is not to suggest that all return migration is based on the success of migrants. As stated initially, migrants are selected because of their youth and health and are thrust into the worst jobs. Their "objective political weakness" to use Castells' term, makes them particularly vulnerable to unregulated workplaces and, disproportionately, to industrial accidents.[20] As Adrian Adams states of the Senegalese workers of France:

> They spend a few years there, living in conditions of extreme deprivation in order to send money to keep the people at home alive. When they return home, either their health is damaged beyond repair or they find that there is nothing for it but to leave again.[21]

It is also the case that migrants rarely learn skills in the host society that may be of benefit to the sending area upon their return. Adams suggests that, in Senegal, "People leave Fata Toro because they have to, not because they prefer it. . . . The most active members must therefore seek work elsewhere; and their departure further weakens the productive resources of the region, endangering the lives of those who are left behind. The work they do in exile does not equip them to break this vicious cycle."[22]

Further, return migration is of obvious benefit to employers as it facilitates the systematic rotation of ethnic groups thereby aiding in their cheapness relative to indigenous workers and to the perpetuation of division within the working class. Points out Castells:

Since the permanence of immigrant workers in each country is only relative, and their degree of subjective identification weaker, the workers' interest in participating in current struggles is limited, and generally concentrated in outbursts linked to their concrete living and working conditions.
Moreover, the racism and xenophobia diffused by the dominant ideology
accentuate the cleavages derived from national cultural particularities and
determine the ideological isolation of immigrants.[23]

Still, return migration may be said to benefit migrants in the following
ways. First, the successful return migrant has achieved at least some of
the security that drove him away in the first place, and the level of his
success need not be high in order for it to be of value to his family left
behind. Writes Portes:

> Through a series of informal economic relationships (i.e., retention of
> land and trade interests in the village), individuals are able to take advan-
> tage of differences in levels of "development." The success of these
> activities depends precisely on the existence of such spatial differences,
> which can be exploited through personal relationships and individual
> effort.[24]

Second, return migration that is recurrent may act as a safety net for
families who suffer deprivation in cycles rather than as a constant. Piore
suggests, for example, that the average undocumented Mexican worker
returns home every six months and that the total length of stay averages
about two and a half years.[25]

Third, return migration may provide the migrant with a degree of independence and control over his life that would not have been possible had
he remained in the sending area. I do not mean this in the psychological
sense of "learning to become modern," although it may be of indirect importance, but in the more direct sense of having the option to leave again
in periods of economic downturn.

And finally, return migration, as suggested in the previous section,
benefits those who do not return. It allows the smaller number who remain to reap the benefits of the host society in an environment of calm
rather than conflict.

In the Great Migration, migrants, though harsh in their criticism of the
South and its peculiar form of "justice," nonetheless retained an attach-
ment to and a longing for the region. Wrote a migrant in Pittsburgh to
his wife in the South, "I like the money O.K. but I like the South bettern
for my pleasure This city is too fast for me."[26] Confessed another, "I were
indeed glad to receive that paper from Union Springs. I saw in this plas
wherse I wrote to ellesfore a 2 horse farm. I have serval nochants of coming back. Yet I am doing well no trouble whatever except I can not raise

my children here like they should be."[27] More frequent were those like the wistful comment from a migrant in Philadelphia, "I would be delighted to have a word from the good old home state."[28]

Thoughts of returning to the South, with the exception of the rather common practice of shipping children "home" for the summer, were rarely translated into action. This was the case even though there were, on occasion, incentives to return. For example, according to the assistant secretary of Associated Charities in Atlanta, "Just after the unspeakable race riot in East St. Louis, Ill., a gentleman from Mississippi agreed to charter a steamboat and return one thousand Negroes to the plantations along the Mississippi River." While the gentleman from Atlanta was unsure if this offer had been accepted, there was plenty of evidence that others like it were rejected emphatically. When asked if he would return, "an unlettered southern 'emigrant'" replied, "Miss, if I had the money I would go South and dig up my father's and my mother's bones and bring them up to this country (Philadelphia). I am forty-nine years old, and these six weeks I have spent here are the first weeks in my life of peace and comfort."[29]

Unfortunately, the "peace and comfort" felt by southern migrants was not always shared by their northern brothers. The small northern black community that had existed before the massive migration resented the newcomers, blaming them for housing segregation and deterioration and for the heightened racism that accompanied their move. Reported the director of the Detroit Urban League, "[The southern migrant] does not receive a warm welcome from the great majority of colored citizens of the better class in the city to which he migrates. They try to decide whether his coming is a benefit or an injury to them," he continued.[30]

In Chicago, points out Spear, "the old settlers began to formulate a myth that became an article of faith in later years. Discrimination, they argued, was minimal before the Migration and it was the behavior of the newcomers that induced it."[31] Even the *Chicago Defender*, which had been instrumental in sparking the migration, chided migrants on "their conduct in public places" and "their ignorance of laws and customs."[32]

Similar problems were noted in Washington. According to George Haynes, of the Department of Labor:

> Only a few weeks before the riots, some leading people of Washington were discussing the fact that in former years the white and colored representatives of various philanthropic and community agencies were accustomed to meet more frequently than now for the exchange of news and places on matters of community interest. The holding of such meetings has grown more difficult and less frequent.[33]

Migrants, for their part, produced very different assessments of the situation, assessments often based on actual achievements. Observed one, "The old Negro settlers have sat on the 'stool of do-nothing' all these many years until the educated hustling southern negro has come. He is filling positions and jobs that negroes have never been known to hold before and getting the best pay." Stated another, "Most of the negro businesses in this city and other northern cities are owned or controlled by southern negroes. Our strongest and most aggressive politicians are in most cases originally from the South."[34]

With all the insults and injuries of the new setting, southern black workers still did not benefit from return migration. Because most who were married were reunited with their families soon after the move, unlike their European counterparts, they did not, in Portes's words, "take advantage of differences in levels of development."[35] For similar reasons, they did not take advantage of the back and forth movement as many undocumented Mexican workers have done more recently. Remaining in the host society also disadvantaged black migrants in that it reinforced their vulnerability and caused a rift to develop not only between them and white workers but, as the last section suggests, within the extant black community as well.

On a hypothetical level, return migration may have been beneficial to the population. Migrants could have worked for part of the year in the North, left their families behind in the South, and returned after a few years or even periodically. They would have formed an independent black working class that could have made significant contributions to the region. By not being in direct competition with white workers in the South, but perhaps proving to be contributors to a secondary economic growth there, blacks could have abated the antagonism between these groups. Thus, if we assume that returning black migrants would not have disrupted the existing labor balances in the South, we can further assume that the southern white power elite would have benefited even more directly from the purchasing power of the migrants and may have, as a result, been inclined to lessen the hardships suffered by the migrants and their families.

Such a suggestion does not ignore the privation endured by black families because of separation. Women, alone for significant parts of the year, would at times have been forced to seek employment to help their families survive. They were forced to do so in the North. The difference would have been the greater buying power of remittances sent South, which would have given them a degree of autonomy unknown before. It is also likely that an independent black working class would have stimulated employment of all kinds within the black community itself.

Children would perhaps have suffered even more than the adults by remaining because of the lack of educational opportunities, although the increased wealth of the community could then have supported a larger number of black academies in the South, educational institutions formed by financially able black parents to offset the discriminatory, segregated southern schools.

The vehemence with which some migrants recounted their personal experiences in the South is, for the moment, sufficient explanation for their desire not to return. It is also true that some migrants, for a host of social and political reasons, may not have been able to return. For all of these reasons, the benefits of migration may hinge on the development of an immigrant enclave.

Immigrant Enclave

The third method by which a migrant may be said to benefit from migration is to participate in an economic enterprise within an immigrant enclave. Alejandro Portes and Alex Stepick have argued that "ethnic enclaves represent a distinct labor market sector" and that "the primary characteristic of ethnic economics is the use of a common cultural bond for economic survival and advancement."[36] Enclaves succeed, according to the authors, because of three interrelated factors: First, enterprises are formed with the consciousness of ethnic solidarity as their base. Second, as a kind of sacrifice for the greater good, migrants agree to be used as cheap labor so that "fledgling enterprises" may survive. And third, migrants willingly accept lower wages initially under the expectation "that employers promote their workers as new positions become open within their firms or support their eventual move into self-employment."[37]

The pattern of migrants using earnings to achieve self-employment has been replicated among many immigrant groups. As Piore has observed, "Typically, [migrants] plan to utilize funds acquired abroad to establish themselves in an activity that will give them independent, entrepreneurial status. . . . The single important exception of which I am aware is the migration of blacks in the United States from the rural South."[38] Piore attributes this shortcoming to lack of opportunity to develop such enterprises in the South.

Ivan Light, in his work *Ethnic Enterprise in America* also notes the important exception of black migration but attributes it to different causes. The most compelling explanation is that urban blacks lack special consumer demands and consequently are made disadvantaged by white competition.[39] Ethnic groups with special diets and language more steadily develop their own small retail enterprises to cater to group demand. Black enterprises are disadvantaged in that, without special demands, they may be routinely undercut by white enterprises who have more capital. The second explanation is that the development of ethnic enterprises requires start-up capital, something the impoverished black community lacks on its own and is prevented from obtaining because of discrimination by banks and other lending institutions.[40] This explanation has been somewhat discredited by comparative analysis that suggests that blacks were no more discriminated against than other ethnic groups. Still, it is not denied that, as a group, blacks have one of the lowest percentages of ethnic enterprise, and poverty and lack of capital within the black community obviously contribute to this failure.

The shortcomings of the second explanation are explained by the third, what Ivan Light has called "culturally defined differences in economic organization."[41] Other ethnic groups, lacking capital from without the community, generate it from within in the form of rotating credit associations. These associations lend community members money on a short-term, no-interest basis to serve as start-up capital. Blacks, who E. Franklin Frazier suggests lacked a "tradition of enterprise" failed to establish such associations and, as a result, had no self-sustaining ethnic enclave.[42]

The black "tradition of enterprise" was, in fact, more prevalent than many have assumed. The National Negro Business League, an organization founded by Booker T. Washington, estimated that there were 20,000 black businesses in 1900 and 40,000 in 1914. According to Robert Higgs, these figures are probably inflated.[43] However, according to the Department of Commerce, there were 25,000 black retail stores, alone, in 1929.

It is possible that the cultural distinction was more prevalent in their character than in their number. Higgs suggests that, "most enterprises were small—so small that they could be operated with little or no hired help."[44] This assessment is supported by the 1929 figures. In that year, there were 25,701 stores owned by 28,243 black proprietors that hired 12,561 employees for an average of .49 employee per store. By comparison, there were 3,865 stores owned by 6,432 Chinese and Japanese proprietors that hired 8,926 employees for an average of 2.3 employees per store.[45] This pattern was also observed in an earlier study by George Haynes, in which he stated, "One of the most important findings is that Negroes form few partnerships and that those formed are rarely of more than two persons. Cooperative or corporate business enterprises are the exceptions."[46]

While cooperative business enterprises were not common, they were

not atypical. Burial societies, health insurance associations, and cooperative banks were particularly prevalent when migrants headed North.
W. E. B. DuBois was particularly interested in the structure of some of
these associations. Observed DuBois, "They were very simple in form:
an initiation fee of small amount was required, and small regular pay-
ments; in case of sickness, a weekly stipend was paid, and in case of
death the members were assessed to pay for the funeral and help the
widow."[47] Even the lowly and despised domestic workers formed "saving
societies" to which savings were directed for future purchases and illness. Fifty-three percent of the domestics studied by Eaton reported
use of saving societies. According to Eaton, "these societies, when they
are bona fide insurance companies, often furnish fair investments to
their contributors."[48]

What ultimately hampered such businesses, however, was not culture,
tradition, or experience so much as the assaults upon ethnic solidarity
within the community itself. As Higgs observed, "black consumers, upon
whom most black businessmen depended for the great bulk of their sales,
gave only grudging support to black enterprises."[49] In large part, this attitude had to do with the previously mentioned, competitive edge of white
businesses but also with the difficulty of unifying a community that had
little more than the color of its skin and its common oppression to keep
it together. Stated George Frederickson, "Despite their participation in a
rich and distinctive folk culture of their own, southern blacks of the Jim
Crow era had much . . . in common with their white oppressors in language, religion, social values, and life-style."[50]

Establishing a universal and distinctive black identity, even in the face
of the dominant society's stigmatized relations with the black population,
was very difficult. Much of what initially passes for ethnic identity in any
multiethnic society is imposed from without, not within. Black migrants
moving North were escaping much more than exploitative economic conditions. The faithful slave, savage child, and sambo-like images that had
been thrust upon them were too vivid a reminder of past oppression to
readily permit a more favorable, counter image to emerge. It took dramatic events like the Garvey movement and the literary flowering of the
Harlem Renaissance and a myriad of undramatic, individual moments of
lesser note but greater significance to remove what Ralph Ellison lamented as "an uncreated consciousness of their color."[51]

Like return migration, the option of an immigrant enclave was more
problematic for the black population. Faced constantly with forces shaped
to divide rather than unite, the group struggled in a fragmented and
piecemeal manner.

Conclusion

Labor migrations typically represent massive movements of vulnerable workers from dependent peripheries to dominant cores. They satisfy a need for cheap labor in the core economy and help to divide the established working class. Both the timing and the direction of these migrant flows are outside the control of those who are induced to move. Still, the migrant himself may be said to benefit from migration in one of three ways. He may be absorbed into the host economy and, in the absence of opposition, achieve a degree of upward mobility. As discussed in this chapter, this "straight-line" pattern of assimilation is increasingly rare in American society and, even in the past, may have only been evident because of its tie to return migration. Return migration, the second alternative, may benefit those who succeed, even at modest levels, in the host society and are able to enjoy these rewards in the more disadvantaged sending area. However, not all labor migrants are able to return regardless of their success and, more significantly, many do not advance. And finally, the migrant may benefit from the relatively protected economy of the immigrant enclave if the population is small and concentrated enough to foster ethnic enterprise.

Black migrants moving North were too many to assimilate, too poor and too vulnerable to return to the South, and too American to support ethnic enterprise. In the aggregate, they reaped none of the possible benefits of labor migration.

CHAPTER EIGHT

Conclusion

Negroes, forever marked by their color,
could only hope for success within a
rigidly delineated and severely restricted ghetto society. No physical wall
has encircled the black belt. But an almost equally impervious wall of hostility and discrimination has isolated Negroes from the mainstream of Chicago
life. Under such conditions, Negroes
have tried, often against impossible
odds, to make the best of their circumstances by creating a meaningful life of
their own. But they have done so, not
out of choice, but because white society
has left them no alternative.[1]

THE GREAT MIGRATION represents a now familiar form of human population movement. Resident in an area where labor displacements occur
because of industrialization, high rural to urban migration, and increased
exploitation and discrimination, migrants are induced to leave for seemingly more lucrative industrial centers. Core employers precipitate this exodus through their penetration of the peripheral economy in search of
the twin pillars of development, raw materials and cheap labor.

Labor migrations are not simply movements of individuals selling their
labor. Migrants do not move, even for only part of a season, merely for
higher wages. Conditions in sending areas must be in a sufficient state
of flux to create uncertainty, intense competition, and eventual displacement. It is only with these unsettling dislocations that populations who
are content, perhaps for centuries, to till the soil or languish in traditional
cottage industries, seem suddenly to rise up en masse and move to another place. They seek the economic opportunity now impossible at
home; they flee the political policies that make them disadvantaged; they
are pulled toward social ideals that were not even dreamed of a few years
before.

In such migrations, it is not plausible to argue that the impetus for leaving lies solely within these persons. Newly found social ideals are imported into areas by the penetration of more advanced centers. Political changes are the products of local governments. Economic displacements represent the articulation of center economic needs and peripheral market hopes. It is, as Burawoy suggests, institutional activity beyond the scope of individual experience that sets the stage for mass migrations.[2]

This is not to imply that the individual is extraneous to the experience. In fact, once set in motion, certain types of migrants leave in fairly predictable patterns. Young literate men, possessing some formal education and previous manufacturing experience are among those most likely to move.[3] They are not alone. For those who are married, women play a direct and necessary role, sustaining their families while their husbands search for work and continuing to supplement meager salaries once they are resettled.

In the Great Migration, migrants were neither an undifferentiated mass nor a displaced rural peasantry. They were rather representatives of a fledgling class of artisans and urban nonagricultural laborers as well as some farm owners and relatively prosperous tenants, all of whom had been deeply and personally affected by the economic transformation of the South. They were the lucky ones. They had the wherewithal to leave when times were bad and prospects worse.

They left the South by selling all they had: land, household goods, anything that could be translated into cash. They did not do these things unconsciously. They did not "pull up and follow almost without a reason."[4]

They were encouraged. Encouraged by powerful institutions whose promises of a better life needed little substance to persuade a population made poor by intense competition for a few, low-paying jobs. Such institutions as the press made arguments that were moral as well as economic. "Your neck has been in the yoke. Will you continue to keep it there because some 'white folks nigger' wants you to? Leave to all quarters of the globe. Get out of the South."[5] The call of a single institution may have seemed merely boastful.

But it was not just one. Labor agents, themselves employees of powerful northern industrialists, roamed the South searching for recruits. Their case was compelling. We need you, they said. If you cannot afford the transportation costs, we will advance it to you. If you do not have the resettlement cash, we will supply it. These offers were ingenious. What transportation was advanced was later deducted from wages. And it was only early on in the migration process that such funds were provided at all. As the movement gained momentum, the inducement was no longer necessary. As for resettlement funds, there is little evidence that these were ever provided. But the importance of labor agents lies not in what they actually provided, but in what they led people to believe.

They were not alone. The Urban League, the black church, even the federal government participated in what became a relatively sophisticated and persistent booster campaign to take new workers North.

In the South, the loss of a significant segment of its labor was not greeted with uniform concern. Floods and boll weevil invasions necessitated a restructuring of labor in agricultural areas; the migration of farm laborers to southern cities was not viewed as a deterioration of conditions or a threat to prosperity. In urban areas, the large influx of rural labor was more than adequate to meet any demand. Relief was felt at what was perceived as the draining off of surplus workers. Added to this was the political advantage in the black belt of diminishing the black majority; an aspect of colonialism that was a constant fear to the white minority.

What seems surprising in their leaving is, in fact, that they waited so long after emancipation to leave the land of oppression. Life in the South had never been good to or for black people. Even in the heyday of the Reconstruction governments, opportunities were few. But blacks did not leave the South at that time because lines of communication had not been established. Northern investors had not yet drawn the South into the orbit of its economic system. At the level of the individual migrant, there were few ties between North and South. The penetration of southern industry by northern investors forever altered the lives of southern black laborers.

Unfortunately, for the migrants, the North was not the hoped for promised land. Drawn as a source of cheap labor, northern industrialists had never envisioned their absorption as equal partners into the mainstream of the American work force. Sometimes imported as strikebreakers, often systematically rotated within firms to produce the maximum ethnic antagonism, they got little in the new system to which they had gained entrance. As Harold Baron suggests, "Black workers were employed on management's own terms."[6]

The continuation of their marginal labor status in the North represented at best a substitution of a precapital for a mature capital labor status. They were, to be sure, better educated than their southern counterparts. Industrial workers often are. They were better clothed. Industrial workers often are. They had greater political participation. Industrial workers often have.[7] But their opportunities for advancement were, in the words of Spear, "rigidly delineated and severely restricted."[8]

The Great Migration in Historical Context

Previous studies of the Great Migration have tied the disappointment of the exodus to individual shortcomings, what Tilly called the antiquated notion of "bewildered country folk," rather than the structure of the system. Commented Robert Park, "America, and perhaps the rest of the world, can be divided into two classes: those who have reached the city, and those who have not yet arrived."[9]

Great Migration participants, however, did not represent a rural peasantry. The significance of this finding lies in the very question of incorporation. Many, it has been shown, came from urban, in some cases skilled backgrounds, and yet their plight was no better than that of their rural counterparts. Indeed, previous level of education and skill made little or no difference to the migrating population. As has been shown, migrants were used to supply an urban-based industrial labor reserve, filling undesirable jobs that whites left in a tight labor market.[10] Whether one assigns greater blame to nonunionization, race prejudice, or employer taste, the fact remains that there was no opportunity to advance and nothing to offset their exploitation.

Others have concluded that the occurrence of the migration at a point when there was an increasing demand for a literate and skilled population left those unskilled and illiterate at a distinct disadvantage. The black rural peasantry, illiterate and unskilled, could not advance, it has been observed. But why, it must be asked, did not the skilled artisan or the semiskilled and unskilled urban worker not advance? It is erroneous to tie such nonadvancement to the personal characteristics of the migrants. Most had previous manufacturing experience, and many were literate. One could perhaps suggest that they had the wrong characteristics; that the skills they possessed could not be translated into modern, industrial needs. Such a proposition is challenged, however, by the fact that employers sought and used workers with what appears to be directly comparable experience, such as in meat packing and iron and steel production.[11]

It is even more difficult to abandon the importance of their literacy. As Lieberson has shown, one out of every six literate blacks left the South during the Great Migration. It was an exodus of a highly selective population. What explanation could be given to explain their immobility vis-à-vis education in comparison with, for example, the European immigrants entering the United States in large numbers right up until 1914? Is it possible that the Europeans were significantly more literate than the southern blacks? Current research suggests, in fact, that they were far less literate.[12]

These explanations neglect the economic moment at which the Great Migration occurred. Black workers were incorporated into a new system built on sustaining profit from an abundant supply of cheap labor that was both substitutable and disposable. Workers were no longer pushed upward in the system but were pushed outward. In the past, successive waves of immigrant groups were advanced to make way for new, more vulnerable reserves. Such a replacement process defined much of the process of assimilation experienced by old European immigration into American society in the mid and late nineteenth century. But by the turn of the century, even before black workers left the South, the old economic system of industrial capital was giving way to the new form of monopoly capital and with it the labor transformation discussed in chapters 4 and 5.

The war demand for unskilled labor that had brought southern blacks North in large numbers for the first time was a necessary but not a sufficient explanation for the transformation. Of more lasting import was the fact that northern capital was prospering because of the circulation of alternate supplies of cheap labor, with circulation as the key element.[13] The use of black labor at that time was related both to the penetration of the southern economy and to the loss of the European supply. Once used, however, the process of cheap labor incorporation was threatened. There was no way routinely to absorb so many potential workers, one tenth of the population of the United States. Blacks, unlike the European and Asian immigrants before them, could not be sent back to the peripheral economies from which they came when the demand for their labor disappeared nor assimilated in smaller numbers at some intermediary level.[14] And blacks did not choose to return to the South. This decision represented something of a crisis for industry. The system worked because workers willingly accepted "bad" jobs. Blacks, by electing not to return, had either to be relegated to a permanent urban-based industrial reserve, called underclass, or absorbed—a solution that would challenge the entire system of profit.

In the 1920s, the belief prevailed that most black workers would be content to remain at the worst jobs on the bottom of the job hierarchy. This notion was reinforced by an ideological climate of racial superiority. Blacks would remain on the bottom because that is where they belonged. Before the migration, small black populations in the North had lived in relative harmony, albeit general poverty, reinforcing the status quo. With the Great Migration, there developed a change in the racial climate. Black demands for civil rights and economic justice were increased and, for their efforts, blacks were more commonly viewed by the white populace as criminal, unsocialized, mentally deficient, and lazy. And as tensions mounted and cities exploded, the labor needs of employers vis-à-vis the migrating black population were advanced.

The ideological roots of these racial distinctions carry, moreover, in fact, an ironic twist. At the turn of the century, Booker T. Washington first warned against immigrant labor, "those of foreign birth and strange tongue and habits" who were displacing black Americans.[15] Other black leaders maintained that immigrants were "socialist agitators undermining the capitalist system and would never adjust to the American way of life."[16] It was all part of the old "divide and conquer" strategy encouraged by those in power who feared that an alliance might form between two exploited and powerless groups. Blacks undoubtedly felt that their participation in such exclusionary movements would reduce competition. However, according to Henri, the "nativism" that resulted became as much "a racist creed as an anti-immigration movement."[17] At first it was sufficient to fear the new immigrants from eastern and southern Europe who were replacing the "sturdy stocks," and were considered stupid, dirty, and dangerously radical. Over time, however, such inferiority and fear was expanded and applied to all non-Anglo-Saxon groups. Blacks, then, had supported ideologies that later became part of their own demise. Henri has pointed out:

> When black Americans line up with white Americans who were pressing for immigration restrictions, believing that their American nativity gave them status of co-equals, they were tightening the chains of racism around themselves. John Higham in his study of American nativism concluded that gradually, "in every section, the Negro, the Oriental, and the Southern European appeared more and more in common light."[18]

Indeed, instead of advancing, they were moved to the very back of the line. Moreover, with that change came a heightened consciousness of inferiority, often supported by scientific discoveries of the bestial and measurements of the brutish.

Once regarded even by the experts as subhuman, blacks could more easily be forced to accept and fill bottom-rung positions. But maintenance of a permanent supply of cheap labor, even with the most virulent of ideologies, is difficult. There was always the danger that blacks would become unionized. As suggested initially, over time even the most visible of groups in the most vulnerable of circumstances may be approached for organization. For blacks there occurred a complete turnaround of labor union policy. Previously barred from membership in almost all industrial and trade unions, they were, in the thirties, for the first time actively recruited by these groups. The reason for the change in union policy seems to be as much political as economic. Because of fears of growing labor unrest associated with the Depression and the gains of movements like "share the wealth" and the Communist party, the administration of Roosevelt began to support protective union legislation.[19] Rights of collective bargaining, job protection, and taxation, which reduced the gaps between rich and poor, were for the first time introduced. With this new set of contingencies, labor unions no longer viewed blacks as antiunion (indeed, the concessions meant that it was more difficult for them to be used by employers as strikebreakers) and welcomed them instead into the fold. Baron observes:

> The trade-union organizing drives of the CIO which actively sought out black workers in heavy and mass-production industry provided a new focus. From 1937 to World War II the CIO conducted the most massive working-class campaign that has ever taken place in America. Its dynamism was so great that it reset the direction of the political activity of the working class, the black community and the left.[20]

Black union members, however, were no longer cheap. By bringing black workers into the fold, union laborers had achieved what they had been attempting through previous exclusion, to make the position of the black worker problematic.

To offset the rising costs of labor, which were threatening the rate of profit, northern capital replaced blacks with more vulnerable, low-wage reserves from developing areas under the orbit of their economic relations. Cheap labor drawn from less developed regions could easily be returned to the sending areas for a host of sins, including attempts at labor organization, should it choose not to return on its own. The status of permanent underclass came to characterize ever larger segments of the black population. Relegating citizens to a redundant status, however, carries its own penalties, and a permanent black underclass is today as much feared as it is needed. Concludes Baron: "The welfare and police costs of maintaining this labor reserve are high, but they are borne by the state as a whole and therefore do not enter into the profit calculations of individual firms."[21]

Assessment of the Great Migration

How, on balance, is the Great Migration to be judged? Many scholars have noted that black migrants left the South uncounseled by the black leadership. Although Booker T. Washington died in 1915 and did not witness the mass exodus from the South, it is clear from his pronouncements that he would have opposed it. He said on one occasion, "the Negro is at his best in the South" and would find there greater economic opportunity and a higher moral life. The *New York Age* warned skilled southern black workmen "to think carefully" before migrating where skilled jobs were hard to get. Professor Kelly Miller, of Howard University, declared that "the Negro's industrial opportunities lie in the black belts" and that the South was his "land of Goshen."[22] Much of the southern black press either remained silent or spoke only in a feeble manner concerning the exodus. W. E. B. DuBois, although not opposed to the migration, certainly understood well that the journey North represented not the end of a struggle but only its beginning.[23]

Some of the opposition to the migration was motivated by fears for personal safety. A black Methodist minister, for example, "was arrested for encouraging some of his parishioners to seek employment with a firm in New York."[24] But most of the black leadership was not in so vulnerable a position. It has been assumed that their appeals were prompted at best by a lack of foresight and at worse by self-gain from those who had sold out to the dominant white society.

Putting aside questions of the failings of the southern black leadership, it is useful to speculate on the impact of the Great Migration on the black community. In 1910, blacks owned over 15 million acres of land in the South; by 1930, it had dwindled to fewer than 10 million.[25] The acreage loss of black farm owners during the ten years, 1920 to 1930, was most significant. Their loss of over 2,700,000 acres was equivalent to 4,296 square miles, or an area more than twice that of the combined areas of Delaware and the District of Columbia.[26] While migration alone did not account for this decline, the combination of it, state policy, declining cotton prices and credit, and the boll weevil certainly did.

Even more dramatic was the plight of black banks. In 1900, there were over 200 black banks in the United States, most of them in the South; by 1930, there were fewer than 20. In 1910, when a vast majority of blacks still resided in the South, there were 17,495 clergymen in the nation as a whole; in 1940, twenty years after the migration, there were 17,102. In 1910, there were 3,077 physicians and surgeons; in 1940, 3,524. In 1910, there were 798 lawyers and judges; in 1940, 1,052.[27] Even where there were slight gains, they did not exceed what could have been expected had blacks remained in a highly segregated South.

But more than issues of ownership, control, or the losses in the professions is the tantalizing suspicion that had the talent and wisdom of that generation of blacks who left the South to become mudsills in northern industry between 1910 and 1930, remained to demand what was rightfully theirs from southern society, the civil rights revolution might have occurred in the 1930s rather than the 1960s.

Emmett Scott, commenting on the causes of the migration observes that "the older generation of blacks avoided much friction by a mutual understanding but their children, who came less frequently into contact with whites, found it difficult to live together on terms accepted by their fathers."[28] Under these circumstances, many parents were, Scott suggests, "not reluctant to send their sons away from home." A woman from Greenville, Mississippi, for example, whose son was in the North, was actually "afraid to invite him home to visit" because, as she stated, "for him to accept the same abuses to which we, his parents, are accustomed, would make him much less than the man we would have him be."[29]

The older generations sent their sons away from home rather than have them sacrificed in what Vincent Harding has called, "the river of our struggle."[30] They could not be expected to know that only another branch awaited migrants in the North.

The Fate of Black Migrants

It is difficult to argue that blacks would have been better off had they never left the South. Migration is a proven stimulant to economic advancement, and blacks fled a South in 1916 that promised to remove what little they had gained since emancipation. As suggested in chapter 1, migrants specifically may benefit from one of three positive alternatives: assimilation, return migration, or development of an enclave society. These options may serve to offset the dominant structure of exploitation.

Assimilation, the path to incorporation for the earliest Europeans, was traditionally the most cherished alternative for the most American of immigrants, the southern black worker. In this, he was disappointed. Assuming the development of an economically secure middle class to be the clearest indication of assimilation, one finds in 1940 that only 7% of the black population could be so defined.[31] Even with the profound change of the 1960s, the black middle class has never exceeded, by generous estimates, 30% of the population, and there are current indications that this group may be shrinking. Moreover, the black middle class has been shown to be more vulnerable than whites of similar age and occupation to the ebb and flow of the market, to earn less income and less promotion, and to have fewer assets. Even with a declining significance of race in America, the black middle class lives, at best, on the margins of the domi-

nant society. As Tilly observed in 1968, "the idea of an inevitable movement toward assimilation faces some difficult facts. The ancestors of most
of America's black population were here well before most of the Europeans on whose assimilation the scheme is based." Moreover, "some forms
of racial discrimination and segregation have worsened several times in
the memory of living men."[32]

Return migration was not an option widely considered. Yet, it may
have been beneficial to the population. Why did not more blacks exercise
this option? I think there are two reasons, both of which have already
been discussed at length in this work. The first is that southern black nonagricultural workers, the bulk of the migrant population, sold all they had
to get to the North and therefore had much less to return to than the usual
return migrant. They broke ties with the South, burned bridges, and
there was no return once done. The second is that as urban workers, there
was less to hold them to the South in any case. They had not lived on
the same piece of land as their fathers and forefathers; were not returning
to time-honored traditions or, in many cases, to institutions, like
churches, which might have bound them. It is far easier for an urban resident to move from one city to another with little loss of continuity in their
lives.

Blacks would also have benefited from the development of an immigrant enclave. That they did not develop one is attributed most directly
to the problem of racial solidarity. "The souls of black folk," W. E. B.
DuBois has observed, carry in them a "double consciousness; a struggle
to be both black and American."[33] The outcome of that struggle was not
always on the side of the race itself. This is not to deny that blacks, like
other immigrant groups, have become part of an ethnicity that is "crystal-
lized" if not created under "frequent patterns of association and identification with common origins."[34] But one must point out, as others have
done, that identification is more readily transferable to common economic
interests in some groups than in others. For blacks, it prevented mobility
within an enclave society.

Blacks neither benefited from the Great Migration as a stepping stone
to industrial advancement nor as minorities filling a special niche within
a dominant society. They could not assimilate because of their perceived
differences from the dominant society; they could not return because they
were too urban; and they could not develop an enclave society because
they were too American. They had, then, nothing to offset their exploitation. Black workers helped to cushion the disquieting effects of early industrialization in the South and to usher in the postindustrial era in the
North. Their contributions were crucial to American economic develop-

ment and prosperity. Their reward was poverty in the North. The Great Migration, like emancipation itself, represented a small step in a struggle to remove the black man's burden. To celebrate it, however, is to praise what DuBois has called "a cry amid a roar of elemental forces."[35]

Notes

I. Migration in Historical and Theoretical Context

1. Ira Katznelson, *Black Men, White Cities* (Chicago: University of Chicago Press, 1973), p. 2.

2. There had been other migrations, most notably the exodus to Kansas in the 1870s (see, for example, Nell Painter, *The Exodusters* [New York: Knopf, 1977]). Blacks in much smaller numbers had also been migrating north since the turn of the century (see Florette Henri, *Black Migration: Movement North 1900–1920* [Garden City, N.Y.: Anchor Press/Doubleday, 1975], and Elizabeth Pleck, *Black Migration and Poverty* [New York: Academic Press, 1979]).

3. Emmett Scott, *Negro Migration During the War* (New York: Oxford University Press, 1920), p. 40.

4. George Haynes, *Negro Migration in 1916–1917* (Washington, D.C.: U.S. Department of Labor, Division of Negro Economics, Government Printing Office, 1919), p. 12.

5. See Alejandro Portes, "Migration and Underdevelopment," *Politics and Society* 7 (1978), pp. 1–48; Manuel Castells, "Immigrant Workers and Class Struggles in Advanced Capitalism: The Western European Experience," *Politics and Society* 5 (1975), pp. 33–66; Michael Burawoy, "The Functions and Reproduction of Migrant Labor: Comparative Material from Southern Africa and the United States," *American Journal of Sociology* 81 (1976), pp. 1050–87.

6. Portes, "Migration and Underdevelopment," p. 3.

7. Robert L. Bach, "Mexican Immigration and the American State," *International Migration Review* 12 (Winter), p. 537.

8. Charles Wood, "Equilibrium vs. Historical-Structural Perspectives on Migration" (Paper presented at a Conference on Immigration and Ethnicity, Durham, N.C., May 1981), p. 2.

9. Portes, "Migration and Underdevelopment," p. 10.

10. Edna Bonacich, "International Labor Migration: A Theoretical Orientation" (Paper presented at a Conference on Immigration and Ethnicity, Durham, N.C., May 1981), p. 11.

11. Ibid., p. 19.

12. Ibid., p. 20.

13. Ibid., p. 12.

14. Portes, "Migration and Underdevelopment," p. 3.

15. Bonacich, "International Labor Migration," pp. 7–9.

16. Ibid., p. 15.

17. Ibid., p. 14.

18. Michael Piore, *Birds of Passage* (New York: Cambridge University Press, 1979) p. 24.

19. Bonacich, "International Labor Migration," pp. 24, 38.

20. Bach, p. 538.

21. Piore, pp. 18–19.

22. Bonacich, "International Labor Migration," p. 38.

23. Ibid., p. 40.

24. Ibid., p. 47.

25. Bach, p. 548.

26. Ibid., p. 549.

27. Piore, p. 169.

28. Portes, "Migration and Underdevelopment," p. 52.

29. Bonacich, "International Labor Migration," p. 48.

30. Ibid., p. 50; Piore, p. 27.

31. Bonacich, "International Labor Migration," p. 52.

32. Robert Blauner, *Racial Oppression in America* (New York: Harper and Row, 1972), p. 23.

33. Bach, p. 543.

34. Portes, "Migration and Underdevelopment," p. 52.

35. Ibid., p. 32.

36. Bonacich, "International Labor Migration," p. 53.

37. Robert T. Averitt, *The Dual Economy* (New York: Norton, 1968), p. 7.

38. Bonacich, "International Labor Migration," p. 52.

39. Castells, p. 370.

40. Quoted in Averitt, p. 127.

41. Averitt, p. 128.

42. Quoted in T. B. Bottomore, *Karl Marx* (New York: McGraw-Hill, 1956), p. 64.

43. Robert Park, *Race and Culture* (Glencoe, Ill: Free Press, 1950), p. 5.

44. Stephen Steinberg, *The Ethnic Myth* (Boston: Beacon Press, 1981), p. 47.

45. Piore, p. 50.

46. Portes, "Migration and Underdevelopment," p. 44.

47. Blauner, p. 63.

48. Haynes, p. 12.

49. Emmett Scott, "Letters of Negro Migrants of 1916–1918," *Journal of Negro History* 4 (July 1919), p. 333.

50. Haynes, p. 47.

51. Ibid., p. 108.

52. Katznelson, p. 31.

53. Gunnar Myrdal, *An American Dilemma: The Negro Problem and Modern Democracy* (New York: Harper and Row, 1944), p. 342.

54. William J. Wilson, *The Declining Significance of Race* (Chicago: University of Chicago Press, 1978) p. 67.

55. Portes, "Migration and Underdevelopment," p. 10.

56. Ibid., pp. 11–12.

II. The Great Migration

1. Scott, "Letters," p. 461.

2. Ray Stannard Baker, *Following the Color Line* (1908; reprint New York: Harper and Row, 1964), p. 101.

3. Melvin Webber, "Order in Diversity: Community without Propinquity," in *Cities and Space: The Future of Urban Land*, ed. Lowdon Wingo, Jr. (Baltimore: Johns Hopkins University Press, 1963), pp. 23–26.

4. Piore, p. 24.

5. Robert Park and Herbert Miller, *Old World Traits Transplanted* (New York: Harper, 1921); John MacDonald and Leatrice MacDonald, "Chain Migration, Ethnic Neighborhood Formation and Social Networks," *Milbank Memorial Fund Quarterly* 42 (1964), pp. 82–97; Sidney Goldstein, "Migration: Dynamics of the American City," *American Quarterly* 6 (Winter 1954), pp. 337–48. MacDonald and MacDonald define "chain migration" as that movement in which perspective migrants learn of opportunities, are provided with transportation, and have initial accommodations arranged by means of primary social relationships with previous migrants. p. 82.

6. Scott, *Negro Migration During the War* (New York: Oxford University Press, 1920), p. 37.

7. Ibid., p. 38.

8. Castells, pp. 33–66. Castells suggests that requirements of age and health represent methods by which employers "by recruiting migrants primarily from among the young and productive, avoid paying the costs of 'rearing' the worker and the maintenance costs after his/her working life has ended."

9. William Tuttle, *Race Riot* (New York: Atheneum, 1974), p. 88; Brinley Thomas, *Migration and Economic Growth*, 2d ed. (Cambridge: Cambridge University Press, 1973), p. 333. Thomas has stated, "So severe was the shortage of labour that many recruiting agents were sent to the South, for example, the Pennsylvania Railroad could not have carried out its essential maintenance work without bringing to the North many thousands of Negro workers."

10. Scott, *Negro Migration*, p. 61.

11. Henri, p. 61.

12. Guychard Parris and Lester Brooks, *Blacks in the City: A History of the National Urban League* (Boston: Little, Brown, 1971).

13. Tuttle, p. 89.

14. Scott, *Negro Migration*, p. 37.

15. Louise Kennedy, *The Negro Peasant Turns Cityward* (New York: Columbia University Press, 1930), p. 53.

16. Ibid., p. 122.

17. U.S. Department of Agriculture, "Report on Study of Negro Migration" (Washington, D.C.: Government Printing Office, 1923), p. 10.

18. Scott, "Letters," p. 331.

19. Scott, *Negro Migration*, pp. 47–48; Kennedy, p. 53; Tuttle, p. 88; Henri, p. 67; Allan H. Spear, *Black Chicago: The Making of a Ghetto, 1890–1920* (Chicago: University of Chicago Press, 1967), p. 133.

20. Scott, "Letters," p. 331.

21. Scott, *Negro Migration*, p. 34.

22. Marta Tienda, "Familism and Structural Assimilation of Mexican Im-

migrants in the United States," *International Migration Review* 14, no. 3 (1980), p. 384.

23. Spear, p. 133.

24. Ibid., p. 134; Tuttle, p. 86; Kennedy, p. 53.

25. Scott, *Negro Migration*, p. 34; Tuttle, p. 86.

26. Scott, *Negro Migration*, p. 98.

27. Scott, "Letters," p. 333.

28. Ibid., p. 334.

29. Tuttle, pp. 84–85; Scott, *Negro Migration*, p. 40.

30. Scott, *Negro Migration*, p. 26.

31. Henri, p. 123.

32. Scott, "Letters," p. 457.

33. Ibid., p. 456.

34. Spear, p. 134.

35. Charles Tilly, "Race and Migration to the American City," in *The Metropolitan Enigma*, ed. James Q. Wilson (New York: Doubleday, 1970), p. 157.

36. Saskia Sassen-Koob, "Formal and Informal Associations: Dominicans and Columbians in New York," *International Migration Review* 13, pp. 319-32.

37. The Urban League had started in 1906 as the Committee for Improving the Industrial Conditions of Negroes in New York City. It held "that the Negro needed not alms but opportunity—opportunity to work at the job for which the Negro was best fitted, with equal pay for equal work, and opportunity for advancement" (Myrdal, 1944). Local branches were soon established in many cities. While the League, which was made up of a nucleus of philanthropists, social workers, and professionals, touched on problems of education, housing, youth, family, and neighborhood of the black community, the primary task of all Leagues was to find jobs for blacks. All offices functioned as employment agencies. They attempted both to open up new jobs and to prevent the loss of jobs already held. Toward those ends, they contacted employers and tried to "sell" black labor—impressing upon the employers that black labor was "efficient and satisfactory" (Myrdal, 1944).

38. Chicago Commission on Race Relations, *The Negro in Chicago* (Chicago: University of Chicago Press, 1920), p. 146.

39. Tuttle, p. 99.

40. Chicago Commission on Race Relations, p. 147.

41. Scott, "Letters," p. 300.

42. Maxine Seller, *To Seek America: A History of Ethnic Life in the United States* (New York: Jerome S. Oker, 1977).

43. W. I. Thomas and Florian Znaniecki, *The Polish Peasant in Europe and America* (Boston: Gorham Press, 1920).

44. Willis Wertherford and Charles Johnson, *Race Relations* (Boston: D. C. Heath, 1941), p. 137.

45. Ibid., p. 138.

46. Theodore Kornweibel, *No Crystal Stair* (Westport, Conn.: Greenwood Press, 1975).

47. Roi Otley, *The Lonely Warrior: The Life and Times of Robert S. Abbott* (Chicago: Henry Regnery, 1955), p. 105.

48. R. H. Leavell, "Negro Migration from Mississippi," in *Negro Migration in*

1916–1917, ed. George Haynes (Washington, D.C.: U.S. Department of Labor, Division of Negro Economics, Government Printing Office, 1919), p. 29.

49. Ibid.

50. Otley, p. 107.

51. Tuttle, p. 89.

52. Thomas Woofter, "Migration of Negroes from Georgia," in *Negro Migration in 1916–1917*, ed. George Haynes (Washington, D.C.: U.S. Department of Labor, Division of Negro Economics, Government Printing Office, 1919), p. 103.

53. Frederick Detweiler, *The Negro Press in the United States* (Chicago: University of Chicago Press, 1922), p. 17.

54. Tuttle, pp. 89–90.

55. Quoted in Scott, *Negro Migration*, p. 17.

56. Scott, "Letters," p. 302.

57. Leavell, p. 30; the *Defender*, for example, told its readers of Robert A. Wilson, formerly of Atlanta, who arrived in Chicago with a nickel and a penny. He spent the nickel for streetcar fare to the *Defender*'s offices and a penny for a bag of peanuts "to satisfy that pang of hunger." The newspaper directed him to the Urban League, which found him work at a foundry. "Since that happy day," the *Defender* added, "Wilson had acquired an automobile, house and bank account and had brought his family from the South, and thus ends the romance of the lone nickel, the Lincoln penny, and the man who made opportunity a realization." Quoted in Tuttle, p. 90.

58. Otley, p. 105; Chicago Commission on Race Relations, p. 92.

59. Scott, "Letters," p. 333.

60. Tuttle, p. 90.

61. Scott, *Negro Migration*, p. 30.

62. Tuttle, p. 91; Scott, *Negro Migration*, p. 30.

63. Tuttle, p. 91; Scott, *Negro Migration*, p. 32.

64. Tuttle, p. 92.

65. Scott, "Letters," p. 330.

66. Ibid., p. 455.

67. Chicago Commission on Race Relations, p. 147.

68. Kennedy, p. 53.

69. Alex Edelstein and Joseph Contris, "The Public View of the Weekly Newspaper Leadership Role," *Journalism Quarterly* 43, no. 1 (1966), pp. 17–24.

70. Piore, p. 3; Burawoy, p. 1051; Portes, "Migration and Underdevelopment," p. 10.

71. Burawoy, p. 1050.

72. Piore, p. 153.

73. Ibid., p. 152.

74. Quoted in Arna Bontemps and Jack Conroy, *They Seek a City* (Garden City, N.Y.: Doubleday, 1945), p. 133.

75. Jorge Balan, Harley Browning, and Elizabeth Jelin, *Men in a Developing Society* (Austin: University of Texas Press, 1973), p. 12.

76. Neil Fligstein, *Going North* (New York: Academic Press, 1981), p. 114.

77. Daniel Johnson and Rex Campbell, *Black Migration in America* (Durham, N.C.: Duke University Press, 1981), p. 79.

78. Kennedy, p. 44.

79. Balan, Browning, and Jelin, p. 12.

80. Portes, "Migration and Underdevelopment," p. 17.

81. Lyonel C. Florant, "Negro Internal Migration," *American Sociological Review* 7 (December 1942), p. 784.

82. Table 2.1 shows a net migration of over 1 million blacks from the rural areas of the South. See Daniel O. Price, *Changing Characteristics—Negro Population* (Washington, D.C.: Department of Commerce, 1965), p. 39.

83. Ibid., p. 11.

84. Florant, p. 785.

85. Henri, p. 66.

86. Abraham Epstein, *The Negro in Pittsburgh* (Pittsburgh: University of Pittsburgh Press, 1919), p. 35.

87. Chicago Commission on Race Relations, p. 95.

88. Quoted in Henri, p. 69.

89. Scott, "Letters," for example, 292, 293, 295, 300; and "Additional Letters of Negro Migrants of 1916–1918," *Journal of Negro History* 4 (October 1919), pp. 413, 416, 417.

90. *New York Age*, August 18, 1916.

91. U.S. Department of Labor, "1923 Report of Migrants in 15 States," *Monthly Labor Review* (January 1924), p. 12.

92. Ibid., p. 13.

93. W. T. B. Williams, "Negro Migration from Alabama," in *Negro Migration in 1916–1917*, ed. George Haynes (Washington, D.C.: U.S. Department of Labor, Division of Negro Economics, Government Printing Office, 1919), pp. 93–113.

94. Haynes, p. 63.

95. Lorenzo Greene and Carter G. Woodson, *The Negro Wage Earner* (New York: Association for the Study of Negro Life and History, 1930), p. 26.

96. Abram Harris, "Negro Migration to the North," *Current History Magazine of the New York Times* 20 (September 1924), p. 921.

97. Scott, *Negro Migration*, p. 38.

98. Charles Johnson, "The New Frontage on American Life," in *The New Negro*, ed. Alain Locke (New York: Albert and Charles Boni, 1925), p. 278.

99. Stanley Lieberson, "Selective Black Migration from the South: A Historical View," in *The Demography of Racial and Ethnic Groups*, ed. Frank D. Bean and W. Parker Frisbie (New York: Academic Press, 1978), pp. 119–42.

100. Ibid., p. 124.

101. Ibid., p. 126.

102. Ibid., pp. 130–131.

103. Ibid., p. 131.

104. Kennedy, p. 1.

105. Tilly, p. 144.

106. C. Horace Hamilton, "The Negro Leaves the South," *Demography* 1 (1964) p. 288.

107. Wilson Record, *Race and Radicalism* (Ithaca, N.Y.: Cornell University Press, 1964), p. 32.

108. Castells, p. 370.

109. W. E. B. DuBois, *The Philadelphia Negro* (1899; reprint, New York: Blom, 1967), p. 25.

110. Betina Aptheker, *Women's Legacy: Essays on Race, Sex and Class in American History* (Amherst: University of Massachusetts Press, 1982), p. 113.

111. Ibid., p. 114.

112. Herbert Aptheker, *A Documentary History of the Negro People in the United States*, Vol. 2 (Secaucus, N.J.: The Citadel Press, 1973), p. 46.

113. Ibid., p. 47.

114. Jacqueline Jones, *Labors of Love, Labors of Sorrow* (New York: Basic Books, 1985), p. 113.

115. Scott, *Negro Migration*, p. 42.

116. Scott, "Letters," p. 333.

117. Scott, *Negro Migration*, p. 42.

118. Rosalyn Baxandall, Linda Gordon, and Susan Reverby, eds., *America's Working Women: A Documentary History—1606 to the Present* (New York: Random House, 1976), p. 133.

119. Gilbert Osofsky, *Harlem: The Making of a Ghetto, Negro New York, 1890–1930* (New York: Harper and Row, 1963), p. 25.

120. Ibid., p. 26.

121. Charles Johnson, "The New Frontage on American Life," in *The New Negro*, ed. Alain Locke (New York: Albert and Charles Boni, 1925), p. 275.

III. The South before the Great War: Economy, Labor, and the Struggle for Power

1. Quoted in Gerald Rosenblum, *Immigrant Workers* (New York: Basic Books, 1973), p. 17.

2. C. Vann Woodward, *Origins of the New South: 1877-1913* (Baton Rouge: Louisiana State University Press, 1951), p. 309; Samuel Hayes, *The Response to Industrialism 1885-1915* (Chicago: University of Chicago Press, 1957), p. 121.

3. Woodward, *Origins of the New South*, p. 310.

4. Ibid., p. 111.

5. Ibid., p. 9.

6. Ibid., p. 111; Hayes, p. 126.

7. Woodward, *Origins of the New South*, p. 113.

8. Stephen Steinberg, p. 28.

9. Roger Ransom and Richard Sutch, *One Kind of Freedom* (New York: Cambridge University Press, 1977), p. 56.

10. Leon Litwak, *Been in the Storm So Long* (New York: Vintage Books, 1980), p. 447.

11. Woodward, *Origins of the New South*, p. 90.

12. Ibid., p. 128.

13. Ransom and Sutch, p. 109.

14. Ibid., p. 110.

15. Ibid., p. 110.

16. Woodward, *Origins of the New South*, p. 183; John D. Hicks, *The Populist Revolt: A History of the Farmers' Alliance and the People's Party* (Lincoln: University of Nebraska Press, 1961), p. 40.

17. Woodward, *Origins of the New South*, p. 113.

18. Ibid., p. 127; Hicks, *The Populist Revolt*, p. 41.

19. Woodward, *Origins of the New South*, p. 150.
20. Ransom and Sutch, p. 157.
21. Woodward, *Origins of the New South*, p. 237.
22. Simkins, *The Old South and the New 1820–1947* (New York: Knopf, 1947), p. 299.
23. Ibid., p. 242.
24. Ibid., p. 242.
25. Ibid., p. 243.
26. Hayes, p. 123.
27. Woodward, *Origins of the New South*, p. 114; Hayes, p. 123.
28. U.S. Senate, Report of the Senate Committee on Education and Labor, *Labor and Capital* (Washington, D.C.: Government Printing Office, 1885), vol. 8, p. 920.
29. Woodward, *Origins of the New South*, p. 291.
30. Ibid., p. 308.
31. Ibid., p. 310.
32. Ransom and Sutch, p. 154.
33. Scott, *Negro Migration*, p. 15.
34. Clyde Kiser, *Sea Island to City* (New York: Columbia University Press, 1932), p. 110.
35. Leavell, p. 17.
36. Woodward, *Origins of the New South*, p. 311.
37. Ibid., p. 114.
38. John Cell, *The Highest Stage of White Supremacy* (New York: Cambridge University Press, 1982), p. 320.
39. Ibid., p. 105.
40. Howard Rabinowitz, *Race Relations in the Urban South 1865–1890* (New York: Oxford University Press, 1978), pp. 61, 66.
41. Woodward, *Origins of the New South*, p. 225.
42. Henderson H. Donald, "The Negro Migration of 1916–1918," *Journal of Negro History* 6 (October 1921), p. 411.
43. Scott, *Negro Migration*, p. 15.
44. Ibid., p. 16.
45. Wilson, p. 56.
46. Carter G. Woodson, *The Negro in Our History* (Washington, D.C.: Association for the Study of Negro Life and History, 1932), p. 21.
47. Scott, "Additional Letters," p. 295.
48. Woodward, *Origins of the New South*, p. 361.
49. Ibid., p. 361.
50. Greene and Woodson, p. 25.
51. Ibid., pp. 98–99.
52. Sterling D. Spero and Abram L. Harris, *The Black Worker: The Negro and the Labor Movement* (1931; reprint, New York: Atheneum, 1969), p. 32.
53. Woodson, *The Negro in Our History*, p. 96.
54. Ibid., p. 99.
55. Donald, p. 434.
56. Scott, *Negro Migration*, pp. 24–25.
57. Woodward, *Origins of the New South*, p. 28; Simkins, p. 434.
58. Simkins, p. 434.

59. Ibid., p. 129.
60. Simkins, p. 435.
61. Ibid., p. 239.
62. Woodward, *Origins of the New South*, p. 221.
63. Spero and Harris, *The Black Worker*, p. 162.
64. Leavell, p. 40.
65. Pete Daniel, *In the Shadow of Slavery: Peonage in the South 1901–1969* (New York: Oxford University Press, 1972), p. 10.
66. Woodward, *Origins of the New South*, p. 221.
67. Ibid., p. 98.
68. Woodward, *Origins of the New South*, p. 226.
69. Simkins, p. 244; Woodward, *Origins of the New South*, p. 224.
70. Scott, "Letters," p. 425.
71. Ibid., p. 330.
72. Ibid., p. 440.
73. Ibid., p. 427.
74. Woodward, *Origins of the New South*, pp. 113–114.
75. Ibid., p. 291.
76. Ibid., p. 308.
77. Lerone Bennett, *Black Power U.S.A.: The Human Side of Reconstruction* (Chicago: Johnson Publishing Co., 1967), p. 330.
78. Woodward, *Origins of the New South*, p. 51.
79. Ibid., p. 226.
80. Carter G. Woodson, *A Century of Negro Migration* (New York: Russell and Russell, 1969), p. 65.
81. Woodward, *Origins of the New South*, p. 219.
82. Ibid., p. 211.
83. C. Vann Woodward, *The Strange Career of Jim Crow* (New York: Oxford University Press, 1966), p. 50.
84. Woodward, *Origins of the New South*, p. 29; Scott, *Negro Migration*, p. 100.
85. Woodward, *Origins of the New South*, p. 30.
86. Ibid., p. 58.
87. Scott, "Letters," p. 414.
88. Wilson, p. 56.
89. Cell, p. 5.
90. Wilson, p. 58.
91. Woodward, *Origins of the New South*, p. 211.
92. Woodson, *The Negro in Our History*, p. 339.
93. Ibid., p. 340.
94. Quoted in Robert T. Kerlin, *The Voice of the Negro, 1919* (New York: Dutton, 1920), p. 56.
95. Ibid., p. 57.
96. Woodson, *The Negro in Our History*, p. 346.
97. Lerone Bennett, *Confrontation: Black and White* (Chicago: Johnson Publishing Co., 1965), p. 78.
98. Woodward, *Origins of the New South*, pp. 350–351.
99. Bennett, *Confrontation: Black and White*, p. 79.
100. Ibid.
101. Woodward, *Origins of the New South*, pp. 361–363.

102. Ibid., p. 363. Herbert Gutman, *Work, Culture and Society* (New York: Vintage, 1976), p. 123.

103. W. E. B. DuBois, *The Nation* 116 (May 9, 1923), p. 590.

104. Piore, pp. 167–168.

105. W. E. B. DuBois, *The New Republic* 33 (January 3, 1923), p. 140.

106. Scott, "Letters," p. 427.

107. Booker T. Washington, *The Rise of the Race from Slavery* (Garden City, N.Y.: Doubleday, 1909), p. 10.

108. Balan, Browning, and Jelin, p. 85.

109. Ibid., p. 85.

110. Painter, p. 44.

111. Woodson, *The Negro in Our History*, pp. 382–88.

112. Ibid., p. 387.

113. Bennett, *Black Power U.S.A.*, p. 332.

114. U.S. Bureau of Education Bulletin, "Statistics of Education of the Negro Race" (Washington, D.C.: U.S. Government Printing Office, 1928), pp. 7–10.

115. N. C. Newbold, "Common Schools for Negroes in the South," *Annals of the American Academy of Political and Social Science* vol. 140 (November 1928), p. 210.

116. Woodson, *The Negro in Our History*, p. 388.

117. *New York Age*, 1915.

118. U.S. Bureau of Education, *Negro Education*, Bulletin #39 (Washington, D.C.: U.S. Government Printing Office, 1916), pp.34–35.

119. Newbold, p. 214.

120. Scott, "Letters," p. 332.

121. Ibid., p. 416.

122. Woodson, *The Negro in Our History*, p. 389.

123. Myrdal, p. 894.

124. Ibid., p. 895.

IV. The North: Labor, the Economy, and the Great War

1. Quoted in Milton Meltzer, *Bread and Roses: The Struggle of American Labor 1865–1915* (New York: Knopf, 1967), p. 95.

2. Quoted in Gutman, *Work, Culture and Society*, p. 30.

3. Rosenblum, p. 70.

4. Steinberg, pp. 35, 40.

5. Rosenblum, p. 45.

6. Steinberg, p. 34.

7. Rosenblum, p. 48.

8. Ibid., p. 56.

9. Ibid., p. 48.

10. Steinberg, p. 34; Rosenblum, p. 75; Hayes, p. 5.

11. Hayes, p. 5.

12. Steinberg, p. 34.

13. Rosenblum, p. 62.

14. Ibid., p. 64.

15. Quoted in Rosenblum, p. 76.

16. Ibid., p. 64.

17. Ibid., p. 66.

18. Hayes, p. 95.

19. Piore, p. 149.

20. Ibid., p. 145.

21. Ibid., p. 150; Rosenblum, p. 125; Hayes, p. 95.

22. Piore, p. 76.

23. U.S. Senate, vol. I, p. 751.

24. Rosenblum, p. 128.

25. Ibid., pp. 127–28.

26. Ibid., p. 128.

27. Ibid., p. 119.

28. Piore, p. 78.

29. Gutman, *Work, Culture and Society*, p. 30.

30. Rosenblum, p. 122.

31. U.S. Senate, p. 752.

32. Hayes, p. 49.

33. Ibid., p. 49.

34. David Gordon, Richard Edwards, and Michael Reich, *Segmented Work, Divided Workers* (New York: Cambridge University Press, 1982), p. 108.

35. Edward C. Kirkland, *Industry Comes of Age: Business, Labor, and Public Policy* (Chicago: Quadrangle Books, 1967), p. 205.

36. Gordon, Edwards, and Reich, p. 107.

37. James Weinstein, *The Corporate Ideal in the Liberal State: 1900–1918* (Boston: Beacon Press, 1968), p. 63.

38. Gordon, Edwards, and Reich, p. 113.

39. Ibid., p. 107; Weinstein, p. 135.

40. Weinstein, p. 111.

41. Gordon, Edwards, and Reich, p. 110.

42. Weinstein, p. 71.

43. Ibid., p. 72.

44. Ibid., p. 71.

45. Gordon, Edwards, and Reich, p. 111.

46. Ibid., pp. 108–111.

47. David Montgomery, *Workers' Control in America* (New York: Cambridge University Press, 1979), p. 20.

48. Gordon, Edwards, and Reich, p. 118.

49. U.S. Senate, p. 415.

50. Ibid., p. 488.

51. Gordon, Edwards, and Reich, p. 113.

52. U.S. Senate, p. 469.

53. Quoted in Montgomery, p. 26.

54. U.S. Senate, p. 136.

55. Gordon, Edwards, and Reich, p. 133.

56. Ibid., p. 135.

57. Ibid., p. 134.

58. Ibid., p. 135.

59. Hayes, p. 32; Gordon, Edwards, and Reich, p. 92.

60. Gordon, Edwards, and Reich, p. 128.

61. Gutman, *Work, Culture and Society*, pp. 29–31.

62. Rosenblum, p. 131.

63. Daniel Nelson, *Managers and Workers' Origins of the New Factory System in the United States, 1880–1920* (Madison: University of Wisconsin Press, 1975), chap. 3.

64. Gordon, Edwards, and Reich, p. 173.

65. Ibid., p. 174.

66. Ibid., p. 140.

67. Ibid., p. 137.

68. Ibid., p. 173.

69. Rosenblum, p. 70.

70. Steinberg, p. 37.

71. Ibid., p. 36.

72. Rosenblum, p. 78.

73. Ibid., pp. 78–79.

74. Ibid., p. 79.

75. Hayes, p. 99.

76. Ibid., p. 102.

77. Ibid., p. 102.

78. Ibid., p. 101.

79. Chicago Commission on Race Relations, p. 357.

80. Ibid., p. 358.

81. Edward P. Hutchinson, "Immigration Policy Since World War One," in *Immigration: An American Dilemma*, ed. Benjamin Munn Ziegler (Boston: Little, Brown, 1953); Dewey H. Palmer, "Moving North: Migration of Negroes During World War I," in *White Racism and Black Americans*, ed. David G. Bromley and Charles Longino, Jr. (Cambridge, Mass.: Schenkman, 1972), p. 30.

82. Bennett, *Confrontation: Black and White*, p. 119.

83. Spero and Harris, p. 13.

84. Steinberg, p. 28.

85. *Survey*, July 1919.

86. "Close Ranks," *Crisis XVI*, July 1918.

87. Henri, p. 276.

88. *Messenger*, March 1919.

89. Henri, p. 271.

90. *Messenger*, October 1919.

91. Henri, p. 271.

92. *Messenger*, October 1919.

93. John Hope Franklin, *From Slavery to Freedom* (1967; reprint, New York: Knopf, 1972), p. 133.

94. Henri, p. 289.

95. Franklin, p. 328.

96. Henri, p. 290.

97. Bennett, *Confrontation: Black and White*, p. 120.

V. Migration and Reaction

1. National Urban League, "Migration Study," doc. no. 31.

2. U.S. Department of Agriculture, p. 24.

3. Spero and Harris, p. 257.

4. Ibid., p. 100.

5. Ibid., p. 97.

6. Piore, p. 29.

7. Castells, p. 34.

8. Ibid., p. 54.

9. Spero and Harris, p. 130.

10. Charles Denby, *Indignant Heart* (London: Pluto Press, 1979), p. 33.

11. Frances Tyson, "The Negro Migrant in the North," in *Negro Migration in 1916–1917*, ed. George Haynes (Washington: Government Printing Office, 1919), p. 125.

12. Charles Wesley, *Negro Labor in the United States, 1850–1925* (New York: Vanguard, 1927), p. 304.

13. Ibid., p. 305.

14. Denby, p. 30.

15. Spero and Harris, p. 145.

16. André Gorz, "Immigrant Labor," *New Left Review* 61 (May-June 1970), pp. 28–31.

17. Chicago Commission on Race Relations, p. 374.

18. Ibid., p. 375.

19. Ibid.

20. Ibid., p. 376.

21. Ibid.

22. Ibid.

23. Ibid.

24. Donald, pp. 383-499.

25. U.S. Department of Agriculture, p. 24.

26. Castells, p. 52.

27. Ibid., p. 53.

28. Henri, p. 153.

29. Spero and Harris, p. 130.

30. Abraham Epstein, p. 36.

31. Ibid., p. 24.

32. Ibid., p. 40.

33. Ibid., p. 41.

34. Document from Migration Study Early Surveys National Urban League Research Department, 1920, microfilm.

35. Epstein, p. 113.

36. Ibid., p. 117.

37. Spero and Harris, p. 132.

38. Tuttle, p. 120.

39. Spero and Harris, p. 135–43.

40. Ibid., p. 136.

41. Ibid., p. 131.

42. Ibid., p. 132.

43. Weinstein, p. xx.

44. Ibid., p. 7.

45. Ibid., p. 9.

46. Ibid., p. 22.

47. Ibid., p. 36.
48. U.S. Department of Labor, Case files on the "U.S. Conciliation Service," microfilm, p. 170.
49. Ibid., p. 119.
50. Ibid., p. 139.
51. Spero and Harris, p. 152; Spear, p. 151.
52. Spero and Harris, pp. 153–54.
53. Scott, *Negro Migration*, p. 114.
54. Spero and Harris, p. 174.
55. Ibid., p. 174.
56. George Haynes, p. 114.
57. Scott, "Letters," pp. 454, 461.
58. Epstein, p. 23.
59. Chicago Commission on Race Relations, p. 97.
60. Henri, p. 139; Spear, p. 157.
61. Henri, p. 150.
62. Chicago Commission on Race Relations, p. 388.
63. Ibid., p. 389.
64. Ibid., p. 390.
65. Spear, p. 158.
66. Ibid., p. 141.
67. David Katzman, *Seven Days a Week* (New York: Oxford University Press, 1978), p. 82.
68. Elizabeth Clark-Lewis, "This Work Had a End: Household Service Employment in Washington, D.C. 1900–1920." Working paper, Center for Research on Women. Memphis State University, 1985, p. 1.
69. Ella Baker and Marvel Cook, "The Bronx Slave Market," *Crisis* 42 (1935), p. 331.
70. Henri, p. 54.
71. Ibid., p. 102.
72. Ibid., p. 43.
73. E. Franklin Frazier, *The Negro in the United States* (New York: Macmillan, 1957), p. 140.
74. Katzman, p. 72.
75. See Davis, *Women, Race and Class* (New York: Vintage, 1983), p. 238; Betina Aptheker, p. 114; and Henri, p. 69.
76. Pleck, p. 178.
77. Spero and Harris, p. 131.
78. Spear, p. 151.
79. Ibid., p. 151; Henri, p. 142.
80. Henri, p. 102.
81. Edward P. Hutchinson, p. 17.
82. Piore, p. 23.
83. Montgomery, pp. 35–36.
84. Ibid., p. 36.
85. Spero and Harris, p. 102.
86. Montgomery, p. 96.
87. Spero and Harris, p. 162.
88. Greene and Woodson, p. 253.

89. Greene and Woodson, p. 131; Spero and Harris, p. 168; Herman D. Bloch, *The Circle of Discrimination* (New York: New York University Press 1969), p. 7.

90. Spero and Harris, p. 161.

91. Greene and Woodson, p. 268; Edna Bonacich, "Advanced Capitalism and Black/White Relations in the United States," *American Sociological Review* 41 (February 1976), pp. 34–51.

92. See Piore, pp. 52–53, for discussion.

93. Gordon, Edwards, and Reich, p. 135.

94. Bloch, *The Circle of Discrimination*, p. 48.

95. Gordon, Edwards, and Reich, p. 136.

96. Bonacich, "Middlemen Minorities," pp. 583–585.

97. Michael Reich, *Racial Inequality: A Political-Economic Analysis* (Princeton: Princeton University Press, 1981), p. 62.

98. Ibid., p. 63. David Brody, *The Steelworkers in America: The Non-Union Era* (Cambridge, Mass.: Harvard University Press, 1960).

99. Ibid., p. 64.

100. Reich, p. 62.

101. Ibid., p. 63. Harold Baron, "The Demand for Black Labor," *Historical Notes on the Political Economy of Racism* series (Somerville, Mass.: New England Free Press, 1971), pp. 29–31.

102. Ibid., p. 34.

103. Piore, p. 44.

104. Ibid., p. 28

105. Ibid., p. 29.

106. Bonacich, "A Theory of Middlemen Minorities," *American Sociological Review* 38 (1973), p. 584.

107. Piore, p. 34.

108. Reich, p. 63.

109. *New York Times*, February 29, 1984.

VI. Migrants in the North: The Political and Social Wars

1. *The Washington Times*, July 23, 1919.

2. Carter G. Woodson, *The Negro in Our History*, p. 464.

3. Harold Gosnell, *Negro Politicians* (Chicago: University of Chicago Press, 1935), p. 17.

4. Ibid., p. 18.

5. Ibid., p. 27; Spear, p. 125.

6. *Survey*, 1920.

7. W. E. B. DuBois, *Writings in Periodical Literature: 1910–1934* (Millwood, N.Y.: Kraus-Thomson Organization, 1982), Vol. II, p. 139.

8. *Chicago Defender*, April 5, 1924, Gosnell, p. 36.

9. Tuttle, pp. 184, 197; Katznelson, p. 89.

10. Tuttle, p. 186; Katznelson, p. 90; Spear, p. 122.

11. Tuttle, p. 187.

12. Katznelson, p. 89.

13. Tuttle, p. 188.

14. Quoted in Katznelson, p. 89; see also Spear, p. 187.

15. Tuttle, p. 189.

16. Gosnell, p. 18.

17. Spear, p. 187.

18. Tuttle, p. 189; Spear, p. 124.

19. Spear, p. 187.

20. Ibid.

21. Tuttle, p. 198.

22. Gosnell, p. 41.

23. Tuttle, p. 200.

24. Ibid.

25. Ibid., p. 201.

26. Ibid., p. 202.

27. Ibid. Such a claim was obviously an overstatement. Gosnell, in *Negro Politicians*, points out that Thompson also had wide support among immigrant voters, p. 42.

28. Tuttle, p. 203.

29. Katznelson, p. 101.

30. Henri, p. 77.

31. Tuttle, p. 194.

32. Spear, p. 189.

33. Tuttle, p. 196.

34. *Messenger*, November 1917, p. 12.

35. Ibid., July 1918, p. 19.

36. Ibid., November 1919, p. 17.

37. Chicago Commission on Race Relations, p. 303–4.

38. Tuttle, p. 370.

39. Katznelson, p. 109.

40. U.S. Department of Agriculture, p. 21.

41. Bennett, *Confrontation: Black and White*, p. 117.

42. Ibid., p. 118.

43. Henri, p. 103.

44. Ibid., p. 102.

45. *Survey*, August 9, 1919, p. 695.

46. Ibid., p. 112; Henri, p. 109.

47. Henri, p. 112.

48. Ibid., p. 119.

49. Ibid., p. 113.

50. Ibid., p. 115.

51. Ibid., p. 119; Chicago Commission on Race Relations, p. 330.

52. Henri, p. 119.

53. Tuttle, p. 22.

54. Elliott M. Rudwick, *Race Riot at East St. Louis* (Carbondale, Ill.: Southern Illinois University Press, 1964), p. 20.

55. Ibid., p. 37.

56. Ibid., p. 49.

57. *Survey*, July 14, 1917, p. 333; Franklin, *From Slavery to Freedom*, p. 398.

58. Bennett, *Confrontation: Black and White*, p. 120.

59. Chicago Commission on Race Relations, p. 1.

60. Tuttle, p. 33; Franklin, *From Slavery to Freedom*, p. 348.

61. Chicago Commission on Race Relations, p. 4.

62. Ibid., p. 9.

63. Franklin, *From Slavery to Freedom*, p. 349.

64. Ibid., p. 349.

65. Tuttle, p. 29.

66. Ibid.; Franklin, *From Slavery to Freedom*, pp. 347–48.

67. Burawoy, pp. 1061–62.

68. Castells, p. 41.

69. Ibid., p. 42.

70. Arna Bontemps and Jack Conroy, *Anyplace but Here* (New York: Hill and Wang, 1966), p. 166.

VII. Migration as a Benefit to the Migrant

1. Ralph Ellison, *Invisible Man* (New York: Harper and Row, 1948), pp. 32–33.

2. Myrdal, p. 1021.

3. Norman Yetman, ed., *Majority and Minority: The Dynamics of Race and Ethnicity in American Life* (Boston: Allyn and Bacon, 1985), p. 219.

4. L. Paul Metzger, "American Sociology and Black Assimilation: Conflicting Perspectives," in *Majority and Minority: The Dynamics of Race and Ethnicity in American Life*, ed. Norman Yetman (Boston: Allyn and Bacon, 1985), p. 341.

5. Yetman, p. 225.

6. Ibid., p. 225.

7. Ibid.

8. Ibid., p. 227.

9. Ibid., p. 256.

10. *Messenger*, March 1919, p. 9.

11. *Survey*, August 18, 1917, p. 443.

12. Ibid., p. 443.

13. Karl Taeuber and Alma Taeuber, *Negroes in Cities* (Chicago: Aldine, 1965), p. 17.

14. Ibid., p. 18.

15. Quoted in Yetman, p. 241.

16. Stanley Lieberson, *A Piece of the Pie: Black and White Immigrants since 1880* (Berkeley: University of California Press, 1980), p. 386.

17. Ibid., p. 387.

18. Nathan Glazer and Daniel Patrick Moynihan, *Beyond the Melting Pot* (Cambridge, Mass.: M.I.T. Press and Harvard University Press, 1963), p. 74.

19. Wilson, pp. 120–21; Sidney Wilhelm, *Who Needs the Negro?* (New York: Anchor Books, 1971), pp. 160–228.

20. Castells, p. 54.

21. Adrian Adams, "Prisoners in Exile: Senegalese Workers in France," in *Peasants and Proletarians: The Struggles of Third World Workers*, ed. Robin Cohen, Peter C.W. Gutkind, and Phyllis Brazier (New York: Monthly Review Press, 1979), p. 324.

22. Ibid., p. 324.

23. Castells, p. 53.

24. Portes, "Migration and Underdevelopment," p. 45.
25. Piore, p. 179.
26. Scott, "Letters," p. 459.
27. Ibid., p. 460.
28. Ibid., p. 460.
29. *Survey*, August 9, 1919, p. 448.
30. Ibid.
31. Spear, p. 168.
32. Quoted in Spear, p. 168.
33. *Survey*, August 9, 1919, p. 448.
34. U.S. Department of Agriculture, pp. 15, 26.
35. Portes, "Migration and Underdevelopment," p. 45.
36. Alejandro Portes and Alex Stepick, "Unwelcome Immigrants," *American Sociological Review* 50, no. 4 (1985), p. 499.
37. Ibid., p. 500.
38. Piore, p. 7.
39. Ivan Light, *Ethnic Enterprise in America* (Berkeley: University of California Press, 1972), p. 11.
40. Ibid., p. 19.
41. Ibid., p. 20.
42. Ibid., p. 21.
43. Robert Higgs, *Competition and Coercion* (Cambridge: Cambridge University Press, 1977), p. 89.
44. Ibid., p. 90.
45. Ibid., p. 497.
46. Ibid., p. 44.
47. W. E. B. DuBois, *The Philadelphia Negro* (1899; reprint, New York: Blom, 1967), p. 221.
48. Isabel Eaton, "Special Report on Negro Domestic Service in the Seventh Ward," in W. E. B. DuBois, *The Philadelphia Negro*, (1899; reprint, New York: Blom, 1967), p. 451.
49. Higgs, p. 90.
50. George Fredrickson, *White Supremacy* (New York: Oxford University Press, 1981), p. 250.
51. Quoted in Yetman, p. 397.

VIII. Conclusion

1. Spear, p. 229.
2. Burawoy, p. 1051.
3. Such selectivity is characteristic of most migrations, although black migration has been thought to be an exception. See Daniel O. Price and Melanie Sykes, *Rural-Urban Migration Research in the United States* (Washington, D.C.: Center for Population Research, Government Printing Office, 1979), p. 6.
4. Quoted in Haynes, p. 101.
5. Quoted in Scott, *Negro Migration*, p. 31.
6. Baron, p. 23.
7. Ibid., p. 29.

8. Spear, p. 229.

9. Park, p. 5.

10. Baron, p. 30.

11. Henri, p. 69.

12. Lieberson, *A Piece of the Pie*, pp. 171–72. Based on rates of literacy between blacks in the North in 1930 and the new European immigrant groups. Lieberson notes that the figure for the total foreign born undoubtedly understates illiteracy among the south, central, and eastern European immigrants.

13. Baron, p. 20.

14. Lieberson, *A Piece of the Pie*, p. 20.

15. Henri, p. 145.

16. Ibid., pp. 145–46.

17. Ibid., p. 147.

18. Ibid., p. 148.

19. Richard Hofstader, *American Political Tradition* (New York: Vintage, 1948), pp. 336–38.

20. Baron, p. 30.

21. Ibid., p. 20.

22. Henri, p. 101.

23. DuBois, *Writings in Periodical Literature*, vol. 4, p. 195.

24. Scott, *Negro Migration*, p. 87.

25. U.S. Department of Commerce, Bureau of the Census, p. 520.

26. Ibid., p. 520.

27. Ibid.

28. Scott, *Negro Migration*, p. 24.

29. Ibid., p. 24.

30. Vincent Harding, *There Is a River* (New York: Vintage, 1983), p. xiii.

31. Steinberg, p. 208.

32. Tilly, p. 101.

33. W. E. B. DuBois, *Souls of Black Folk* (New York: Fawcett, 1961), p. 16.

34. William Yancey, Eugene Eriksen, and Richard Juliana, "Emergent Ethnicity," in *Majority and Minority: The Dynamics of Race and Ethnicity in American Life*, ed. Norman Yetman (Boston: Allyn and Bacon, 1985), p. 186.

35. Quoted in Katznelson, p. 3.

Bibliography

Adams, Adrian. "Prisoners in Exile: Senegalese Workers in France." In *Peasants and Proletarians: The Struggle of Third World Workers*, edited by Robin Cohen, Peter C. W. Gutkind, and Phyllis Brazier, pp. 307–30. New York: Monthly Review Press, 1979.

Alba, Francisco. "Mexico's International Migration." *International Migration Review* 12 (1978), pp. 502–13.

Alexander, Will. "The Negro in the New South." *Annals of the American Academy of Political and Social Science* (November 1928).

Aptheker, Betina. *Women's Legacy: Essays on Race, Sex, and Class in American History*. Amherst: University of Massachusetts Press, 1982.

Aptheker, Herbert. *A Documentary History of the Negro People in the United States*. Vol. 2. Secaucus, N.J.: The Citadel Press, 1973.

Averitt, Robert T. *The Dual Economy*. New York: Norton, 1968.

Bach, Robert L. "Mexican Immigration and the American State." *International Migration Review* 12 (1978), pp. 536–38.

Baily, Samuel. "The Role of Two Newspapers in the Assimilation of Italians in Buenos Aires and Sao Paulo, 1893–1913." *International Migration Review* 12 (1978), pp. 321–40.

Baker, Ella, and Cook, Marrel. "The Bronx Slave Market." *Crisis* 42 (1935), pp. 330–31.

Baker, Ray Stannard. *Following the Color Line*. 1908. Reprint. New York: Harper and Row, 1964.

Balan, Jorge; Browning, Harley; and Jelin, Elizabeth. *Men in a Developing Society*. Austin: University of Texas Press, 1973.

Baron, Harold. "The Demand for Black Labor." *Historical Notes on the Political Economy of Racism*. Series. Sommerville, Mass.: New England Free Press, 1971.

Baxandall, Rosalyn; Gordon, Linda; and Reverby, Susan eds. *America's Working Women: A Documentary History—1606 to the Present*. New York: Random House, 1976.

Bennett, Lerone. *Confrontation: Black and White*. Chicago: Johnson Publishing Co., 1965.

———. *Black Power U.S.A.: The Human Side of Reconstruction*. Chicago: Johnson Publishing Co., 1967.

Blair, Lewis Harvie. *A Southern Prophesy: The Prosperity of the South Dependent upon the Elevation of the Negro.* Edited by C. Vann Woodward. 1889. Reprint. Boston: Little, Brown, 1964.

Blauner, Robert. *Racial Oppression in America.* New York: Harper and Row, 1972.

Block, Herman D. "Labor and the Negro, 1866–1910." *Journal of Negro History,* vol. 50 (July 1965).

Bonacich, Edna. "A Theory of Ethnic Antagonism: The Split Labor Market." *American Sociological Review* 37 (1972), pp. 547–59.

———. "A Theory of Middlemen Minorities." *American Sociological Review* 38 (1973), pp. 583–99.

———. "Abolition, the Extension of Slavery, and the Position of Free Blacks: A Study of Split Labor Markets in the United States, 1830–1863." *American Journal of Sociology* 81 (1975), pp. 601–28.

———. "Advanced Capitalism and Black/White Relations in the United States: A Split Labor Market Interpretation." *American Sociological Review* 41 (February 1976), pp. 34–51.

———. "International Labor Migration: A Theoretical Orientation." A paper presented at a Conference on Immigration and Ethnicity, Durham, N.C., May, 1981.

Bontemps, Arna, and Conroy, Jack. *They Seek a City.* Garden City, N.Y.: Doubleday, 1945.

———. *Anyplace but Here.* New York: Hill and Wang, 1966.

Bottomore, T. B. *Karl Marx.* Glencoe, Ill.: Free Press, 1950.

Bressler, Marvin. "Selected Family Patterns in W. I. Thomas's Unfinished Study of the Bintl Brief." *American Sociological Review* (1952), pp. 563–73.

Brody, David. *The Steelworkers in America: The Non-Union Era.* Cambridge, Mass.: Harvard University Press, 1960.

Burawoy, Michael. "The Functions and Reproduction of Migrant Labor: Comparative Material from Southern Africa and the United States," *American Journal of Sociology* 81 (1976), pp. 1050–87.

Campbell, Daniel M., and Johnson, Rex. *Black Migration in America: A Social Demographic History.* Durham, N.C.: Duke University Press, 1981.

Cash, Wilbur J. *The Mind of the South.* New York: Knopf, 1941.

Castells, Manuel. "Immigrant Workers and Class Struggles in Advanced Capitalism: The Western European Experience." *Politics and Society* 5 (1975), pp. 33–66.

Castles, Stephen, and Kosack, Godula. *Immigrant Workers and Class Structure in Western Europe.* London: Oxford University Press, 1973.

Cell, John. *The Highest State of White Supremacy.* Cambridge: Cambridge University Press, 1982.

Chicago Commission on Race Relations. *The Negro in Chicago.* Chicago: University of Chicago Press, 1920.

Clark-Lewis, Elizabeth. "This Work Had a End: Household Service Employment in Washington, D.C. 1900–1926." Working paper, Center for Research on Women. Memphis State University, 1985.

Coles, Robert. *Farewell to the South.* Boston: Little, Brown, 1972.

Daniel, Pete. *In the Shadow of Slavery: Peonage in the South 1901–1969.* New York: Oxford University Press, 1972.

Denby, Charles. *Indignant Heart*. London: Pluto Press, 1979.

Detweiler, Frederick. *The Negro Press in the United States*. Chicago: University of Chicago Press, 1922.

Dollard, John. *Caste and Class in a Southern Town*. Garden City, N.Y.: Anchor Books, 1957.

Donald, Henderson H. "The Negro Migration of 1916–1918." *Journal of Negro History* 6 (October, 1921), pp. 383–499.

Drake, St. Clair, and Cayton, Horace R. *Black Metropolis*. New York: Harper and Row, 1962.

DuBois, W. E. B. *The Negro Artisan*. Atlanta Study No. 7. Atlanta: Atlanta University Press, 1902.

————. *Souls of Black Folk*. New York: Fawcett, 1961.

————. *The Philadelphia Negro*. 1899. Reprint. New York: Blom, 1967.

————. *Black Reconstruction in America*. Cleveland: World Publishing Co., 1969.

————. *Writings in Periodical Literature: 1910–1934*. 4 vols. Millwood, N.Y.: Kraus-Thomson Organization Limited, 1982.

Duncan, Otis D. "The Theory and Consequences of Mobility of Farm Population." In *Population Theory and Policy: Selected Readings*, edited by Joseph J. Spengler and Otis D. Duncan. Glencoe, Ill.: Free Press, 1956.

————, and Duncan, Beverly. *The Negro Population of Chicago: A Study of Residential Succession*. Chicago: University of Chicago Press, 1957.

Eaton, Isabel. "Special Report on Negro Domestic Service in the Seventh Ward." In W. E. B. DuBois, *The Philadelphia Negro*, pp. 427–509. 1899. Reprint. New York: Blom, 1967.

Edelstein, Alex, and Joseph Contris. "The Public View of the Weekly Newspaper Leadership Role." *Journalism Quarterly* 43, no. 1 (1966), pp. 17–24.

Ellison, Ralph. *Invisible Man*. New York: Harper and Row, 1948.

Epstein, Abraham. *The Negro Migrant in Pittsburgh*. Pittsburgh: University of Pittsburgh Press, 1919.

Fligstein, Neil. *Going North*. New York: Academic Press, 1981.

Florant, Lyonel C. "Negro Internal Migration." *American Sociological Review* 7 (December 1942), pp. 782–91.

Fox, Stephen R. *The Guardian of Boston: William Monroe Trotter*. New York: Atheneum, 1970.

Frank, André Gunder. *Capitalism and Development in Latin America*. New York: Monthly Review Press, 1967.

Franklin, John Hope. *From Slavery to Freedom*. 1947. Reprint. New York: Knopf, 1967.

Frazier, E. Franklin. *The Negro in the United States*. New York: Macmillan, 1957.

Fredrickson, George. *White Supremacy*. New York: Oxford University Press, 1981.

Furtado, Celso. *Development and Underdevelopment*. Berkeley: University of California Press, 1965.

Garrison, Vivian, and Weiss, Carol. "Dominican Family Networks and U.S. Immigration Policy: A Case Study." *International Migration Review* 13 (1979), pp. 264–83.

Glazer, Nathan, and Moynihan, Daniel Patrick. *Beyond the Melting Pot*. Cambridge, Mass.: M.I.T. Press and Harvard University Press, 1963.

Goldstein, Sidney. "Migration: Dynamic of the American City." *American Quarterly* 6 (Winter 1954), pp. 337–48.

Goodwyn, Lawrence. *The Populist Moment*. New York: Oxford University Press, 1978.

Gordon, David; Edwards, Richard; and Reich, Michael. *Segmented Work, Divided Workers*. New York: Cambridge University Press, 1982.

Gorz, André. "Immigrant Labor." *New Left Review* 61 (May-June 1970), pp. 28–31.

Gosnell, Harold. *Negro Politicians*. Chicago: University of Chicago Press, 1935.

Gossett, Thomas F. *Race: The History of an Idea in America*. Dallas: Southern Methodist University Press, 1963.

Greene, Lorenzo, and Woodson, Carter G. *The Negro Wage Earner*. New York: Association for the Study of Negro Life and History, 1930.

Gutman, Herbert. *Work, Culture and Society*. New York: Vintage, 1976.

———. *The Black Family in Slavery and Freedom 1750–1925*. New York: Vintage, 1977.

Hall, Charles E. *Negro in the United States 1920–1932*. New York: Arno Press, 1969.

Hamilton, C. Horace. "The Negro Leaves the South." *Demography* 1 (1964), pp. 273–95.

Handlin, Oscar. *Immigration as a Factor in American History*. Englewood Cliffs, N.J.: Prentice-Hall, 1959.

Harding, Vincent. *There Is a River*. New York: Vintage, 1983.

Harris, Abram. "Negro Migration to the North." *Current History Magazine of the New York Times* 20 (September 1924), pp. 920–25.

Harrison, Shelby M. *Public Employment Offices*. New York: Russell Sage Foundation, 1924.

Hayes, Samuel. *The Response to Industrialism 1885–1914*. Chicago: University of Chicago Press, 1957.

Haynes, George. *The Negro at Work in New York City: A Study in Economic Progress*. New York: Columbia University Press, 1912.

———. "Negro Migration." *The Survey* 4 (May 4, 1918).

———. *Negro Migration in 1916–1917*. Washington, D.C.: U.S. Department of Labor, Division of Negro Economics, Government Printing Office, 1919.

Hendricks, G. L. *The Dominican Diaspora: From the Dominican Republic to New York City—Villagers in Transition*. New York: Columbia University Teachers' College Press, 1974.

Henri, Florette. *Black Migration: Movement North 1900–1920*. Garden City, N.Y.: Anchor Press/Doubleday, 1975.

Hicks, John D. *The Populist Revolt: A History of the Farmers' Alliance and the People's Party*. Lincoln: University of Nebraska Press, 1961.

Higgs, Robert. *Competition and Coercion*. Cambridge: Cambridge University Press, 1977.

Higham, John. *Strangers in the Land: Patterns of American Nativism 1860–1925*. New Brunswick, N.J.: Rutgers University Press, 1955.

Hofstader, Richard. *American Political Tradition*. New York: Vintage, 1948.

"How the War Brings Unprophesied Opportunities of the Negro Race." *Current Opinion* 61 (December, 1916), pp. 399–412.

Hutchinson, Edward P. "Immigration Policy Since World War One." In *Immigra-*

tion: American Dilemma, edited by Benjamin Munn Ziegler, pp. 16–21. Boston: Little, Brown, 1953.

Johnson, Charles. "The New Frontage on American Life." In *The New Negro*, edited by Alain Locke, pp. 268–98. New York: Albert and Charles Boni, 1925.

Johnson, Charles. *The Negro in American Civilization.* New York: Henry Holt, 1930.

Johnson, Daniel, and Campbell, Rex. *Black Migration in America.* Durham, N.C.: Duke University Press, 1981.

Jones, Jacqueline. *Labors of Love, Labors of Sorrow.* New York: Basic Books, 1985.

Katzman, David. *Seven Days a Week.* New York: Oxford University Press, 1978.

Katznelson, Ira. *Black Men, White Cities.* Chicago: University of Chicago Press, 1973.

Kennedy, Louise. *The Negro Peasant Turns Cityward.* New York: Columbia University Press, 1930.

Kerlin, Robert T. *The Voice of the Negro, 1919.* New York: Dutton, 1920.

Kirkland, Edward C. *Industry Comes of Age: Business, Labor, and Public Policy.* Chicago: Quadrangle Books, 1967.

Kiser, Clyde. *Sea Island to City.* New York: Columbia University Press, 1932.

Kornweibel, Theodore. *No Crystal Stair.* Westport, Conn.: Greenwood Press, 1975.

Leavell, R. H. "Negro Migration from Mississippi." In *Negro Migration in 1916–1917*, edited by George Haynes, pp. 15–49. Washington, D.C.: U.S. Department of Labor, Division of Negro Economics, Government Printing Office, 1919.

Lieberson, Stanley. "Selective Black Migration from the South: A Historical View." In *The Demography of Racial and Ethnic Groups*, edited by Frank D. Bean and W. Parker Frisbie, pp. 119–42. New York: Academic Press, 1949.

———. *A Piece of the Pie: Black and White Immigrants since 1880.* Berkeley: University of California Press, 1980.

Light, Ivan. *Ethnic Enterprise in America.* Berkeley: University of California Press, 1972.

Lipset, Seymour Martin. "Social Mobility and Urbanization." *Rural Sociology* 20 (1955), pp. 220–28.

Litwak, Leon. *Been in the Storm So Long.* New York: Vintage Books, 1980.

Lynd, Staughton. *Reconstruction.* New York: Harper and Row, 1967.

MacDonald, John, and MacDonald, Leatrice. "Chain Migration, Ethnic Neighborhood Formation and Social Networks." *Milbank Memorial Fund Quarterly* 42 (1964), pp. 82–97.

Mandle, Jay. *The Roots of Black Poverty.* Durham, N.C.: Duke University Press, 1978.

Marks, Carole. "Split Labor Markets and Black-White Relations, 1865–1910." *Phylon* 42 (1981), pp. 293–308.

———. "Lines of Communication, Recruitment Mechanisms, and the Great Migration of 1916–1918." *Social Problems.* 31, no. 1 (October 1983), pp. 59–83.

Meltzer, Milton. *Bread and Roses: The Struggle of American Labor 1865–1915.* New York: Knopf, 1967.

Metzger, L. Paul. "American Sociology and Black Assimilation: Conflicting Perspectives." In *Majority and Minority: The Dynamics of Race and Ethnicity in*

American Life, edited by Norman Yetman, pp. 346–51. Boston: Allyn and Bacon, 1985.

Montgomery, David. *Workers' Control in America*. New York: Cambridge University Press, 1979.

Myrdal, Gunnar. *An American Dilemma*: The Negro Problem and Modern Democracy. New York: Harper and Row, 1944.

National Urban League. "Migratory Study." Doc. no. 31.

Nelson, Daniel. *Managers and Workers' Origins of the New Factory System in the United States, 1880–1920*. Madison: University of Wisconsin Press, 1975.

Newbold, N. C. "Common Schools for Negroes in the South." *Annals of the American Academy of Political and Social Science*. Vol. 140 (November 1928).

O'Connor, James. *The Fiscal Crisis of the State*. New York: St. Martin's Press, 1973.

Odum, Howard W. *Social and Mental Traits of the Negro*. New York: Columbia University Press, 1920.

Osofsky, Gilbert. *Harlem: The Making of a Ghetto, Negro New York, 1890–1930*. New York: Harper and Row, 1966.

Otley, Roi. *The Lonely Warrior: The Life and Times of Robert S. Abbott*. Chicago: Henry Regnery, 1955.

Ovington, Mary White. *Half a Man: The Status of the Negro in New York*. New York: Longmans, Green, 1911.

Painter, Nell. *The Exodusters*. New York: Knopf, 1977.

Palmer, Dewey H. "Moving North: Migration of Negroes During World War I." In *White Racism and Black Americans*, edited by David G. Bromley and Charles Longino, Jr. Cambridge, Mass.: Schenkman, 1972.

Park, Robert. *Race and Culture*. Glencoe, Ill.: Free Press, 1950.

———, and Miller, Herbert. *Old World Traits Transplanted*. New York: Harper, 1921.

Parris, Guychard, and Brooks, Lester. *Blacks in the City: A History of the National Urban League*. Boston: Little, Brown, 1971.

Piore, Michael. *Birds of Passage*. New York: Cambridge University Press, 1979.

Pleck, Elizabeth. *Black Migration and Poverty*. New York: Academic Press, 1979.

Portes, Alejandro. "Migration and Underdevelopment." *Politics and Society* 7 (1978), pp. 1–48.

———. "Modes of Structural Incorporation and Present Theories of Labor Migration." Belagio, Italy: Revised version of paper delivered at the Conference on International Migration Studies. The Rockefeller Foundation, 1979.

———, and Stepick, Alex. "Immigrant Enclaves," *American Sociological Review* 8 (1985), pp. 493–514.

———. "Unwelcome Immigrants," *American Sociological Review* 50, no. 4 (1985).

Price, Daniel O. *Changing Characteristics—Negro Population*. Washington, D.C.: Department of Commerce, 1965.

Price, Daniel O., and Sykes, Melanie. *Rural-Urban Migration Research in the United States*. Washington, D.C.: Center for Population Research, Government Printing Office, 1979.

Rabinowitz, Howard. *Race Relations in the Urban South 1865–1890*. New York: Oxford University Press, 1978.

Ransom, Roger, and Sutch, Richard. *One Kind of Free*. New York: Cambridge University Press, 1977.

Record, Wilson. *Race and Radicalism*. Ithaca, N.Y.: Cornell University Press, 1964.

Reich, Michael. *Racial Inequality: A Political-Economic Analysis*. Princeton: Princeton University Press, 1981.

Rosenblum, Gerald. *Immigrant Workers*. New York: Basic Books, 1973.

Rudwick, Elliott M. *Race Riot at East St. Louis*. Carbondale, Ill.: Southern Illinois University Press, 1964.

Sandburg, Carl. *The Chicago Race Riots*. New York: Harcourt, Brace and Rowe, 1919.

Sassen-Koob, Saskia. "Formal and Informal Associations: Dominicans and Columbians in New York." *International Migration Review* 13, pp. 319–32.

Scheiner, Seth M. *Negro Mecca: A History of the Negro in New York City, 1865–1920*. New York: New York University Press, 1965.

Scott, Emmett J. "Letters of Negro Migrants of 1916–1918," *Journal of Negro History* 4 (July 1919).

———. "Additional Letters of Negro Migrants of 1916–1918." *Journal of Negro History* 4 (October 1919).

———. *Negro Migration During the War*. 1920. Reprint: New York: Arno Press and New York Times, 1969.

Seller, Maxine. *To Seek America: A History of Ethnic Life in the United States*. New York: Jerome S. Oker, 1977.

Shugg, Robert W. *Origins of Class Struggle in Louisiana*. Baton Rouge: Louisiana State University Press, 1939.

Simkins, Francis Butler. *The South Old and the New 1820–1947*. New York: Knopf, 1947.

Snavely, T. R. "The Exodus of Negroes from the Southern States." In *Negro Migration in 1916–1917*, edited by George Haynes, pp. 51–79. Washington, D.C.: Government Printing Office, 1919.

Spear, Allan H. *Black Chicago: The Making of a Ghetto, 1890–1920*. Chicago: University of Chicago Press, 1967.

Speare, Alden; Goldstein, Sidney; and Frey, William. *Residential Mobility, Migration and Metropolitan Change*. Cambridge, Mass.: Ballinger, 1975.

Spero, Sterling D., and Harris, Abram L. *The Black Worker: The Negro and the Labor Movement*. 1931. Reprint. New York: Atheneum, 1969.

Stampp, Kenneth. *The Era of Reconstruction, 1865–1877*. New York: Knopf, 1966.

Steinberg, Stephen. *The Ethnic Myth*. Boston: Beacon Press, 1981.

Strickland, Arvarh. *History of the Chicago Urban League*. Urbana, Ill.: University of Illinois Press, 1966.

Taeuber, Karl, and Taeuber, Alma. *Negroes in Cities*. Chicago: Aldine, 1965.

Thomas, Brinley. *Migration and Economic Growth*. 2d ed. Cambridge: Cambridge University Press, 1973.

Thomas, Dorothy S. *Research and Memorandum on Migration Differentials*. New York: Social Science Research Council, bulletin no. 33, 1938.

Thomas, W. I., and Znaniecki, Florian. *The Polish Peasant in Europe and America*. Boston: Gorham Press, 1920.

Tienda, Marta. "Familism and Structural Assimilation of Mexican Immigrants in the United States." *International Migration Review* 14, no. 3 (1980), pp. 383–408.

Tilly, Charles. "Race and Migration to the American City." In *The Metropolitan*

Enigma, edited by James Q. Wilson, pp. 124–46. New York: Doubleday, 1970.

Tindall, George Brown. *Emergence of the New South, 1913–1945*. Baton Rouge: Louisiana State University Press, 1967.

Todaro, Michael P. *Internal Migration in Developing Countries*. Geneva: International Labor Office, 1976.

Tuttle, William. *Race Riot*. New York: Atheneum, 1974.

Tyson, Frances. "The Negro Migrant in the North." In *Negro Migration in 1916–1917*, edited by George Haynes, pp. 115–56. Washington, D.C.: Government Printing Office, 1919.

U.S. Bureau of Education Bulletin. "Statistics of Education of the Negro Race." Washington, D.C.: Government Printing Office, 1928.

U.S. Department of Agriculture. "Report of Study of Negro Migration." Washington, D.C.: Government Printing Office, 1929.

U.S. Department of Commerce, Bureau of the Census. *Current Population Reports*. ser. D-20, no. 154: "Reasons for Moving." March 1962 to March 1963. (1966).

U.S. Department of Labor. "1923 Report of Migrants in 15 States." *Monthly Labor Review* (January 1924).

————. Case files on the U.S. Conciliation Service. Microfilm.

U.S. Senate. Report of the Senate Committee on Education and Labor. *Labor and Capital*. Washington, D.C.: Government Printing Office, 1885.

Vickery, William. *The Economics of the Negro Migration, 1900–1960*. New York: Arno Press, 1977.

Washington, Booker T. *The Rise of the Race from Slavery*. Garden City, N.Y.: Doubleday, 1909.

Weatherford, Willis, and Charles Johnson. *Race Relations*. Boston: D. C. Heath, 1941.

Webber, Melvin. "Order in Diversity: Community without Propinquity." In *Cities and Space: The Future of Urban Land*, edited by Lowdon Wingo, Jr., pp. 23–59. Baltimore: Johns Hopkins University Press, 1963.

Weinstein, James. *The Corporate Ideal in the Liberal State: 1900–1918*. Boston: Beacon Press, 1968.

Wesley, Charles. *Negro Labor in the United States 1850–1925*. New York: Vanguard, 1927.

Wilhelm, Sidney. *Who Needs the Negro?* New York: Anchor Books, 1971.

Wilkening, E. A. et al. "The Role of the Extended Family in Migration and Adaptation in Brazil." *Journal of Marriage and Family* 30, no. 4 (1968).

Williams, W. T. B. "Negro Migration in Alabama." In *Negro Migration in 1916–1917*, edited by George Haynes, pp. 93–113. Washington, D.C.: U.S. Department of Labor, Division of Negro Economics, Government Printing Office, 1919.

Williamson, Joel. *After Slavery*. Chapel Hill: University of North Carolina Press, 1965.

Wilson, William J. *The Declining Significance of Race*. Chicago: University of Chicago Press, 1978.

Wood, Charles. "Equilibrium vs. Historical-Structural Perspectives on Migration." Paper presented at a Conference on Immigration and Ethnicity, Durham, N.C., May 1981.

Woodson, Carter G. *The Rural Negro*. Washington, D.C.: Association for the Study of Negro Life and History, 1930.

———. *The Negro in Our History*. Washington, D.C.: Association for the Study of Negro Life and History, 1932.

———. *A Century of Negro Migration*. New York: Russell and Russell, 1969.

Woodward, C. Vann. *Origins of the New South: 1877–1913*. Baton Rouge: Louisiana State University Press, 1951.

———. *Reunion and Reaction: The Compromise of 1877 and the End of Reconstruction*. Boston: Little, Brown, 1951.

———. *The Strange Career of Jim Crow*. New York: Oxford University Press, 1966.

Woofter, Thomas. "Migration of Negroes from Georgia." In *Negro Migration in 1916–1917*, edited by George Haynes, pp. 75–91. Washington, D.C.: U.S. Department of Labor, Division of Negro Economics, Government Printing Office, 1919.

———. *Negro Migration: Change in Rural Organization and Population of the Cotton Belt*. New York: W. D. Gray, 1920.

Yancey, William; Ericksen, Eugene; and Juliana, Richard. "Emergent Ethnicity." In *Majority and Minority: The Dynamics of Race and Ethnicity in American Life*, edited by Norman Yetman. Boston: Allyn and Bacon, 1985.

Yetman, Norman, ed. *Majority and Minority: The Dynamics of Race and Ethnicity in American Life*. Boston: Allyn and Bacon, 1985.

Index